Authenticating Ethnic Tourism

PEFC
PEFC/16-33-111
CATG-PEFC-052
www.pefc.org

TOURISM AND CULTURAL CHANGE
Series Editors: Professor Mike Robinson, *Centre for Tourism and Cultural Change, Leeds Metropolitan University, Leeds, UK and* Dr Alison Phipps, *University of Glasgow, Scotland, UK*

Understanding tourism's relationships with culture(s) and vice versa, is of ever-increasing significance in a globalising world. This series will critically examine the dynamic inter-relationships between tourism and culture(s). Theoretical explorations, research-informed analyses, and detailed historical reviews from a variety of disciplinary perspectives are invited to consider such relationships.

Full details of all the books in this series and of all our other publications can be found on http://www.channelviewpublications.com, or by writing to Channel View Publications, St Nicholas House, 31-34 High Street, Bristol BS1 2AW, UK.

TOURISM AND CULTURAL CHANGE
Series Editors: Professor Mike Robinson, *Centre for Tourism and Cultural Change, Leeds Metropolitan University, Leeds, UK* and Dr Alison Phipps, *University of Glasgow, Scotland, UK*

Authenticating Ethnic Tourism

Philip Feifan Xie

CHANNEL VIEW PUBLICATIONS
Bristol • Buffalo • Toronto

Library of Congress Cataloging in Publication Data
A catalog record for this book is available from the Library of Congress.
Xie, Philip Feifan.
Authenticating Ethnic tourism/Philip FeifanXie.
Tourism and Cultural Change:26
Includes bibliographical references and index.
1. Tourism–China–Hainan Sheng. 2. Culture and tourism–China–Hainan Sheng.
3. Ethnic groups–China–Hainan Sheng. 4. Hainan Sheng (China)–Social life and customs.
I. Title. II. Series.
G155.C55X52 2010
338.4'7915129–dc222010026362

British Library Cataloguing in Publication Data
A catalogue entry for this book is available from the British Library.

ISBN-13: 978-1-84541-158-9 (hbk)
ISBN-13: 978-1-84541-157-2 (pbk)

Channel View Publications
UK: St Nicholas House, 31-34 High Street, Bristol BS1 2AW, UK.
USA: UTP, 2250 Military Road, Tonawanda, NY 14150, USA.
Canada: UTP, 5201 Dufferin Street, North York, Ontario M3H 5T8, Canada.

The policy of Multilingual Matters/Channel View Publications is to use papers that
are natural, renewable and recyclable products, made from wood grown in sustainable
forests. In the manufacturing process of our books, and to further support our policy,
preference is given to printers that have FSC and PEFC Chain of Custody certification.
The FSC and/or PEFC logos will appear on those books where full certification has been
granted to the printer concerned.

Typeset by Datapage International Ltd.
Printed and bound in Great Britain by the MPG Books Group

Contents

List of Illustrations

Figures

Plates

Tables

Acknowledgments

I am indebted to many people for their generous contributions to the writing of this book. The funding for the fieldwork for my doctoral dissertation was provided by Canadian International Development Agency, due in large part to studying under my academic advisor, Dr Geoff Wall. He enlightened me to the potential research values of folk villages on Hainan Island, China, as an entry point to understand ethnic tourism.

Dr Richard Pearson, Professor Emeritus of Syracuse University, did an outstanding job copyediting the manuscript, and he made many helpful suggestions for improving both the writing and the content. Dr Kai Gu, Lecturer in the School of Architecture and Planning at the University of Auckland, New Zealand, helped with the figures and maps of Hainan. I especially want to thank Bernard Lane, co-editor of *Journal of Sustainable Tourism*, for his persuasive judgment in the life cycle of authenticity in ethnic tourism. Dr Lynn Pearson, Associate Professor of Spanish at Bowling Green State University, read over the first draft of the manuscript and encouraged my thinking at all stages of the book's progress. She remains sine qua non for the completion of this book.

I owe a debt of thanks to Dr Kaye Chon and Dr Cathy Hsu, who invited me to spend a sabbatical at the School of Hotel and Tourism Management at Hong Kong Polytechnic University in Fall 2009. I had an opportunity to conduct more fieldwork and to update the findings on Hainan during my stay in Hong Kong. It was an unforgettable moment, working on the final portion of the manuscript, watching the glittering lights of the Central shining on Victoria Harbor in front of my office window.

Finally, I appreciate Dr Mike Robinson and Dr Alison Phipps, editors of the Tourism and Cultural Change book series, for helping me to clarify my ideas to better structure this book. I am grateful for the assistance of Sarah Williams, the commissioning editor, in the process of the publication. For all the extraordinary help I have received, any limitations in the book's thought, structure or scope are, of course, entirely my own.

Preface

My interest in the issue of authentication in ethnic tourism goes back to my time as a doctoral student in planning at the University of Waterloo, Ontario, Canada. After teaching at Bowling Green State University, Ohio, USA, from 2001 to the present, the question of authentication remains some of the most stimulating research in my mind. The book is the culmination of this endeavor to trace the changes of tourist folk villages, people and tourism landscapes on Hainan Island, the largest tropical island located off the southern coast of China, from 1999 to 2009.

This book is a product of its context, both authentication and ethnic tourism. The previous research engenders a kaleidoscope of findings, ranging from tourists' search for genuineness to ethnic minorities' resistance to be commodified. In this book, I propose that ethnic tourism closely resembles an 'ethnic panopticon' in which ethnicity is often viewed as a distant object in a structured power relationship played by various stakeholders when tourism occurs spatiotemporally. Tourists look for something 'real', 'truthful' and 'authentic' as a predominant trend driving ethnic tourism. Potter (2010) calls this kind of pursuit a 'perpetual coolhunt' since authenticity is 'a positional good, which is valuable precisely because not everyone can have it'. What tourists can get is 'a dopey nostalgia for a non-existent past' as ethnicity becomes an imagined entity owing to the malaise of modernity.

The discourse of authenticity attracts endless debates by pointing to what it is not. It is fraught with contradictions that stem from the lack of a set of criteria with which to measure, compare and deconstruct. MacCannell (2008) wittingly raised a question to deride the authenticity debates in tourism studies – 'Why it never really was about authenticity?' This book is a shifting of emphasis away from authenticity of ethnic culture, an issue widely discussed by tourism researchers, to the processes of authenticating ethnic culture. It focuses on what authentication is, how it works, who is involved and what are the problems in the process. It aims to examine who authenticates ethnic tourism rather than to assess adherence to some absolute and arbitrary standard of authenticity of tourism products and experiences. In order to do so, I put forward a conceptual framework on the issue of authentication by identifying key stakeholders involved in ethnic tourism. I suggest that the identified stakeholders, in their evaluation and attribution of authenticity, may be assessed according to their positions on a range of five continuums. It is critical to clarify the perspectives of authenticity as seen by different stakeholders as well as the permutations of authenticity that have taken place in the ongoing discourse. In that way, authenticity's nature evolves from a static into a more dynamic concept, which can be formulated according to the different stages of development relating to all the parties involved. Authentication should be viewed as an interactive process in which a balance of forces defines a state of equilibrium.

Hainan Island was chosen to compare these identified stakeholders when authenticating ethnic cultures in different, if not, contrasting ways. Ethnic tourism, when put into practice, can create a series of paradoxes between conservation of tradition and change in the process of development. The aboriginal Li, having resided on the island for hundreds of years, recently used the purpose-built folk villages to commodify their culture. The Indonesian-Chinese population fled Indonesia and resettled on the island during the anti-Communist insurrection in 1960s, and has preserved its distinctive diasporic culture. An Indonesian village was born out of a desire to portray its culture to passerby tourists. All these folk villages scattered along the highways to increase their visibility and to provide convenient access to mass tourists. The view of authentication presented here explores the multiple layers of reality, experienced by stakeholders using different yardsticks. Village managers, dance performers, governments and tourists are among the key players in authenticating ethnic cultures and serving as a process of translating 'originary' for tourist consumption. It is like the game of 'rumor', where a communication line of several people is formed to verbally pass a sentence from one person to the next, each whispering into the other's ear. The original sentence is often dramatically changed, both in terms of its form and content. The result of authentication can never bring back the 'originary', but it does convey a message through different people, albeit the point of departure and last iteration will never be the same.

This book will fill a gap in tourism studies by answering questions pertaining to the authentication of ethnic tourism in an island setting. By using the study of folk villages, a form of ethnic visitor attractions, I hope to draw attention to authentication as an alternative way of avoiding personal value-laden judgments of authenticity. The key outcome is to develop possible strategies for mitigating the tourism-ethnicity paradoxes and tensions through more sensitive and informed planning. The conceptual framework presented in this book could be applied to other situations. Academic interest in such studies may include learning whether or not this conceptual framework and its methodology is useful in understanding authentication of other destination areas. In addition, this type of research could reveal similar or dissimilar constraints to the application of the framework to socio-cultural, political and economic environments in other parts of the world.

Introduction: Lo auténtico aún existe

In 2005, the Ministry of Tourism in Bolivia launched a new tourism campaign with the slogan *'Lo auténtico aún existe'* (authenticity still exists), featuring ethnic Quechuas and Aymara, the descendents of the Incas and the Tiwanaku culture. The slogan implies a strong desire for 'real' experiences in tourism to interact with ancient cultures. Ethnic identity, albeit somewhat fluid, has determined the social hierarchy in Bolivia. The publicity campaign typifies these ethnic groups in Bolivia, which have maintained their cultures, languages and folk traditions. The tourism video showed that the popular festivals and rituals have been rediscovered and revived after being forgotten for centuries. Colorful ethnic images have been used to embellish the attractiveness of Bolivia as a tourism destination. It claimed that Bolivia is indeed a 'lost world' with untouched ethnic cultures and unspoiled natural scenery. Traveling in Bolivia is an opportunity to re-live history where tradition is maintained and inspired by ancient Incas and Aymaras. Potential tourists can view scenes of pre-Columbian and colonial architecture in places such as Potosi, Sucre and Cochabamba. Ethnicity was a driving force in the social relations of individuals and communities, but now it plays an important theme to attract tourists by showing the ancient ruins of the Incan civilization and their descendants, by playing music and dancing in traditional dress. The pursuit of authenticity, therefore, can be a powerful marketing tool for tourism as tourists seek real and meaningful experiences in their travels.

As evidenced in Bolivia, ethnic tourism has become a worldwide phenomenon that not only showcases ethnic distinctiveness, but also attracts visitors for cross-cultural experiences and provides pleasurable environments for their gaze (Urry, 2002). Ethnicity has been increasingly promoted as a tourist attraction and as a strategy to generate income and foreign exchange for ethnic communities. Historically, tourism involves the movement of people outside their normal places of work and residence. As such, it provides participants with novel experiences, often

1

bringing them in contact with unknown places and people. For many tourists, this is a search for the Other, which is judged in relation to the Self and one's usual behaviors and settings. Ethnicity is arguably the most fundamental basis of perceived distinction between human groups, which can be generally defined as 'the existence of culturally distinctive groups within a society, each asserting a unique identity on the basis of a shared tradition and distinguishing social markers such as a common language, religion, or economic specialization' (Winthrop, 1991: 94). A variety of terms, such as 'indigenous', 'tribal', 'aboriginal' and 'native', are extensively used in the tourism literature to describe the original inhabitants of a country. Although usage of the terms is elastic and often vague, scholars normally choose a specific term to describe a particular group, which reflects its ethnic identity and the potential responses of the readers with respect to the research studies (Hinch & Butler, 2007). In this book, I have chosen to use the word 'ethnic' to refer to the groups of people who share the same heritage, including 'their material artifacts, belief systems, religions, forms of government, customs, language, recreation, housing, commercial activity, forms and places of work, education, and science and technology' (Smith, 1990: 87).

The advent of ethnic tourism started as the pursuit of the exotic 'other', the differentness and the authentic experience. It is commonly regarded as part of cultural tourism, which is a form of recreation combining cultural and natural resources that is marketed to the public in terms of 'quaint' customs of indigenous and often exotic peoples. Cole (2006) distinguished ethnic and cultural tourism as the former is used for the 'primitive other' and the latter for the high arts in the developed nations. Ethnic tourism also refers to tourism activities in which ethnic people are directly or indirectly involved either through control and/or by having their culture served as the center of the attraction. The modern explosion of interest in ethnic tourism is multifaceted in cause, ranging from supply factors (such as heritage planning, economic need and cultural revival), to demand factors (such as the desire for creative, cultural pride, authentic experiences and entertainment by and for visitors). It is assumed that, as majority peoples, who are usually the tourists, observe and experience minority cultures, their understanding and appreciation of ethnic positions on major issues may improve. Those issues may be cultural; they may also be more general. Increased understanding can result in changed attitudes and behaviors that lead, in turn, to a more just and equitable relationship between minority and majority peoples (Cohen, 2002).

The popularity of ethnic tourism has also created a series of tensions and conflicts when ethnic culture is commoditized as a tourism source. The anthropologist, Van den Berghe (1994: 8), described ethnic tourism as activities in which 'the tourist actively searches for ethnic exoticism', primarily when so-called First World peoples seek contact with Third World peoples. Ethnic tourism has traditionally been viewed as 'utopia of difference', a by-product of imperialism or the new product of neo-colonialism. Historically, meetings with ethnic group members became the stuff of romanticized visions and the basis of conscious or unconscious oppression by colonizers or members of the majority society. The process of ethnic tourism could create acculturation and value changes undermining the core of ethnic traditions. The mentality of 'I'll give you something, but you haven't got anything that I would want' (Morgan, 1994: 185) expressed toward ethnic minorities is evidently documented in the history of the West and colonial expansion. Examples such as the cultural assimilation of aboriginal people in Australia until the early 1970s, and the authentic 'noble savage' of African countries under British rule, where 'spectatorial lust' (Erlmann, 1999: 109) motivated the tours of African landscapes, are typical in the early stage of ethnic tourism. Numerous studies have implied that ethnic tourism may not serve as a catalyst for the changing relationships between minority and majority; rather, it tends to undermine the indigenous places and identities intentionally and unintentionally. Hall and Tucker (2004: 12) write that:

> The role that [ethnic] tourism can play in transforming collective and individual values is inherent in ideas of commoditization, which implies that what were once personal "cultural displays" of living traditions or a "cultural text" of lived authenticity become "cultural products" that meet the needs of commercial tourism, as well as the construction of heritage. Such a situation may lead to the invention of tradition and heritage for external consumption that meet visitor conceptions of the other.

Ethnic culture, or 'tradition', is transformed into a set of things that are at once symbolic of the Western pursuit of the exotic 'other', and the commodities of modernization. The emphasis of ethnic tourism, such as visits to native homes and folk villages to observe and/or participate in native customs, rituals, ceremonies and other traditional activities has a profound impact on the host culture and environment. Edward Bruner (2005), in his book, *Culture on Tour: Ethnographies of Travel*, delineated his involvement as a tour guide for a deluxe tour of Indonesia in order to study ethnic tourism from the inside. 'I was an anthropologist', he wrote, 'but also, in effect, one of the tourists'. But Bruner's director, who accompanied the group, was not pleased by his photographing of tourists as they photographed Indonesians, nor his attempt to explain that a folk ballet at a princess's home was a performance constructed purposely for tourists. Instead of making his fellow tourists more self-aware of the authenticity of the performance, as he anticipated, he got himself fired. The episode underlined a striking contrast between a 'master tourist tale' that sees ethnic tourism as representations of an authentic culture and what Bruner (2005: 17) coined the 'touristic borderzone' – a point of conjuncture where tourists encounter locals in performance. Ethnic tourism, for Burner (2005; 18) is, 'improvisational theatre... where both tourists and locals engage in a coproduction: they each take account of the other in an ever-shifting, contested, evolving borderzone of engagement'. The tourist gaze in ethnic tourism is a 'questioning gaze' within limits. It is a cultural imagery, a fantasy and a constructed theatrical setting.

The socio-cultural models that saw ethnic tourism as another aspect of neo-colonialism are steadily ceding to more nuanced approaches since the nature of ethnicity is more complex than it may appear at first sight. In the field of anthropology, for instance, ethnicity does not constitute a new domain of research, but tourism is a new form to challenge the adequacy of conventional cultural theories. Two fundamental perspectives regarding the relationship between ethnicity and culture were put forward: primordial and situational (Hitchcock, 1999). The former views ethnic cultures as static and leads to the assumption that any change imposed by contact with a politically dominant state must result in irreversible acculturation. The primordial perspective involves understanding the processes by which ethnic identities and boundaries are created, modified and maintained. Geographic and historic isolation, and cultural differences are all seen as important in creating and sustaining ethnic identities. This perspective stresses the endurance of ethnic identities and distinctive traditions as cultural enclaves even within multicultural states. Ethnic culture is viewed as tribal with identity support and maintenance as central. The development of tourism encroaches on traditional cultures and bears an analogy to the 'billiard ball model' (Wood, 1980: 565), where a static sphere (ethnic cultures) is relentlessly hit by a mobile one (tourism). The very existence of the ethnic boundary creates the visitor attraction.

By contrast, a situational perspective (also called constructivism) regards ethnic cultures as 'a set of processes and social relations, which may be invoked according to circumstances' (Hitchcock, 1999: 21). A situational approach provides positive views of identity and presents ethnic communities as being far from passive victims of the visitors' gaze. Tourism turns culture into a commodity and ethnic communities are encouraged or sometimes even forced to modify traditional cultures to accommodate the needs of both visitors and the local people. The concept of ethnicity is seen more as a set of cultural differences that are continuously communicated. Clifford (1986: 9–10), therefore, described cultural identity as 'an ongoing process, politically contested and historically unfinished', and as 'always mixed, relational and inventive'. The existence of an ethnic boundary does not necessarily create tourist attractions, rather, the concept of pluralism is of importance. In this perspective, ethnic tourism should be recognized as being shaped by contemporary global processes, rather than by traces of the past (Wood, 1997). The salient feature of the situational perspective is that ethnic identity is assumed to be ambiguous and subjective: culture has not been conceived as a concrete entity acted on by forces from outside, but rather as sets of symbols, or as webs of significance and meaning. These symbols are variable, relative and conditional. In his seminal work, *The Location of Culture*, Bhabha (2004) argued that cultural presentations are hybridized, ambiguous and interstitial. Many destinations, peoples and cultural experiences are located in what Bhabha calls the 'third space', which is an existence that is under-recognized, displaced and in-between forms of assumed differences. As Ryan and Aicken (2005) noted, 'if a characteristic of post-modernism is the de-differentiation of fantasy and fact, history and myth, and the affective and cognitive, then, too, the boundaries between theory and practice also become blurred to create some hybrid product which often, in tourism, emphasizes the experiential'. Hollinshead (1998) reviewed Bhabha's theory by suggesting that culture and ethnicity are the results of dynamic processes that produce, reproduce and transform. Instead of learning about ethnicity and its representation, this construct is experienced and lived. Culture and its interpretation are ever-changing and imaginative phenomena in all stages of development – creation, renewal and fabricated rather than static entities. Ethnic identity turns out to be a feeling 'subject to ebb and flow' (Poole, 1997: 133).

Tourism research related to ethnicity has concentrated on describing and understanding the impacts of tourism on host societies (Moscardo & Pearce, 1999). The existing work on ethnic tourism mainly focuses on the normative issue of whether tourism was beneficial or detrimental for its hosts (Wood, 1998). Perspectives of ethnic tourism *inter alia* have varied from the host–guest nexus of tourism impacts (Hinch & Butler, 1996), to the conflicts and tensions between ethnic culture and tourism encroachment (Robinson & Boniface, 1999; Ryan & Aicken, 2005), to the debates on authenticity and commodification of ethnic cultural performance (Cohen, 1988, 2002; MacCannell, 1973). Areas of ethnic tourism, among many, include extensive ethnographic research on the Balinese in Indonesia (Picard, 1996); the challenges and opportunities of tourism development in Northern Territory in Australia (Ryan & Huyton, 2000); the situational adaptation of ethnic performance to re-signify aesthetic forms of traditional meaning in Canada (Mason, 2004); and the contested interpretation of Maori identity in New Zealand (Taylor, 2001). The research on ethnic tourism has traditionally been regarded as a mild oxymoron by tourism researchers and practitioners. The prevailing assumption is that any attempt to use cultural elements to accommodate tourists will cheapen or trivialize the presentation and interpretation of ethnic culture and heritage. The marketing of ethnic tourism often emphasizes the 'primitive', 'exotic', 'adventure' or the 'savage', such as talking about headhunting and cannibalism, practices that ceased long ago. The result is an inaccurate and harmful portrait of a complex and ever-changing people. Ethnic tourism practice may destroy the host's culture or calcify a culture into a 'frozen' picture of the past. Cultures are named and stereotyped. The visitors seek to see representations of the culture and the host society provides access to the expected symbols. The terms 'touristic culture' and 'touristification' were proposed by Picard (1990) in reference to situations where tourism is so pervasive that it has become an integral part of everyday life. In such situations, the interaction with tourists may be a central component in the definition of ethnic identity. Picard showed that the Balinese have come to objectify their culture in terms of the arts and to evaluate tourism impact in terms of whether the arts are flourishing or not. The convergence of tourism and culture in the late 20th century was presented by Richards (1996: 12) as a realistic *fait accompli*, and he suggested that 'in spite of reservations about the potential negative impacts of tourism on culture, it seems that tourism and culture are inseparable'.

On the other hand, research on ethnic tourism also unveils positive impacts: tourism can promote the restoration of arts, revitalize skills, foster creativity and provide a platform for communities to present themselves confidently. Using the same research setting in Bali, Indonesia, McKean (1989) concluded that tourism was strengthening the local arts by providing opportunities for more dancers, musicians, wood carvers and other crafts-persons. Furthermore, he suggested that the Balinese were quite successful in maintaining the boundary between what belonged to their culture and what could be presented to tourists. 'Cultural involution' was proposed as a term to indicate that ethnic culture is mutable and that tourism infuses new meanings, adding value both economically and psychologically to cultural expressions previously largely taken for granted. McKean further suggests that local communities as objects of exploitation were unfounded. There are multiple and competing meanings in individual sites, contrasting meanings in different sites in the same country, and changes in the meaning of sites over time.

The purpose of this book is not to argue for or against ethnic tourism, as previous research has done. There is a glaring deficiency in ethnic tourism research, namely, the needs of stakeholders are often under-emphasized. When this occurs, decisions may be made without adequate consideration of key impacts when tourism strategies are being developed. Furthermore, little research has been undertaken to review the roles of stakeholders who authenticate ethnic resources, because the tourism–ethnicity relationship has long been associated with cultural tensions and the use and misuse of ethnic resources. It has become increasingly important to understand who authenticates culture and how this occurs in the negotiation of cultural authenticity. By borrowing Bruner and Kirshenblatt-Gimblett's (1994: 459) provocative question, 'who has the power to determine what will count as authentic?' in the critique of cultural anthropology, this book focuses on what authentication is, how it works, who is involved and what are the problems in the process. It aims to examine who authenticates ethnic tourism rather than to assess adherence to some absolute and arbitrary standard of authenticity of tourism products and experiences. To do so, I propose a strong conceptual framework to analyze and evaluate the authentication by different stakeholders of ethnic tourism in a specific setting – the ethnic Li minority on Hainan Island, which is the largest tropical island located off the southern coast of China. Ethnic tourism, when put into practice, can cause a series of paradoxes between conservation of tradition and change in the process of development. These paradoxes can also serve as yardsticks to evaluate tourism–ethnicity relationships in a Chinese context. The key outcome is to develop possible strategies for mitigating these paradoxes and tensions through more sensitive and informed planning of ethnic tourism development. By using the study of folk villages, a form of ethnic visitor attractions, on Hainan, China, the book shows that the concept of authentication not only provides a way of avoiding personal value-laden judgments of authenticity, but also a practical way of addressing issues of authenticity. It is critical to clarify the perspectives of authenticity as seen by different stakeholders as well as the permutations of authenticity that have taken place in the ongoing discourse. In that way, authenticity's nature evolves from a static into a more dynamic concept, which can be formulated according to the different stages of development relating to all the parties involved. The book is based on research and fieldwork on Hainan Island, China, from 1999 to 2009. It contributes valuable information to the research on ethnic tourism in developing areas and, at the same time, tests the utility of the conceptual framework for authentication.

The Practice of Ethnic Tourism

According to Hinch and Butler (1996), the more focused study of ethnic tourism, in various forms, has been characterized by four general phases: (1) legitimization as a scholarly study; (2) critical advocacy for ethnic people; (3) analysis from a policy and economic development strategy perspective; and (4) pragmatic cross-cultural education. The concept of ethnic tourism may simply refer to ethnic people's involvement in the tourism industry as owners of tourism businesses, such as hotels and casinos, but is more commonly understood as referring to a tourism product whose focus is native culture (Notzke, 2004). The practice of ethnic tourism centers on the issue of control in terms of ownership and management interests in ethnic attractions. There are three major forms of ethnic tourism: (1) ethnic-controlled businesses that do not feature ethnic culture, e.g. casinos, golf courses; or (2) tourist activities that feature ethnic culture with little or no control by ethnic people, e.g. Walt Disney World, theme parks; or (3) ethnic-controlled businesses featuring ethnic presentations, e.g. ethnic folk villages. The latter generally refers to cultural ethnic tourism, a tourism product that focuses on native culture that has a direct impact on ethnic communities. Zeppel (1998) termed 'community-based ethnic tourism', in order to distinguish ethnic tourism that is controlled by ethnic people from tourism using ethnicity as a marketing tool. Smith (1989) proposed that, in general, ethnic tourism involves four interrelated elements: the geographic setting (habitat), the ethnographic traditions (heritage), the effects of acculturation (history) and the marketable handicrafts. As the four S acronym (sun, sea, sand and sex) encapsulates beach resort tourism, the four Hs – habitat, heritage, history and handicrafts – similarly describe the ethnic tourism phenomenon.

The corollary phenomenon of modernity is the weakening of political borders that has let people and goods pass in and out of the homogenized societies. In the context of globalization, the 'death of distance' (Cairncross, 1997: 2) is becoming the norm, while tradition and 'fixed modernity' are transformed into a kind of 'liquid modernity' (Bauman, 2000: 1). The growing economic prosperity provides 'cultural exchanges' or 'interactional experiences' (Taylor, 2001) by people from different regions and countries. The 'global modernity' and 'tourism mobility' has modified culture and heritage so that it becomes imaginative discourse constructed out of available intelligence about the past (Sheller & Urry, 2004). Simultaneously, ethnic culture is constantly evolving in the face of change within the environment in which it exists. Cultural change is not governed only by tourism impacts: a whole series of other change engines are at work, even in remote ethnic communities, fuelled by economic and technical transitions, the spread of the mass media and broadcasting, and the globalization of knowledge and ideas. McKercher and du Cros (2002: 97) wrote in a similar vein, arguing 'culture is not a static concept. Over time, every culture changes, sometimes radically, sometimes imperceptibly. At stake is the rate of change, the purpose of change, the instigator of change, and its relationship to the context of the core values of the culture'. These changes, reflected in commodification of ethnic tourism, can be widely seen in local festivals, theme parks, visitor folk villages and other cultural events. A classic example described by Greenwood (1977) revealed that a traditional Alarde festival in the Basque town of Fuenterrabia, Spain, representing ethnic identity was severely compromised when the local municipal authority attempted to make the celebration more accessible to tourists by holding two performances on the same day. This widely cited example illustrated the adverse impacts of tourism on the ethnic culture in that 'a vital and exciting ritual became an obligation to be avoided' (Greenwood, 1977: 135). However, the follow-up research indicated that tourism per se had little to do with the apparent decline of the Alarde. The problem was that the Spaniards who controlled the municipality under the Franco dictatorship had little interest in Basque culture. Once the officials had been replaced by Basques, the locals were willing to perform twice a day. The traditional festival, far from being an obligation to be avoided, remained a vibrant and exciting ritual. Nowadays, the festival performance can even be exported as a tour, sometimes forming part of a regional or national marketing effort. Ethnic cultures are not unchanging traditions that have been handed down, but have always been subject to fashion and market forces beyond the boundaries of the local community. These forces do not grow organically from environment and communities, instead, they may be developed in marketing agencies and media reports.

Most importantly, ethnic tourism is facing an endless debate on the issue of authenticity and commodification. The concept of authenticity has featured prominently in tourism studies, which can be simply defined as 'a desired experience or benefit associated with visits to certain types of tourism destinations. It is presumed to be the result of an encounter with true, uncommercialized, everyday life in a culture different than that of the visitor' (Smith, 1990: 31). The concept implies that tradition is authentic if it is passed down without change through the generations. The term 'commodification' is used to refer to situations in which a price is placed on artifacts or experiences that were previously not for sale so that cultural expressions become marketable tourism products. Early critical theorists (Cohen, 1988; Graburn, 1984; Pitchford, 1995) juxtaposed two versions of ethnic and traditional cultures: one pure and authentic and another an artificial and inauthentic representation created for and sold to an increasingly homogenous consumer society. The Frankfurt School's critical theories (Friedman, 1981) posited that the rising influence of modernization, industrialization and bureaucratization on social and cultural life has led to the mass production and consumption of products guided by bland and standardized formulas, which refers to commodification. Cultures have lost their historical specificity and become increasingly 'theme-parked' (Sorkin, 1992). As argued by Swedish ethnologist, Orvar Löfgren (1999), a tour package for ethnic tourism almost invariably involves the same devices: the welcoming reception, the 'local' cocktail, the 'exotic' tour with time for souvenir shopping, the 'folk dance,' the beach barbeque with roast pig and the final party where tourists are invited to try on ethnic headwear and dance with the entertainers.

Despite standardization and globalization, one of the first issues to be considered is: what is the 'authentic' form of ethnic tourism? Or does commodification degrade the ethnic cultures, or is it a form of cultural revival? (Daniel, 1996) since touristic performances have been staged, prepared and packaged to frame ethnic cultures. This conventional dualism between authenticity and commodification has been identified as a central orienting principle in tourism studies. Concern with authenticity and commodification is prevalent in many areas of endeavors, and is seen by some as an attribute of postmodernity and the growing pursuit of heritage of all kinds (Conran, 2006; Kim & Jamal, 2007). The approaches vary, for example, Boorstin (1961) saw tourists as being duped and seduced to visit contrived attractions; MacCannell (1973, 1984, 1992a) viewed tourists as modern pilgrims in search of the authentic. Belhassen *et al.* (2008) recognized three different facets of authenticity. (1) Objectivist approach, which assumes that authenticity emanates from the originality of the object. It presupposes that the existence of authenticity as an entity can be measured and evaluated. (2) Existential approach, raised by Wang (1999, 2000), that authenticity dwells on the feelings of tourists rather than the toured objects. (3) Constructivist approach, focusing on the process of the discourses, where authenticity is viewed as symbolic embodied with imagery, expectations and powers. Authenticity is, therefore, a slippery and contested term. Jack and Phipps (2005) pointed out that it has become 'a perennial cul-de-sac' in tourism research since 'intercultural communication' is constantly changing. Nonetheless, authenticity discourses have proliferated, since they inherently embody a myriad of concepts, such as tradition, culture, heritage, legacies, commodification, performance and many others.

There is a growing consensus (Cohen, 2002; Taylor, 2001) that authenticity is a negotiable concept depending on state regulations, the visitors, tourism businesses and the host communities and their knowledge of, and belief in, their 'own' past. Each stakeholder can create their own subjective framework of what constitutes the authentic aspects of ethnic tourism. The pursuit of authenticity is what Michel Foucault (1980: 109) refers to as 'regimes of truth', made by authorized stakeholders and accepted by society as a whole and which are then distinguished from false statements by a range of different practices. The pursuit inherently involves tensions between authority and autonomy, localization and globalization, evolution and museumification, etc. However, given the verisimilitude nature of authenticity, it is necessary to shift the discussion to a more traceable dimension, rather than asking what is or is not to be considered authentic in tourism, or what represents an authentic reconstruction of culture and heritage, it would be better to ask questions such as: who benefits from authenticity? (Barthel-Bouchier, 2001). Shepherd (2002: 196) argued that the current research on authenticity should have 'less focus on identifying what has been commodified and hence no longer counts as "authentic" and more attention on the question of how authenticity is constructed and gets decided'. Jackson (1999: 101) proposed to 'abandon the search for "authenticity" and to examine more tractable question of "authentification" (identifying those who make claims for authenticity and the interests that such claims serve)'. Reisinger and Steiner (2006) echoed that the focus on object authenticity, a term used for the genuineness of cultural presentations, should be discontinued, since there is no common ground as to its the existence, meaning or importance. The debate on authenticity is what German philosopher, Immanuel Kant, refers to as 'subjective universal' judgments – meaning that judgments are subjective and are not tied to any absolute and determinate concept. Ryan (2003) further queried whether 'authenticity' is an adequate framework of analysis and proposes 'authorization' as a more appropriate term. As commented by Grünewald (2002: 1018), 'authenticity in whose eyes?' will be more important to discuss in the field of tourism. All these arguments are very similar to my perspective in advocating an emphasis on *authentication*, which is a negotiated attribute with multiple dimensions whose status is evaluated differently by different assessors. The goal of this book is to investigate the processes of authentication through which the identified groups and interests make claims for authenticity and attempt to legitimate their constructions of ethnicity and culture. Meanwhile, commodification could be 'the necessary evil' of cultural revival, further suggesting a more complex perspective: that commodification and authenticity are not a dichotomous pair of concepts. Commodification does not necessarily destroy the meaning of cultural products, either for the locals or for the tourists (Cohen, 1988). Commodification of cultural expressions can be interpreted as a means of marking and valuing identity and a step in the finding of the true self through the appropriation of heritage.

The Approach of this Book

The common thread of this book is a shifting of emphasis away from authenticity of ethnic culture, an issue widely discussed by tourism researchers, to the processes of authenticating ethnic culture. Instead of asking whether a particular dance performance or ethnic artifact is authentic or not, the study of authentication asks whose interests are served by a specific version of ethnic tourism. In short, the focus is not on what ethnic tourism is, but why it is that way, not on what it does as much as what has been done to it.

The process of preparing this book has been bracketed by two major factors: (1) the booming economy in China has reshaped the landscape of ethnic communities; and (2) the status of ethnic communities during the process of ethnic tourism development. My first fieldwork on Hainan Island was undertaken in the early 1990s, when tourism was a burgeoning business and the ethnic Li minorities had yet to realize its potentials. The first folk village opened in 1992 near the city of Tongzha (now Wuzishan) in response to increased demand on the part of tourists to experience ethnic cultures when driving down the central route. The first folk village, called '*Fan Mao*', was an actual Li minority residential community. Tourists spent an hour or so touring the village and experiencing the 'back-stage' life of the Li minority people. A primitive thatched hut was built for ethnic dance performances. It is worth noting that the original idea for the folk village was not commercially oriented. Rather, it was designed to showcase ethnic culture and life, to satisfy tourists' curiosity. Thus, the initial tourist village was strong on authenticity with minimal commodification of culture. In the late 1990s, with the development of the economy, commercial activities were dominant in each of the ethnic villages and little attention was given to sustainable development. Ethnic tourism was perceived as a 'gold rush' with a sharp rise in these purpose-built folk villages. Ethnic Li clothing became a business uniform and the 'traditional' dance perfor-mances were seen as 'manufactured' routines. In recent years, the development of ethnic tourism has gradually changed the social structure of the ethnic minority and caused the relocation of expressions of their culture. Instead of touring several folk villages, tour guides select only one village on the tour route. Consequently, opportunities for interaction between tourists and ethnic minorities have been influenced by transport planners and tour operators, as well as the managers of the folk villages.

Although the relationships between ethnic tourism and political power have been widely discussed in a variety of contexts and locations, they are the most influential factor in China. Ethnic minorities are peripheral to the national class system since the power is not evenly distributed within the nation. Minorities are often perceived as being lower than the lowest ranking, with individuals assigned to the bottom rung of the hierarchy in a stratified society (Swain, 1993). Harrell (1995a: 3) labeled these ethnic minorities as 'peripheral people' since the Chinese government has for a long time developed a 'stigmatized identity' to create a sense of ethnic minorities as being backward, uncivilized, dirty, stupid, and so forth. Ethnic minorities are generally depicted as women (i.e. erotic, promiscuous having not yet learned the proper civilized morals of sexual repression); as children (i.e. childlike and desperately needing civilizing education); and as ancient (i.e. primitive, unchanged or living fossils) (Harrell, 1995a). The term 'ethnicity' is also defined based on cultural distance from the Han Chinese (Oakes, 1997). The objective in identifying ethnic groups and fostering regional autonomy was to determine which areas and people were underdeveloped and most in need of efforts to upgrade their cultural, economic and social conditions. Ethnic minorities in China 'are expected to ultimately evolve into assimilated members of the majority patriarchal socialist society' (Swain, 1993: 9). Therefore, authentic tradition is interpreted as 'a dominant culture's expectations of a subordinate group's traditions' (Oakes, 1992: 12), and the Chinese government continues to play a fundamental role in deciding ethnic identity. The greater authenticity does not imply greater benefits for the ethnic communities, but implies greater social control over ethnic representation and interpretation by the authorized stakeholders. The government in China serves as a promoter, regulator and purveyor of cultural forms, while also validating ethnic group awareness and legal rights. State policies on the ethnic minorities can positively or negatively influence tourism development. On the other hand, the unevenly distributed powers in lower levels, such as provincial and local governments, provide differing views on authenticating ethnic tourism. Lukes (2005) proposed three aspects of the decision-making process: (1) a one-dimensional view focuses on conflicts and decision making; (2) a two-dimensional view acknowledges both decisions and non-decisions in favor of special interests of one group over others; and (3) a three-dimensional view centers control over the political agenda and identifying latent conflicts. Perhaps ethnic tourism in China is still in the one-dimensional view where decision making is firmly controlled by the governments at various levels (e.g. national, provincial and local). Ethnic communities have little or no say in terms of the development and community participation is virtually non-existent. However, the top-down system also provides a fertile ground for various levels of governments to exhibit different attitudes toward ethnic tourism development, e.g. the national government pays more attention to the autonomy control, while the provincial government is more interested in economic development by using the ethnic resources and the local government knows better to exercise cultural power to attract tourists. As asserted by Richter (1989: 2), '[ethnic] tourism is a highly political phenomenon, the implications of which have been only rarely perceived and almost nowhere fully understood'.

While this book uses a specific tourist destination in a region in China as its analytical focus, it would be misleading to say that this work is a 'case study' per se, or a work about Chinese ethnic minority to the exclusion of other considerations. Indeed, one of the central assertions of the work is that to discuss ethnic Li minority is inherently to draw connections, comparisons, articulations and overlaps with other places, because that is what ethnic tourism is: an activity that involves various stakeholders, each with competing goals and desires.

The book is comprised of eight chapters that describe and analyze different aspects of ethnic tourism in the Li community on Hainan Island, China. Each chapter begins with an anecdote from news reports or academic books to illustrate tensions in the relationship between tourism and various ethnic groups. Not limited to the Chinese context, but also international topics, such as the use of *Lo auténtico aún existe* at the beginning and the end to highlight the contested meanings of authenticity.

Chapter 1 provides the broad intellectual context for the work as a whole as it considers the variability and the mutability of the concept of authenticity generally and ethnic tourism in particular. I examine a theoretical background for ethnic tourism and argue the need for ambiguity and hybridity to understand the complexity of ethnic tourism. Chapter 2 focuses on the concepts of authenticity and commodification as the definitive problems. The argument for seeking the definition of authentication I espouse throughout this book is: a negotiated attribute with multiple dimensions whose status should be evaluated differently by different assessors. I have proposed a conceptual framework on the issue of authentication by identifying key stakeholders involved in ethnic tourism and describing these stakeholders based on the existing literature, particularly in the Chinese context. Among many groups of people with interests in ethnic tourism, four key stakeholders were identified for investigation: (a) governments at various levels, (b) ethnic communities, (c) tourists and (d) tourism businesses. I suggest that stakeholders, in their evaluation and attribution of authenticity, may be assessed according to their positions on five continua. These continua constitute paradoxes and tensions within ethnic tourism, and they occur because of the inherent contradictions between stability and change that are found in processes of development:

(1) Authenticity versus commodification: this is essentially an indicator of contemporary performances of authenticity in ethnic tourism. The dichotomy between authenticity and commodification provides an endless debate on how to use ethnic resources and how to development tourism in a balanced way.

(2) Economic development versus cultural preservation: development implies change and although many changes may be desired, not all are desirable. This dimension thus suggests a possible tension and trade-off between economic enhancement and cultural maintenance.

(3) Cultural evolution versus museumification (the 'freezing' of culture): dynamic cultures are not static but evolve. Thus, although

there are signs and symbols with strong associations with particular ethnic groups, this perspective suggests a more 'situational' view of culture, with ethnicity being continually renegotiated.

(4)   Ethnic autonomy versus state regulation: in the case of ethnic minorities, this dimension contrasts the common desire of minority peoples to control their own destinies in the face of the power that is commonly vested in the majority and the state.

(5)   Mass tourism development versus sustainable ethnic tourism: this dimension contrasts a desire to seek tourism development at almost any cost against a perspective that sees tourism as one possible means of contributing to the well-being of communities, economically, environmentally and socially.

Chapter 3 builds on the theoretical framework detailed in Chapter 2 by focusing on Hainan Island. I examine how the typical images of this place, and in particular the growing tourism industry, can occlude tensions between ethnic communities and other stakeholders. I trace the history of tourism development on Hainan Island and examine the involvement of ethnic Li minorities in the tourism industry. I discuss Hainan's unique geographic characteristics, environment, economy, the growth of tourism and its ethnic culture. Tourist-oriented folk villages have been identified as a significant convenient point of access for investigating the tensions in authenticating ethnic resources. In this longitudinal study, all folk villages were visited, photographed and inventories of their tourism offerings were made during 10 years (1999–2009). A map of comparison was provided to show the changing distribution of villages. Managers of the folk villages were interviewed to ascertain information on their perceptions of authenticity. Interviews were also conducted with employees of folk villages and interviews and a survey were undertaken with tourists at three selected villages.

Chapters 4–7 analyzes the findings by arraying stakeholders on five pairs of paradoxes that constitute a conceptual framework for the examination of authentication and to test the utility of this framework. I study the perspective on authenticity at three different levels (e.g. national, provincial and local) in Chapter 4, interview the perspectives of the Li dance performers as part of the ethnic minority on the authentication of their culture, heritage and identity in Chapter 5, survey tourists' perspectives on the authenticity of folk villages in Chapter 6, and analyze the perspectives from tourism businesses on the authenticity of folk villages in Chapter 7.

If the central assertion of this work, then, is that authentication of ethnic tourism must be interpreted in light of stakeholders' relationships, I suggest in Chapter 8 that different stakeholders have differing positions on ethnic tourism. Considering the discourse of the involvement, I encounter a particular problem, namely, the five proposed continua, which are interacting and overlapping during the process of authentication. It can be understood as 'mazeway resynthesis' (Wallace, 1956: 266) whereby stakeholders' involvement is inextricably intertwined. Authentication is, in fact, a system for managing equilibrium in order to maintain the degree of cultural tensions by identified stakeholders. I also suggest that economic activity in ethnic tourism involves these stakeholders whose views should be considered when development takes place: the vulnerabilities need to be taken into account when strategies are forged. Strategies for development should focus on fine tuning these imbalances to ensure optimal results. For example, the governments should work closely with tourism businesses to avoid negative implications of economic development. Tourism businesses should be involved with ethnic communities to set up a sustainable development agenda. Furthermore, village businesses need to provide an informative introduction for tourists so that they become acquainted with ethnic cultural development.

In the epilogue, I consider the recommendations for future tourism development on Hainan Island, outline the broader theoretical implications of the research and suggest additional avenues that can be taken for future research in ethnic tourism. This book aims to expand the possibilities for an ongoing dialogue in the study of authenticity. I offer perspectives on how the views of the traditional ways of authenticity should be modified. A new emphasis on authentication is a necessary goal of ethnic tourism, which demands that both tourism researchers and practitioners address inherent cultural tensions by identifying those who are involved during the process of the movement and those who construct a progressive relationship. Giddens (1984), tracing French historian Fernand Braudel's terminology, refers to the goal as a *longue durée* with respect to the impacts of tourism on ethnic communities in the myriad shapes and this is the objective that will be pursued throughout this study.

Chapter 1
Tourism and Ethnic Peoples

Introduction

The Opening Ceremony was the highlight of the 2008 Olympic Games in Beijing, China. It started at 8:08 pm on 8 August, reflecting the Chinese belief that eight is a lucky number. One of the most exciting parts of the ceremony was a group of children marching together with the Chinese flag. The children were dressed in the elaborate costumes of China's 56 ethnic groups, including the Han majority (about 90% of the population). The intent of the ceremony was to showcase ethnic harmony and to foster patriotism toward China as one nation. A little girl standing on the top of the podium sang 'Ode to the Motherland' as the 56 children smiled and paraded slowly around the stadium.

It was a powerful portrayal of the multi-ethnicity and the unity of the nation. The audience roared with cheers and the Chinese media enthusiastically announced to the world that '56 children from 56 Chinese ethnic groups cluster around our Chinese national flag, we are one family'. However, a week after the Opening Ceremony, news leaked that the little girl chosen for her appearance was lip-syncing to a recording of another girl, deemed not pretty enough and so replaced. Perhaps even more significantly, it was also revealed that the 'ethnic' children were all members of China's dominant Han population, not from the other 55 ethnic groups as claimed. According to a British newspaper, *The Independent* (15 August 2008), the apparent fakery did not trouble Chinese officials, as one bluntly told the press that 'it is typical for Chinese performers to wear different apparel from different ethnic groups, there is nothing special about it', and most importantly, 'they will wear different apparel to signify [ethnic] people are friendly and happy together'.

The ethnic children's performance during the 2008 Olympics Opening Ceremony provides an excellent example to illuminate the dimensions of two basic concepts in this chapter: ethnicity and authenticity. Perhaps both are a Pandora's Box containing the paradoxes of all mankind. An abiding concern has been the implications of ethnicity viewed as a fixed and absolute attribute. The issue of authenticity is of concern to postmodernism in general and is easily applied to tourism. It is assumed that authenticity is a positive attribute, opposed to commodification, fakery and consumerism. Contrary to these views of ethnicity and authenticity, the Opening Ceremony in Beijing demonstrated that neither ethnicity nor authenticity seemed to be important as long as the event succeeded and the spectators had a good time. As Nyiri (2006: 80) commented, in China, 'authenticity has not been a concern of the modern, and theming is not necessarily a product of the postmodern. "Culture" and "development" are seen as synergetic rather than antithetical'. The official's rebuttal highlighted that ethnicity is a mere cultural display, albeit a complex one, that can be reconstructed or reproduced. It is a tool used by the government to 'otherize' groups whose appearances are different from the Han majority. Authenticity is important only to the extent that its markers, e.g. performance imagery and ethnic costume, can be used to achieve a desired effect. There is an urgent need to have an in-depth understanding of ethnicity and authenticity, particularly to locate both notions in a wider system in relation to the postmodern literature. Some larger concerns here are the [re]structuring and [re]presentation of ethnicity and the contestation of authenticity in the field of ethnic tourism.

The use of the term ethnicity is a complex and problematic one. Ethnicity inherently embodies an undertone of 'minority issues' and 'race relations' (Eriksen, 2002) that include aspects of group relationships: how they view themselves and how others regard them. Tambiah (1995) suggested that ethnic identities are composed of inheritance, ancestry, place of origin, skin color, language, religion and any combination of these. Most importantly, ethnic identity is a conscious construct that can substantiate many elements of an ethnic system for political and social purposes. McLean (1997) argued that the term ethnicity carries a markedly pejorative connotation. He pointed out that its original meaning from Greek and Latin denoted those beyond the borders, the uncivilized and the barbarians. In the USA, ethnicity came to be used as a civil term to describe those non-White Anglo-Saxon Protestant (WASP) individuals during WWII and its use continues to describe a certain 'racial' characteristic. In this vein, West (1999) has argued that discourse on ethnic differences from a Western perspective has been undeniably racist, guided by a philosophy of identity, which serves to devalue multiplicity and heterogeneity. The concept of ethnicity is largely dependent on the assumptions of identity, uniformity, universal discourses, fixed centers, established authority and order (Bredin, 1993).

What is commonplace and persistent in discourse about ethnicity is the recurring argument as to whether it is a fundamental distinction among human groups or a constructed formulation that continually changes. The former view is central to those theorists who hold that ethnicity can be identified and categorized. The diversity among human groups, with regard to such variables as race, language, religion and heritage, serves as differentiating criteria. However, ethnic classifications have increasingly come into question, particularly when origins are mapped onto differential access to resources (Levine, 1999). Ethnic identities often have crucial consequences when important resources are allocated on the basis of ethnic classification. The establishment of the Native American Reservations in the USA and Canada, for example, represents a typical method of administratively controlling the identities and resources of ethnic groups. Boundaries between the reservations and the lands belonging to the majority culture can be maintained; thus, assimilation or amalgamation is not ideal for preserving the ethnic identities. Emphasis on aspects of group life that are primitive and uncontaminated, such as unexploited or undestroyed resources, reinforces a sense of ethnic particularity. Tensions between retaining a closed or 'pure' ethnic identity and exchanging cultures with others persist because they ultimately reflect the struggle to determine the basis on which 'self' and 'belonging' are defined.

A growing body of research on the restructuring of ethnicity has been carried out by anthropologists and sociologists. Fredrik Barth's (1969) 'boundary maintenance'; Abner Cohen's (2004) 'instrumentalist' and 'circumstantialist' position; and Clifford Geertz's (2000) 'primordialist' view of ethnicity are examples of such research. Eriksen (2002: 4) proposed that ethnicity is fundamentally 'an aspect of a relationship, not a property of a group'. Cultural distinctiveness and racial categorizations that seek to present ethnicity as an absolute defining criterion for identity face a number of challenges. The first such challenge is the reality that ethnicity can be negotiated, emerged, hybridized and syncretized. Not only can it be the result of a process of self-identification from within a group given a multiplicity of social groups in modern societies, ethnic identity is often shaped from without the groups themselves. In 2000, the US Census allowed respondents to declare two or more races for the first time and it is estimated that mixed-race individuals number 7.3 million nationwide (US Census Bureau, 2000). A second challenge to the view of ethnic identity as an absolute, distinct characteristic is the reality that multi-ethnic societies have emerged in many contexts, making it difficult to formulate a static framework for ethnicity. Hyder (2004) claimed that despite calls for a reassertion of ethnicity and cultural authenticity, new multi-accented and syncretic identities become increasingly hard to ignore. A third challenge to an essentialized view of ethnic identity is reflected in the reality. Identity itself can be disrupted, reassembled and intermingled over the course of individuals' experience. The thrust of this scholarship is to assert that cultural authenticity and 'pure' ethnic identities are patently exposed.

Furthermore, cross-cultural interaction does not erode the specificity of ethnicity. Ethnicity has increasingly become a commodity that is relentlessly focused on, since purity is an illusion for sale. A salient example can be seen in the words, *pure laine*, literally meaning 'pure wool' in French, employed in Québec, Canada, as a way to determine a Québécois identity. The words reflect a desire to establish a connection with ancestors from France and a desperate longing to be an independent nation. Nonetheless, the concept of *pure laine* has taken on a pejorative and discriminatory flavor given the shifting demographics in Québec because of the immigration of other ethnic groups. It has become increasingly difficult to define the *Québécois de souche* (old stock Québécois) given immigration and a broader desire for multiculturalism in Canada. Immigrant culture can both reinforce and add to the traditional Québécois culture. Although there is a concern about the identity crisis in Québec over the future of the French language, culture and the integration of immigrants, being Québécois is composed of the ambiguities and complexities of multi-accented identities, much closer to what Pierre Nora (2001) called *'les lieux de mémoire'*, environments of intimate memories of the past.

The political use of cultural symbols and commodification of ethnic identities to amplify nationalism is widespread in multi-ethnic countries. As Anderson (1991) has pointed out, a nation is 'an imagined political community' and ethnicity is considered as a 'structure of feeling' embodied in material practice and lived experience. State-organized social activities, such as special events or tourism, tend to seek the unity and harmony of different ethnic groups or to exhibit the success of assimilation and acculturation. Eriksen (2002) coined the term 'ethno-genesis', meaning the emergence of ethnic relations and identities through historical changes or political interferences. There are several conceptualizations that have shaped ethnogenesis in various countries: the Chicago School's metaphor of the 'melting pot' has been widely accepted in the USA when dealing with ethnic groups from various backgrounds; Joseph Stalin's emphasis on a common language, territory, economic life and psychological make-up to forge a national identity was adopted in the former Eastern Bloc countries and China; and the metaphor of a 'cultural mosaic' has been used in Canada, Australia and the UK as a framework for relationships among ethnic groups. Although each of these conceptualizations appears to affirm the importance of ethnic differences, an examination of the official discourse of ethnic policies of these countries reveals an ambivalent, often contradictory, attitude toward ethnicity. Although models, such as the 'melting pot' or multiculturalism, have the objective of fostering tolerance and equality for different ethnic groups, often they end up as divisive efforts for social control by the majority culture. The self-declared independence of Kosovo in Europe in February 2008 provides a vivid example that ethnicity remains a thorny issue in determining the national identity despite a persistent assimilation policy and the economic benefits offered by the majority. The dichotomous dynamics of nationalism and localism, globalization and localization, identities and loyalties, ethnicity and nationhood often cause tremendous tensions when ethnic groups strive to define their relationship to Otherness.

Issues of contestation and representation are constantly recognized as central to ethnical bases of tourism contexts where ethnic minorities are dominated by a metropolitan core of the majority. In a world of global homogeneity, the desire for an encounter with the Other has allure since it can promote a sense of cultural absolutism where the Other is supposed to be distinctively unique and seemingly authentic. Ethnic identity can be manipulated to fit the contemporary needs of the society or those of so-called 'authentocrat' tourists who staunchly adhere to all things authentic. The commodification of ethnic groups' histories and heritage may result in differing interpretations: 'specific pasts' and 'rewritten pasts' (Hollinshead, 1997: 179). Similarly, Baudrillard (1995), in the book *Simulacra and Simulation*, distinguished between what he called 'dissimulation' and 'simulation' for modern tourism: dissimulation involves the masking of reality by presupposing its absolute existence; simulation, on the other hand, 'devours' reality, leaving nothing except signs that merely refer to each other. Given the ubiquity of the mass media, simulation becomes the most prominent source and purveyor of 'reality'. The notions of 'deconstruction', 'invention of tradition', 'recycling of tradition' and 'authenticity' once again become buzz words to explore the impacts of exogenous forces, such as tourism encroachment on ethnic communities. The key issue is how to conceptualize ethnic tourism in such complicated circumstances and how to find linkages among ethnicity, culture, tradition and heritage.

There is a dearth of literature about ethnicity, authenticity and tourism from different philosophical approaches, particularly from a postmodernist perspective (Wang, 1999). This chapter will aims to examine contemporary debates around ethnicity and tourism and focus on the important understanding of ambiguity and hybridity by using Foucault's (1976) eye-of-power, Saïd's (2003) Orientalism and the 'third space' concept of Bhabha (2004). Ethnic tourism involves the technologies of gazes, what I call 'ethnic panopticon', where tourists and ethnic minorities interact in a rational-disciplinary matrix with the time-space compression. I will argue that the notion of ethnic ambiguity and hybridity is of critical utility in challenging the assertion of essentialized ethnicity. Ethnic culture is a *bricolage* of mixing, melding and merging with other cultures in various periods of time. I analyze the concepts of authenticity and commodification, a traditional dichotomy in tourism studies from a postmodern perspective.

Ethnic Panopticon

Michel Foucault's exploration of the relationship between knowledge and power in his book, *Discipline and Punish: The Birth of the Prison*, marks a shift in the traditional research in the social sciences. The metaphoric idea of 'technology' and internalized disciplinary practice, as demonstrated by Foucault (1980), posits a control that combines both detachment and mastery of forces. A number of 'technologies' manage and discipline prisoners who are under the continual surveillance of a gaze that has the power to punish them. The technologies of power encompass the relationships between individuals, the organizations, and even the State. Foucault draws on the work of the 18th-century philosopher Jeremy Bentham's prison concept of panopticon, to conceptualize the interactions among power, technology and observation. Foucault described Bentham's panopticon as:

A perimeter building in the form of a ring. At the centre of this a tower, pierced by large windows opening on to the inner face of the ring. The outer building is divided into cells each of which traverses the whole thickness of the building. These cells have two windows, one opining onto the inside, facing the windows of the central tower, the other, outer one allowing daylight to pass through the whole cell. All that is then needed is to put an overseer in the tower and place in each of the cells a lunatic, a patient, a convict, a worker or a schoolboy. The back lighting enables one to pick out from the central tower the little captive silhouettes in the ring of cells. In short the principle of the dungeon is reversed; daylight and the overseer's gaze captures the inmate more effectively than darkness, which afforded after all a sort of protection. (Foucault, 1980: 147)

As one can imagine, panopticon is a remarkable prison model in which the power of the gaze results in self-control and self-regulation by the prisoner. The panopticon is an apparatus, a 'machine of the visible' based on a 'brutal dissymmetry of visibility' (Friedberg, 1994: 17) that permeates the guard–prisoner relationship. The structure of the panopticon is designed to permit the guards to see their prisoners without their being seen. Even though there might be no guards working in the central tower, Foucault pointed out that the effect of lighting and the carefully placed blinds prevent prisoners from knowing that at the given moment they feel under observation. This combination of observation and power dominance gives the gazer (guards) a sense of omnipresent voyeurism and the gazee (prisoners) a feeling of inescapable surveillance.

Foucault's conception of *le regard* has induced a special type of gaze – 'panoptic gaze' — wherein the subject is placed in a condition of inescapable visibility. The subject thus can only imagine that everything he/she does is viewed by the guard. The panopticon's purpose is to create a highly efficient mechanism to control prisoners, and has a reflective impact on the prisoners' psychological behavior. Strain (2003: 27) characterized the technology of panoptic gaze as 'the constant push and pull of distanced immersion, by the desire to be fully immersed in an environment yet literally or figuratively distanced from the scene in order to occupy a comfortable viewing position'. Foucault's discernment is that the creation of a gazer–gazee relationship characterized by an imbalance of power and distance between the two, results in an immensely powerful control system. Surveillance ought to occur involuntarily whenever distance separates the functioning of the subjugated (i.e. those supposedly receiving the power) and the dominating (i.e. those supposedly wielding the power). The distinctiveness of the roles reinforces the sense of identity because each must fit in the designated construct. The process prompts the prisoners in the cells to self-regulate consistent with the rules or the standards of conduct set by the prison. Foucault called this conformity with the rules, *practique de soi*, a self-directed process designed to meet societal expectations. An advantage of the panoptic model is that it tends to make corporeal punishment unnecessary because confinement can be successfully maintained by just the structure of the prison and the prisoners' expectation that they may always be under scrutiny.

The significance of the gazer-gazee construct has had a profound impact on research in many fields. Almost all institutional settings can, as Hollinshead (1999a) has suggested, be conceptualized from a panopticon perspective; that is the eye-of-power/eye-of-authority/the new-power-of-universal-surveillance. The gazer–gazee perspective entered the discourse of tourism studies with the publication of John Urry's book, *The Tourist Gaze*, in 1990. Urry masterfully applied Foucault's *le regard* to the context of modern tourism by problematizing the interrelated complex roles: tourists and tourees. The eye-of-power construct has become institutionalized within the tourism industry by viewing the tourist role as a dominant one, driven by the expectation of receiving pleasurable (through distance) experience with less advanced tourees. From a distance, tourists cast a privileged 'eye' on tourees as they see, understand and appropriate desired things, although there is a clear segregation between 'front stage' and 'back stage'. Tourees are encouraged to act or behave exactly according to what tourists expect, so that smiling faces are shown and photos can be snapped.

Most importantly, the gaze of tourists ensures the sustainability of power structures since various stakeholders stay involved in tourism development. Urry suggested that tourees as ethnic minorities are aware of being observed by tourists and they are requested to 'perform' in ways that emphasize their difference from tourists. The tourist/touree relationship centers on 'romantic gazes' that are systematically constructed on the participants' beliefs that there are racial, linguistic, cultural and historical differences between the two groups. The ocularcentrism in tourism, as proposed by Urry (2002), authenticates tourist gazes in order to allow tourists to gratify their needs.

I argue that Foucauldian *le regard* can serve to highlight two critical aspects of ethnic tourism, which I call 'ethnic panopticon': (a) the Other as a distant object within a structured power relationship and (b) the structuring of the Other as a consumable product spatially and temporally. The first of these aspects involves defining some behavior as normal and some as deviant by the gazers. There is a tendency for gazee–gazer (or host–tourist) relationships to be unequal and unbalanced in character. The panopticon as a model for incarceration is based on perspectives of power and the 'subject of power' (Foucault, 1980) to control the relationship between gazers and gazees. Tourists (the Self) and the ethnic minorities (the Other) are allowed to interact within a matrix of rational-disciplinary relations characterized by time-space compression. The life of ethnic minorities is viewed as remote, exotic, sensual, primitive and servile, and dependent on tourists for survival and modernization.

Nagel (2003: 14) suggested that ethnicity and sexuality are interrelated in the process of commercialization. Erotic locations and exotic destinations, such as ethnic folk villages, are 'surveilled and supervised, patrolled and policed, regulated and restricted, but that are constantly penetrated by individuals forging sexual links with ethnic Others across ethnic borders'. Ethnic tourism uses the technologies of gaze to enable tourists to take possession of ethnic minorities from a distance. It can be noted that the distance between tourists and ethnic minorities can be perceived, imagined, reconstructed and phantasmagoric. Ethnic tourism provides an excellent opportunity to compress time-space in order to validate a healthy definition of Self through visiting ethnic villages and attractions. The socio-cultural gap between tourists and the host cultures is clearly manipulated since distinct differences are required to define social relationships, history and identities.

According to Bauman (2000), the voyeuristic gaze on the Other is deemed to be optimal since tourist–host interactions tend to be fleeting and fluid. Such transience of contact favors and promotes distance and casts the Other as an aesthetic object to be viewed from different angles. Tourists visiting ethnic sites experience various times and sites of ethnic progression (or regression). To some extent, the tourists and the Other come together, though at a distance in an artificial space. In this sense, tourists are like the prison guards in the central tower of the panopticon while ethnic minorities are the prisoners confined in the cells, the objects of an imagined scrutiny, where the internalized expectation of surveillance changes the imposition of external power, in this case, tourism. The eye-of-power can exist due to the perceived distance where both tourists and tourees consciously and effectively follow the *practique de soi*. Bruno (1993: 201) described tourism as 'lust of the eyes'. Curiosity about the Other motivates tourists to visit the division between the ordinary (mainstream culture) and the extraordinary (minority culture). However, the vigor of that curiosity reinforces the notion that 'such gazes cannot be left to chance. [Tourists] have to learn how, when and where to "gaze"' (Urry, 2002: 10). Borrowing Foucault's concept of *heterotopias* (places outside all places), ethnic tourism fosters the location of tourists' contact with ethnic minorities in settings different from the tourists' everyday experience. Globalization and commodification of ethnic culture, as tourism impinges on the communities, induces tourists to superimpose their imagination on the Other, and to create nostalgic representations of the past for contemporary consumption.

The simulation of Other as a consumable product closely resembles the lighting effect in the panopticon: the prisoners are prevented from seeing the guards in the central tower but believe they are regularly watched perennially. Such one-way vision works perfectly well in the context of power and dominance. Tourism turns out to be an imagined landscape, including sensescape, soundscape, smellscape, tastescape and dreamscape, manufactured for consumption (Spang, 2000; Strain, 2003). Tourees may be unaware of social change or tourist tastes (as obstructed by the lights and blinds in the panopticon), however, it goes without saying that an exotic 'Other' is most likely to attract tourism business. Romanticized primal or undeveloped ethnic people are most effective in stimulating the fantasy of tourists. In modern society, the mobility of tourism allows tourists to travel to distant ethnic destinations, many of which are not ready to accommodate them. Through the gaze, ethnic tourism in this case, becomes marked and ritualized as an open text, hence evoking 'the idea of dynamic construction, of an open and complex organization' (Casetti, 1998: 8). Ethnicity henceforth becomes the decoded message while tourists become the spectator and the decoder. As a decoded message, the meaning of ethnicity is 'read' by many tourists from different cultures, languages, genders, races, social classes, to name just a few. Hunter (2001: 43) suggested that the tourists in a panopticon setting are 'trapped in an invisible glass cage, able only to gaze out at the "other's" body, an indecipherable text, a confusing, foreign combination of signifiers'. The tourist–host relationship is context-bound and embedded in barriers of differences. Ethnic performance is socially and spatially regulated to varying extents. The 'encountering space' between tourists and tourees is staged and contrived for the convenience of consumption. Ethnic culture should be frozen since museumified heritage will arouse the interests of the tourists. Tourism as an industry manipulates social power and is a key factor for the construction of culture and heritage.

Ambiguity and Hybridity

Influenced by Foucault's work on power and knowledge, Edward Saïd's (2003) magnum opus, *Orientalism*, introduced the binary structure of ethnicity in an increasingly complex world. According to Saïd (2003), orientalism is a corporate institution where the West can dominate, restructure and exert power over the Orient. Inspired by Foucauldian conception of discourse, Saïd focused on a dialectic of dominant/dominated, colonizer/colonized, hegemony/resistance and majoritarian/minoritarian. Rather than 'discourse of the same', the social constructs rely on the division to justify the oppression or control of the Other. Orientalism uses categories dividing the world into the West and the East, or Orient, thereby becoming 'a powerful tool for one part of the world to validate, institutionalize and privilege the Other' (Bryce, 2007: 167). The East is characterized as mysterious, exotic, backward and despotic in order to justify acts of colonialism. Power imbalance existing on economic and ideological levels between two worlds is the root cause of civilization. The line of reasoning defines mainstream culture (or Eurocentrism) as a construction, anyone who does not fit instantly becomes the Other.

Modern cosmopolitanism spans geography and cultural differences that are not bound by political boundaries of the societies. It is a dominant psychological feature in the developed world to position things in and of the world (Hollinshead, 2004). The recent television program entitled 'Living with the Kombai Tribe', aired by the Discovery Channel, reveals the striking contrast between the Self and the Other in terms of civilization and neo-colonization. The program features a group of White male adventurers living with the Kombai tribe in the jungles of West Papua, New Guinea. The advertisement claimed that the tribe's lifestyle, dubbed as 'stone-age', has remained unchanged for 15,000 years. The White adventurers had to go around naked, except for wearing leaves or penis gourds. They live in treehouses above the ground and eat food that no member of Western society would imagine ingesting. The narrative also mentioned that cannibalism is still believed to take place among the tribes, therefore, these adventurers were at risk of being eaten. The 'Living with the Kombai Tribe' program can be seen as reinforcing Saïd's view of 'The Other question', in which stereotypes and the discourse of colonialism are necessarily inseparable, creating a fantasy world of cultural differences to consume.

Although Saïd's *Orientalism* has drawn criticism for its simplistic dyadic view of the world; especially in light of the recent trend of reverse-Orientalism, in which the rising incomes of an Asian middle class demand 'Westernness' on display. Nonetheless, it has received a positive reception in tourism studies because the majority of research is taking an etic and often Eurocentric view of cultural authenticity and commodification (Cole, 2007). Hall and Tucker's (2003) work, *Tourism and Postcolonialism*, echoed Saïd in asserting that tourism per se encompasses contested discourses, identities and representations. They held that tourism in postcolonial times can be interpreted as a form of 'leisure imperialism', 'the hedonistic face of neocolonialism' or 'a new colonial plantation economy' within which the tension between identity and authenticity occurs concomitantly. The bifurcation of 'developed' and 'underdeveloped', or 'traditional' and 'modern', has established the Other as a commodity for consumption. Hall and Tucker (2004) suggested that the binary structure proposed by Saïd has a profound influence on ethnic tourism since tradition and change, authentic difference and cultural homogenization are critical issues in postmodern and postcolonial times. Tourism researchers have argued about the impacts of tourism on 'traditional' and 'authentic' cultures and have discussed ways to preserve heritage. The binary perspective serves to make the critical point that ethnic culture can be renegotiated in its entirety. For example, cultural preservation will be advocated when commercialization becomes pervasive; or economic development will be prioritized when the community endeavors to capitalize on the cultural heritage as a means of tourism resources. The dichotomy identified by Saïd serves to further our understanding of cultural differences under the influences of postcolonial existence.

Saïd's *Orientalism* also exemplifies the power of discursive authority in the process of tourism development. By determining itself to be the holder of reason and modernity, the West separates itself from the Orient and becomes the standard to which all other cultures must be compared (Bryce, 2007). Hechter's (1999) 'internal Colonialism', identified two types of struggles between ethnic minorities and majorities in terms of assimilation and acculturation. 'Diffusion' leads to ethnic homogenization while 'internal colonial' heightens unique ethnicity. The latter has become a conscious process to reify cultural differences, unique customs and distinctive cultures. Ethnicity is an imagined construct designed to substantiate Western or the majority's needs. In other word, the West or the majority of the population hold 'flexible positional superiority' (Saïd, 2003: 7) to control the East or the minority. Harrell (1995) used the term 'civilizing projects' to describe governments' policies toward ethnic minorities – a systematic cultural assimilation and acculturation over the periods of time. Ethnicity is viewed as feminized and infantilized in public that civilization is a pretext for control ethnic minorities.

In a homogeneous nation, such as China, ethnic minorities are asked to re-enact the past in order to accommodate the needs of the majority for diversion. Jacques Lacan (2006: 75–81) labels this phenomenon as a 'mirror stage'. The purpose of the mirror stage is to establish historical identities that justify majority domination over minority Others, or to allay narcissistic anxiety about the Self. Lacan (2006: 197–268) puts forward three categories to describe this type of human psychoanalysis: (a) the Imaginary, (b) the Symbolic and (c) the Real.

Imagined category illusions are characterized by synthesis, autonomy and similarity. Tourists are in pursuit of the dreamed Shangri-La, the lost horizon where encounters with ethnic minorities are supposed to be spontaneous and idyllic. The majority of tourists are excited minority performances as they travel. Tourism provides a theater of memory to represent these historically displaced minorities to the majority.

Ethnic tourism in the Symbolic category consists of a series of markers and signifiers of transformed ethnicity, conducive to the limited gaze of tourists. It is a fantasy journey of signs, impressions and aesthetic consciousness. Many ethnic performances for tourists are truncated, simplified and rendered less dissonant to cater to the visitors. Tourists can get what they want to see and know by filtering untreated strangeness, or reinforcing the nostalgic images they hold.

The Real, an original category synonymous with authenticity, is identified by Lacan as 'the impossible' in postmodernity because it is impossible to imagine, to integrate what into the Symbolic, and to be achievable. Given this situation, ethnic tourism turns into a cultural pilgrimage and tourists are in search of 'hyperreality' (Eco, 1986: 1). Thus, the pursuit of the Real in ethnic tourism becomes centered on desire, instead of reality. It focuses on seeking a stamp of approval from the ethnic minority. Zizek (2000) has argued that the desire of the Real is not to realize its goal, but to transform itself into desire since authenticity cannot be achieved but needs to be continually quested. Zizek called this quest a 'monster of desire' because the search for something non-existent can be overwhelmingly powerful.

Foucault's *le regard*, Saïd's critique and Lacanian psychoanalysis are clearly points of departure for my discussion of ethnic tourism, but I also draw directly on Homi Bhabha's (2004) thesis on *Location of Culture*. Bhabha has another important postcolonial theory that incorporates hybridity, mimicry, difference and ambivalence. Bhabha acknowledged that traditional colonial discourses, such as the Self and Other, promote a powerful stereotype of the colonized as the fixed Other inferior to the colonizer. Once this polarization is accepted, it serves to legitimize conquest, surveillance and control. In Saïd's Orientalism model, the processes of assimilation and acculturation are products of one-way contact, e.g. colonizer to colonized. In reality, ethnicity is an ambivalent concept that should not be regarded as solidly distinct or as pervasively particular. The symbolic elaborations of ethnicity require separate from reductionism, such as the dyad of Orientalism. Bhabha directs the attention to what happens on the borderlines of cultures, to ascertain what occurs in-between cultures (Huddart, 2006). There is a need to transgress the boundaries of colonial discourse and re-examine the Self/ Other dichotomy. Bhabha uses a metaphor of the 'third space' as a stairwell, the corridor that connects difference:

> The stairwell as liminal space, in-between the designations of identity, becomes the process of symbolic interaction, the connective tissue that constructs the difference between the upper and lower, black and white. The hither and thither of the stairwell, the temporal movement and passage that it allows, prevents identities at either end of it from settling into primordial polarities. This interstitial passage between fixed identifications opens up the possibility of a cultural hybridity that entertains difference without an assumed or imposed hierarchy. (Bhabha, 2004: 4)

The 'in-between' space of liminality truly reflects the dilemma in modern tourism that the tourist gaze has increasingly become mobile, portable and culturally promiscuous (Strain, 2003). The idea of liminality is transformational, where practices, cultures and identities are positioned between the global and local, the public and private, and fluid and solid spaces. The process of liminality views cultures on a border or a threshold and exoticizes extreme cultural differences or conflicts as a source of beauty. The 'in-between' people, such as ethnic minorities, previously marginalized and suppressed, suddenly find they can empower themselves through showcasing their ethnic culture and heritage. Tourism becomes a new channel for these in-between people to legitimize themselves in public. 'Split locations' or 'fractured identities' (Hollinshead, 2004) can produce new definitions of peoples, places and pasts; therefore, ethnic culture is viewed as inherently hybrid and socially constructed. It is a nostalgic form of remembering ethnic discourse, but does not necessarily define what ethnicity is. Hollinshead (2004) has summarized that cultural hybridity is (a) a liminal space or interstitial passage between fixed identifications; (b) a 'third space' to avoid the politics of polarization and radicalization; (c) an emergent cultural knowledge that resists unitary and ethnocentric notions of diversity; (d) a space between received rules of *a priori* cultural engagement and antagonistic forms of cultural representation; (e) a fantastic location of cultural difference where identities continually open up for changes; (f) a social utterance that undergoes historical transformations; and (g) a continuous negotiation and encounter over differential meanings of culture. Hybridity holds that cultures are not discrete phenomena existing on an island; instead, they are always in contact with one another, and this contact leads to cultural mixed-ness (Huddart,

2006). Ethnic tourism is a collage, an assemblage of different forms of ethnic presentations, and an eventual creation of a new ethnic identity.

Hybridity typifies a poststructuralist approach, which asserts that differences and complexities are the key aspects to be researched. One academic contention is hybridity and mixed-ness are the antithesis of purity. 'Impurity' of cultures is commonly seen as being inauthentic within a loss of provenance. The presentation of ethnic cultures, e.g. in arts performance, is constantly questioned as authentic due to the popularity of mass tourism. Nederveen-Pieterse (2001) countered that the problem does not lie with hybridity, but the fetishism of boundaries that has marked history. An 'authentic' culture favors the unexpected, fortuitous and hybrid. The significance of the debate of authentic culture depends on what Bahbah (2004) called 'an active agency', where cultural meaning should be negotiated by a variety of parties. In that case, the complexities of a world become a form of resistance, played by different stakeholders, in order to find a suitable equilibrium, i.e. the location of the culture, as in the title of Bhabha's book. In addition, hybridity and liminality are not only spatial entities, but also temporal ones as they relate to the perceived modernity or backwardness of certain cultures. Stereotyping discourse of processes and performances captured in exhibitions tend to be inaccurate.

Vergès (2001) presented a case study on the term 'ethnic Creole' throughout the world. He noted that the term takes different meanings with regard to its geographical, linguistic and historical location. The term 'creolization' is widely used to describe processes of deterritorialization, hybridity and mixing, since Creole identity is characterized by a variety of changes and fluidity and constant re-adaptation. Creole can be viewed as a polemical character of colonialism and an ethnic identity without a home. Although Creole can be narrowly interpreted as the mix of New World and African slavery, it is rarely used to identify a single identity owing to the range of how it is defined in Latin America. For example, in Brazil, Creole is a term for a dark-skinned group that has predominantly African ancestry, while in Haiti it refers to light-skinned persons of partial European ancestry. Vergès (2001: 179) has offered the general view that creolization is not multiculturalism, nor the paradoxes of postmodern subjectivities, rather, it is a condition that produces rootless identities that grow as rhizomes. It is more important to focus on the relationships rather than on affiliations, ancestry, blood and land. The Creole identity reflects what Bhabha called 'third space', a translocal circuit of culture and heritage born 'in-between' with a context of cosmopolitanism (Gilroy, 2000). The multiplicity of Creolization demonstrates that ethnic identity reflects a desire for tourism consumption, but it has little meaning for social reality. In a similar vein, Françoise Lionnet's (1995) theory of *métissage*, a process of cultural mixing between Indians and French through marriage in Canada, results in 'transculturation'. The Métis have long been treated as Franco-Canadian even though they would more appropriately be viewed as an ethnic minority belonging neither to Franco- nor to Anglo-Canada. As Lionnet has pointed out, *métissage* demonstrates that

> a process of cultural intercourse and exchange, a circulation of practices which creates a constant interweaving of symbolic forms and empirical activities among the different interacting cultures... reciprocal influence is the determining factor here, for no single element superimposes itself on another; on the contrary, each one changes into the other so that both can be transformed into a third. (Lionnet, 1995: 11–12)

Therefore, hybrid culture is a moving culture having a holistic character including a set of changing values and beliefs. Those values and beliefs are associated with differences attributed to national, regional or local identity. The increasing mobility of contemporary globalization facilitates the transient encounters between tourists and the host communities and fosters cross-cultural communication. In tourist–host encounters, cultural forms, which do not belong to any particular culture, may be viewed as hybrids (Rojek & Urry, 1997). Meethan (2003) further criticized the definition of the local as unitary and essential while the translocal is considered to be simply 'outside', 'other' and 'in-between'. In reality, the museumified local is an illusion whereas the mixing of cultural forms is a constant. Meethan (2003: 19) has argued that 'rather than solving the problem of essentialism or transcending boundaries as it may first appear, hybridity, and for that matter creolization and other cognate terms simply confuses [ethnic identities]'. Concerns about the decay of ethnic cultures due to the influx of tourists should not be viewed as a threat. Ethnic cultures have been continuously deterritorialized and deconstructed at various periods of time. The hybridizing process is the localizing or indigenization of cultural forms that are the systematic conditions of maintaining cultural distinctiveness. The concept of hybridity is a red herring since hybrid culture may already become an authentic culture, *ipso facto*. Nederveen-Pieterse (1995) suggested that cultures can no longer be thought of as exclusively territorial in their scope since locality is not diminished in its importance despite all forms of tourism encroachment. Culture is not a static container insulated from the real world, it is a self-definitive process in order to achieve socio-economic and political benefits.

Chapter 2
Authenticity and Commodification

Introduction

On 23 January 2008, *The Wall Street Journal* published an interesting report on how Disney localized the Mickey Mouse character to boost its Hong Kong theme park. Mickey Mouse is undoubtedly an authentic American cultural icon even though it was artificially created by Walt Disney in 1928. The globalized Disney has built Disneylands on various continents. Hong Kong Disneyland was one of the latest expansions. It targets Chinese consumers who were expected to understand Disney, or so it seemed. Unfortunately, Chinese tourists, unfamiliar with Disney's traditional stories, were sometimes left bewildered by the Hong Kong park's attractions. Products shipped directly from the USA often lacked interpretations and were confusing for people without a knowledge of Mickey Mouse. In order to accommodate Chinese tourists, Disney decided to change several characters, e.g. the bearded Chinese God of Wealth was introduced. The contrast of having an ancient Chinese character standing side-by-side with Mickey Mouse was amusing, but was readily accepted by the tourists and park staff alike. The authentic American icon, Mickey Mouse, also appears to be shaped to meet the taste and demands of the Chinese tourists. For example, modifications of Mickey Mouse's personal traits were made to reflect Chinese culture. Since cheese is not popular in Chinese cuisine, a showcase inside the kitchen of 'Mickey's House', a new attraction at the Hong Kong park, displayed his favorite cheeses from Europe and North America and a steamed rice-flour cake from China.

Disneyland is an example of a purpose-built theme park constructed in the era of postmodern culture. It provides an ideal setting for tourists to enjoy contrived presentations and created characters. Disneyland is a microcosm of fantasy and imagery where Mickey Mouse and Snow White dance hand-in-hand on Main Street. Perhaps Disneyfied theme parks are such an oxymoron in the lexicon of tourism studies that few researchers find them authentic. Disneyland is in the tourism business, selling the experience that tourists want. It does not try to indoctrinate tourists, rather, it strive to illustrate the 'real' past. Ritzer and Liska (1997) concluded that

Disney's theme parks came of age in the same era as McDonald's fast food, that McDisneyization is the product of postmodernism. The principles of McDisneyfied tourism require a highly controlled, efficient and predictable system, therefore the search for authenticity in a Disneyland is necessarily a futile one. On the flip side, Disneyland is indeed widely regarded as a commodified authenticity. Mickey Mouse was a fictitious character originally created by Walt Disney, but he has become an authentic American icon after years of marketing and promotion. It is a classic example of 'emergent authenticity' because something is produced for the sake of tourists' needs but eventually becomes the authentic thing. The steamed rice-flour cake display in Mickey's House is another challenge to Mickey's authenticity because as an American mouse, this food should be totally foreign to him. It would be inauthentic to place the rice cake in the house pretending that he would enjoy it as much as the cheese. The juxtaposition of American cheese and Chinese rice as a creative idea is obviously de-territorial and misplaced. However, tourists are receptive to the display that heightens their involvement with the theme park. In addition, taking pictures with the Chinese God of Wealth and Mickey Mouse is a popular thing to do during a visit to Hong Kong's Disneyland. Tourists seek 'experiential authenticity' where the original objects are no longer meaningful. The authenticity centers on being believable rather than being original. What is taken to be authentic in a Disneyland does not remain static, but is continually renewed in different contexts and nations. Gardner (2005) pointed out that the problem of authenticity in the postmodern period is that 'the authentic' has collapsed and has been replaced with a 'logic of inauthentic authenticity'. Grossberg (1992: 201) espoused the idea that in capitalist societies, there is no true, authentic folk culture against which to evaluate the 'inauthenticity' of popular culture.

Stephen Fjellman's (1992) book entitled *Vinyl Leaves: Walt Disney World and America*, is an in-depth analysis of the authenticity of Disney's theme parks. From Fjellman's perspective, the Walt Disney enterprise creates a utopian antidote for daily life, like the vinyl leaves that beautifully adorn the artificial trees in the park. The pretend authenticity in which the Disney products are packaged makes it impossible to analyze the experience objectively. Not only is Disney specialized in marketing the product to attract tourists, but it is also capable of converting the fake into the authentic. The Disney approach decontextualizes the original context that prevents people from a coherent understanding: Mickey Mouse and American history, the fake and the authentic, are given an equal foothold in the Magic Kingdom; the Moroccan tent and the

Chinese pavilion, the fake and the fake, are erected side by side as 'touristic icons' in Epcot Center. Disney manipulates history into 'distory' or 'historicide' (Fjellman, 1992: 87) of the past while tourists are immersed in an 'imagineered' world where authenticity is not important. Fjellman (1992: 9) argued that corporate capitalism heightens the attractions so that 'the commodity form is natural and inescapable'. A Disney park, like any other amusement park, realistically performs what tourists want to experience, rather than what tourists need to know.

The intriguing thing about Disney's culture is that inauthenticity emerges out of the very attempt to retain or regain authenticity. The growing preponderance of the fakery, as presented on the massive scale of the theme park, does not necessarily detract people or diminish the interest of the tourists. If Fjellman's 'distory' is indeed a disaster, why are tourists still willing to engage in these activities? If the 'imagineered' world of Disney is widely viewed as inauthentic, why does it continue to attract tourists from far and wide? Perhaps the answer lies in the perception of an authenticity that derives from 'the property of connectedness of the individual to the perceived, everyday world and environment, and the processes that created it' (Hall, 2007: 1140). In this case, the Disney enterprise's tendency to 'reproduce' culture in staged settings as an integral part of commodification is identified as a major marketing tool to attract tourists. Perceived authenticity is the key whereas enclavic tourist space offers the connection with an out-of-everyday environment. Kirshenblatt-Gimblett (1998) suggested that in the context of theme parks or special events, the access to authenticity lies in a moment of aesthetic reception, rather than in the objects presented. The only time tourists experience the authentic is when they encounter things that they do not understand, thus requiring them to make up their own minds about what they see.

As noted at the end of the introduction, I suggest that the discourse of authenticity be viewed as *longue durée*, an ongoing process resulting in multiple layers of hybridity. The current concept of authenticity essentially ignores the evolutionary nature of culture and heritage. By putting forward a life cycle for authenticity within the context of ethnic tourism, I endeavor to demonstrate a distinctive feature of the ethnic cultures; that is a process of mixing, which accelerates and becomes wider in scope as time passes (Nederveen-Pieterse, 2001). The proposed life cycle for authenticity shows the power plays of various stakeholders as they attempt to influence the course of ethnic tourism development. Tourism research needs to shift the attention on how authenticity is constructed and who influences the decisions about that construction. As

Duval (2004: 72) commented, 'when tradition and identity are invented, the differences between the sacred and the profane become moot, just as the argument for authentic/inauthentic does little to capture the process or meaning behind culture tourism'.

I propose that it is important to shift the direction of research from authenticity to authentication. In other words, it is more useful to identify the positions of the stakeholders who authenticate ethnic tourism and its resources. The focus of this chapter includes identification of stakeholders according to their relationships with ethnic tourism development in China, assessment of the implications of power and paradoxes, and management strategies and practices related to their position on authenticity. After reviewing the ethnic tourism literature about China, four key stakeholders are identified: (a) governments, (b) tourism businesses, (c) tourists and (d) ethnic communities. Five paradoxes, modified from Swain's (1989) work, serve as yardsticks to measure the perspectives of these stakeholders regarding authentication. A conceptual framework is developed to present the perspectives of the four identified stakeholder groups on authentication.

The Definitions of Authenticity and Commodification

Defining authenticity has proved to be enduringly problematic, if not pointless. Research on authenticity confirms the difficulty of defining something that is complex and contested and is fraught with contradictions and paradoxes. In addition, authenticity is a loaded word used in daily discourse and may carry a variety of different meanings. According to Bhabha's poststructuralist approach, authenticity is the quandary of the stereotype; that is, a false representation of a given reality. It is a Eurocentric view of the process inextricably intertwined with power and culture (Cole, 2007). Saïd's *Orientalism* illuminates that authenticity is negotiated and reconstructed by various cultures, notably by those who can exercise the colonizer's control. That model of authenticity is a static representation that does not have the complexity of differences and is limited in its ability to account for the importance of psychological and social relationships. It is suggested that authenticity stands in opposition to the commodification of modern society and the advancement of industrialization, where pre-modern is regarded as authentic and modern as inauthentic. However, authenticity is not an entity, but a feeling, referred to by Jean-Jacques Rousseau as *'sentiment de l'existence'*, central to the power relationship and anchored by self-affirmation and discovery (Damrosch, 2005). In the context of ethnic tourism, the pursuit of authenticity is to reify the past in terms of a nostalgic yearning for the Other and to deny the present in order to establish a distinctive Self. Ethnicity has been transformed into an army of semiotics, labels and markers that need to be certified as authentic. Without these markers, ethnic tourism could not be experienced as authentic.

The concept of authenticity has long been discussed *ad nauseam* across many intellectual fields, and can be seen in German philosopher Johann Gottfried Herder's enlightening declaration that 'we each have an original way of being human' (Goldberg, 1994: 78). A preoccupation about authenticity has gradually crept into tourism because of the field's interdisciplinary nature. Authenticity presupposes a quality of the object that can be assessed and examined by different groups. For tourism, authenticity can be seen as objectivism, which imposes both distance and truth. There exists an interaction in authenticity between object and subject, there and here, past and present (Taylor, 2001). While tourism establishes contacts between individuals, disconnect between tourists and residents remains a dose of reality. Tourist attractions, such as theme parks and folk villages, market authenticity but may thwart the tourists' assumed desire for genuine experiences. Perhaps the challenge within the 'tourist–the Other' relationship is lack of 'intimacy' (Conran, 2006; Trauer & Ryan, 2005) required to fully appreciate the intricacy of minority culture and heritage. For instance, ethnic dance performances take place in a given tourism encounter and generally allow for little personal contact between guests and ethnic hosts. Cultural performance tends to rely on caricature and stereotype. Often, the more structured the event and the shorter the visit, the less opportunity tourists have to make genuine contact with local communities. Because tourists are denied contact with the performers who, for the most part, remain on stage, such performances transmit the over-signification of an identity of difference (Taylor, 2001). Palmer (1994) suggested that ethnic tourism should be viewed as 'enclave tourism' in which cross-cultural understanding is discouraged in favor of voyeurism through a clear demarcation between the tourists and locals. As I have proposed earlier, ethnic tourism can be viewed as an 'ethnic panopticon', which applies temporal and spatial distance between subject and object in an effort to present something culturally 'authentic' in order to make the products valuable and unique. Authenticity has its value only where there is perceived inauthenticity.

Goffman (1959) first divided authenticity of experience into 'front' and 'back' regions. The front region represents and presents inauthentic, contrived experiences while the back region represents and presents authentic, intimate experiences. In the modernist critical tradition, culture 'on stage' is viewed as culture out of context because 'the moment that culture is defined as an object of tourism, or segmented and detached from its indigenous sphere, its aura of authenticity is reduced' (Taylor, 2001: 15). The first complete debate on authenticity in tourism was initiated in MacCannell's (1976) book entitled *The Tourist: A New Theory of the Leisure Class*. MacCannell (1976) asserted that tourees, the ethnic communities confronted with the arrival of visitors, guard their culture by dividing their lives into 'back stage', where they continue traditions away from the gaze of visitors; and 'front stage', where they perform a limited range of activities for a visitor audience. The argument assumes that touristic cultural performance, which MacCannell called 'staged authenticity', is less authentic than practices not performed for visitors or for the commercial purpose. MacCannell described tourists are interested in penetrating the marginal communities, such as the Hill Tribes of Thailand. They want their visits to be 'authentic', not 'packaged'. However, their quest for authenticity is always doomed to failure because tourists seek superficial and manufactured experiences, described by Boorstin (1961) as 'pseudo-events'.

In his sarcastic chapter entitled 'Cannibalism Today', MacCannell (1992a) proposed the terms 'ex-primitive' and 'performative primitive' to designate what he calls 'a special ethnological class or category'. Similar to the thesis of Saïd's *Orientalism*, the cannibalism of culture is defined as a feature of capitalism, a Western ideology that has abandoned its authenticity in the quest for modernity and technology. However, MacCannell (1992) insisted that tourism is a perpetual quest for the authentic where 'the distinction between the authentic and the inauthentic, the natural and the touristy, is a powerful semiotic operator within tourism' (Culler, 1981: 131). The search for authenticity remains a major driving force behind modern tourist behavior since tourism permits the release of more 'authentic' selves. However, the quest can never be fulfilled because the 'ex-primitive other' is in diametric contradiction to modernity. MacCannell pessimistically predicted that there is no salvation in modern tourism to resolve this paradox. At best, there is the creation of a 'false touristic consciousness', a product of a commodity-driven industry that would trick tourists into accepting that contrived attractions are, in fact, authentic.

With the concept of authenticity being widely applied in tourism studies, its ambiguity and limitations have been increasingly exposed. In recent years, tourism scholars have suggested that cynical tourism commentators, such as MacCannell and Boorstin, have probably overstated the importance of authenticity. This argument challenges the traditional divide between authenticity as objective, passively inherited, embodied and transmitted, versus authenticity that is solely the result of human self-consciousness in the contemporary context. The case study of Disneyland in Hong Kong indicates that the binary of the front and back stages is not as distinctive or important as originally anticipated. Oakes (1998), following his fieldwork with the ethnic minority in Guizhou, China, concluded that cultural tourism is the 'misplaced search for authenticity', which represents a false conception of modernity. Bruner (2005: 146) rejected MacCannell's view of authenticity as 'an essentialist vocabulary of origins and reproduction' because a single real authentic culture does not exist. He also challenged Baudrillard's concept of simulacra that 'what is presented in tourism is new culture constructed specifically for a tourist audience', by arguing that, 'there is no simulacrum because there is no original' (Bruner, 2005: 5).

Cohen (1988, 2002) argued that 'authenticity' is socially constructed and its social connotation is not given but is 'negotiable' with various stakeholders and that authenticity and falseness are not dichotomous concepts; rather, he asserted, authenticity is spurious essentialism because all culture is mere social construction, constantly re-invented to serve present purposes, in our completely heteroglot milieu (Handler & Linnekin, 1984). Authenticity is not equal to historical accuracy, and tradition is not equal to truth (Preston, 1999). The quest for authenticity should be judged against varying types of visitor profiles (c.f. experimental visitors, experiential visitors, recreational visitors, and diversionary visitors). Wang (1999) criticized the constructivist perspective that authenticity is often viewed as object-related and applied only to a narrow range of tourism. Instead, he categorized three types of authenticity in terms of tourist experiences: (a) 'objective authenticity', which refers to the authenticity of original and authentic experiences in tourism equated to an epistemological experience (i.e. cognition) of the authenticity of originals; (b) 'constructive authenticity', which refers to the authenticity projected onto toured objects by tourism producers in terms of their imagery, expectations, preferences, beliefs, powers, etc., thus, the authenticity of toured objects is in fact symbolic authenticity; and (c) 'existential authenticity', which refers to a potential existential state of being that is to be activated by tourist activities and can have nothing to do with the authenticity of toured objects. Wang (2000) asserted that existential authenticity can be examined at intra-personal and inter-personal levels. The former relates to bodily feelings of pleasure, spontaneity and control, while the latter is a sense of togetherness in families, among friends and other social networks. Authenticity can be experienced when tourists meet 'authentic' people in certain contexts that are not necessarily related to a front stage or a back stage setting. Wang (2000) suggested that it is an over-generalization to claim that all tourists are searching for authenticity. Rather, it can be viewed as a factor in tourism motivations composed of two elements: behavioral and situational. Authenticity implies a combination of an appropriate setting, representing a back stage social environment, and a set of appropriate actions by the visitor, such as eating local cuisine and meeting local residents. At the same time, inauthenticity is not inherent in the touristic experience, but a variable that depends on the expectations and goals of the tourist.

A major dilemma for tourism research has been the endless debate about the availability, validity, reliability and comparability of authenticity as determined by a variety of measures. Existing research has acknowledged authenticity as having a substantial role in the discipline and in critical cultural practice. Nonetheless, there is no consensus among researchers on how to measure the concept of authenticity, which is elusive and often illusive. Academic endeavors have been made in recent years to develop a framework for indicators of authenticity (Jamal & Hill, 2004) by using objective (real), constructive (socio-political) and personal (phenomenological) measures to describe the relationship between tourists and tourism businesses or to define authenticity by seeking the determinants (Chhabra, 2005). Because authenticity is not a 'primitive given' (Cohen, 1988: 379), but something that emerges in the social processes, it will be more useful to understand the stakeholders in social development, what I refer to as 'authentication'. To avoid the confusion, research should focus on how authentication is carried out as a particular culture's form of expression by institutionalizing and authorizing social practices and knowledge. Bruner (1994), Wood (1997) and Taylor (2001) have raised the important question: 'who has the right, authority, or power to define what is authentic?' Power relationships in tourism are dynamic and periodically changing. I would argue that power relations are the essential ways to probe authentication and that authenticity should be examined through a life cycle where stakeholders are actively involved in each stage.

The following section (Xie & Lane, 2006) proposes the idea of applying a life cycle model to the impact of tourism on the authenticity of ethnic cultures, including arts, music, dance, etc. It is noted that vibrant cultures are subject to change and may evolve in response to both internal and external stimuli. Since tourists are unlikely to have been a part of traditional societies, their mere presence is a catalyst for change. Ethnic cultures, as presented by a variety of arts performance, can be viewed as an amalgamation of different stages with the concept of authenticity as relative rather than absolute. A five-stage process of change is put forward from organically evolved primordial conditions to a complex multi-authenticity situation in which management rather than organic growth is the dominant feature. The life cycle model seeks to help understand an increasingly complex world in which ethnic tourism can decline, survive or change, and in which tourism's demands and opportunities have powerful roles. Most importantly, it demonstrates that authenticity is a mutable concept that evolves in various stages of ethnic tourism development. In the process of authentication of ethnic cultures, various stakeholders play an important part.

The Life Cycles of Authenticity

Wallace (1956), employing an anthropological approach, proposed a processual model of revitalization movements. It portrays an initial steady state followed by various external changes that trigger a period of revitalization, eventually returning to a new form of steady state. Wallace's model has proved to be a good tool for understanding ethnohistory and cultural movement (Harkin, 2004). According to Wallace's model, ethnic cultures are subject to a revitalization process that consists of five stages: (a) a steady state, when cultural forces exist in a dynamic equilibrium; (b) a period of increased individual stress, when the society has been pushed out of equilibrium owing to external events; (c) a period of cultural distortion, when native cultures have been inadequately adapted; (d) a period of revitalization, when a new plan rises to cope with a distorted culture and a new culture is established with its own methods for handling change; and (e) a new steady state, where new codes are enforced and a fresh equilibrium evolves. The whole movement can be understood as a process of 'mazeway resynthesis' (Wallace, 1956: 266), whereby exogenous factors, such as tourism development, may affect the ethnic culture and create a new type of arts performance catering to tourists. Ethnic tourism is a system for managing equilibrium and maintaining cultural authenticity. It can 'fail' or 'die out', but still continue to influence ethnic cultures for long periods.

In a similar vein, Willis (1994), through extensive research on ethnic arts performance, provided a paradigm of the development of expressive culture from its indigenous beginnings to mass culture commodification. By utilizing folklore and neo-Marxian frames (Hebdige, 1988), Willis delineated the first level, or 'folk culture', as a 'tribal mode of production with traditional practices that enhance people's spiritual or secular lives' (Willis, 1994: 179). Here a 'tribe' is any group of people having the same habits and ideas, etc. She called the intermediary stage of expressive culture, 'popular culture'. It is this stage where indigenous producers continue to be the primary consumers of the practices, but the culture is often taken outside the original site of its production. The arts performance, at this point, transitions the culture from its folk origins to a popular level of consumption. Finally, cultural practices grow so popular that they become a part of mediated 'mass culture' where a 'distinct separation between those who control and produce the cultural commodity and those who buy it' takes place (Willis, 1994: 179).

Giddens' structuration (1984) theory adequately addresses what Wallace's mazeway resynthesis and Willis's (1994) paradigm mean in sociological research. His underlying assumption is that social structure and action are evolving and constantly influenced by individual agents. A social structure including the elements of tradition, heritage, culture, etc., can be transformed when people start to ignore, replace or reproduce them. The transformation cannot happen overnight, but can be done by an incremental social force. These gradual changes, i.e. *longue durée*, take place at a micro level with a traceable and identifiable cycle. Although Giddens has not used tourism as a case study to substantiate the theory of structuration, it is a typical social force impacting the everyday world and changing the way people think. It is evident that the debate on authenticity in the context of tourism will not be complete without an embodiment of social forces, both internal and external, which could be random, ephemeral, contradictory and fluid. I believe that *longue durée* is essential to understanding the complex of authenticity, which has gone through various stages of evolution, culturally and historically, within a dynamic context. Since the concept of ethnicity is hybrid and liminal, there is no stable referent on which authenticity is based. The meaning of authenticity is not history, rather, it is a nostalgic process realized in material objects, such as performing arts or craft, sites, special places and even whole landscapes. Through the pursuit of authenticity by a variety of stakeholders, the present touches the past, the modern glorifies the ancient. Bruner (1994: 408) commented that authenticity should be seen as 'a struggle, a social process, in which competing interests argue for their own interpretation of history'.

The theoretical framework of the present study (Figure 2.1) draws mutually compatible ideas from the literature in the above fields, particularly from Wallace (1956), Giddens (1984) and Willis (1994). The argument presented here incorporates the notion of a life cycle. This life

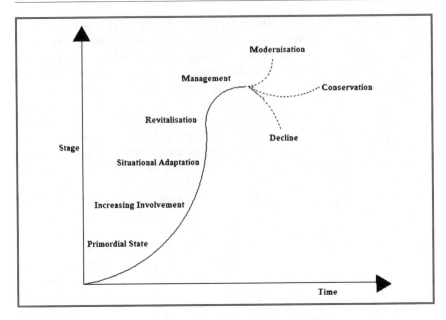

Figure 2.1 The cycle of authenticity (after Butler, 1980)

cycle is based on the classic S-shaped product life cycle, widely accepted for most consumer products (see, e.g. Wilson *et al.*, 1992) and translated into relevance for the world of tourism destinations by Butler (1980). It is recognized that there are criticisms of this basic life cycle concept (see Doyle, 1976; Lumsdon, 1997); these will be discussed later in this chapter.

It is proposed that the relationship between ethnic tourism and authenticity is subject to a change and potential revitalization process that consists of, at least, five stages:

(1) The primordial state, when tourism is in a primitive stage with few external influences.
(2) Increasing involvement, when tradition is pushed out of equilibrium owing to external forces, such as the development of ethnic tourism, or political pressures, or local population movements, inward or outward.
(3) Situational adaptation, when ethnic tourism has gone through 'cultural involution' (McKean, 1989: 126): here the forces of tourism can inject new meanings and/or values into current cultures, and eventually culture and tourism become inseparable.

(4) Revitalization, when ethnic performers and performances rise to cope with a stressed/distorted culture and a new culture is established with its own methods for handling change that turns the commodified ethnicity into an 'authentic' cultural expression. To some extent, the original meaning, however defined, may have been lost.

(5) Management, where new codes are introduced and a new equilibrium evolves. Conscious management in Stage 5 contrasts with unmanaged organic growth in Stage 1. Under management, the ethnic arts performance can change in three ways. It may be rejuvenated to further restructure, 'improve' and make the performance 'new'; it may strive to return to an earlier 'authentic' stage; it may stagnate as a result of social or economic transition and/or changes in visitors' tastes.

The purpose of the proposed life cycle is twofold. Firstly, it combines the concepts of authenticity and commodification encompassed by each stage of the model, in order to construct a progressive relationship, a *longue durée* with respect to the impacts of ethnic tourism. Here, the varying significance of authenticity may lead to the invention of a new cultural performance for the purpose of attracting visitors and turning it into something 'inauthentic'. Authenticity and the forces of commodification necessarily operate within this conflictive arena (Greenwood, 1989). Secondly, the proposed life cycle aims to be a basis for a form of management tool, which can further understanding and monitoring ethnic cultural change. The implementation of a more sustainable tourism is not a spontaneous and unplanned phenomenon. Management is the hallmark of both sustainable tourism and the fifth stage of the proposed cycle.

The primordial state

Ethnic cultures in this stage reflect strong identity as primordial sentiments. The performances are the product of spontaneous improvisation depending on the quality and quantity of ethnic community experiences, especially the intimate relationships between individuals and nature, history and beliefs (Diamond *et al.*, 1994). The primary focus of the performances is group affiliation rooted in a primordial sense of shared descent (Van den Berghe & Keyes, 1984). Cultural knowledge based on real or assumed ancestry is used to explore the symbolism of sound and image in the performance. Ethnic performances are used to express a strong cultural identity that becomes symbolically, emotionally, religiously and politically significant to ethnic people. One example is the 'Ghost Dance' in the USA at the end of the 19th century, when Native Americans used dance performances to reunite with friends and relatives in the ghost world. This dance form eventually turned into a strong political movement against white settlers (Kehoe, 1989).

The concept of authenticity in this stage can be summarized as a set of symbols that are interpreted as concrete embodiments of ideas, attitudes, identities, religions, etc. Ethnicity can serve as a model for 'cultural functionality' because it supplies symbols after which other non-symbolic processes can be patterned (McLean, 1997). Ethnicity provides templates for producing and reinforcing cultural authenticity. In general, dances and ritual performances 'give meaning or objective conceptual form, to social and psychological reality both by shaping themselves to it and by shaping it to themselves' (Geertz, 1973: 39). Tradition, defined as those ideas and practices before the arrival of outsiders (Kaeppler, 2004), is the central focus of ethnic arts performance. For the outside observers, an ethnic arts performance has an air of reality, which derives from a traditional perspective and can be analyzed scientifically and appreciated for its aesthetic features; for performers, it is a way to realize their ethnic identity through re-enactment and materialization. Arts performances become rituals by following entrenched cultural conceptions and directives (McLean, 1997). For example, ethnic rituals and dances performed by shamans in Asia and Central America are devoted to telling the patient the cure, or to communicating with dead ancestors (Cauquelin, 2004). Within the performance, emotions and objectives are stimulated by both sacred symbols and the belief systems of the culture (Anderson, 1991).

This unity of the cultural ethos is evident in the more sophisticated ceremonial performances. These types of ceremonies are not only models of, but also models for, how '[ethnic] men attain their faith as they portray it' (Greetz, 1973: 46). Visual and written documentation provides fragmented glimpses of the presence of the ethnic arts performance, therefore, the concept of authenticity can be perceived as a generic and uncontestable attribute of primary ethnic manifestation. Ethnic arts performances at this stage normally consist only of 'pure' traditions, possibly of great time depth, and are not commercially oriented. Rather, they are designed to showcase ethnic culture in order to satisfy local people and perhaps the curiosity of a small number of visitors. The impact of tourism for the performances in this primordial stage appears to be negligible, directly or indirectly.

Increasing involvement

This stage shows increasing initiatives to market to, and provide accommodation for visitors, resulting in an increased number of outsiders attending the ethnic attractions. It is at this stage that the concept of commodification surfaces with the arrival of tourists to ethnic performances. The process of commodification starts when objects begin to be evaluated primarily in terms of their exchange value, in a context of trade, thereby becoming goods (Best, 1989; Cohen, 1988; Dupre, 1983). Many tourism researchers have been concerned about whether an ethnic performance loses meanings for the communities once it has been commodified (Watson & Kopachevsky, 1994). Authenticity appears, however, to be a flexible notion molded into *ad hoc* resources to be spent in order to achieve economic priorities. MacCannell (1984) has referred to this process as 'reconstructing ethnicity'. Although visitors may be aware that certain ethnic performances are unique, they typically fail to see beyond this façade and hardly ever comprehend profound insights or differences. Ryan and Huyton (2000) suggested that tourists attending ethnic performances are, at best, lay anthropologists and their perceptions of authenticity are a judgment or a value placed on the destination as a whole.

Ethnic performance can be influenced not only by tourists who seek authentic ethnic presentations, but also by other stakeholders, such as governments, local communities and tourism businesses (Xie, 2003a). For example, political interests, in general, view authenticity as a negotiable, not a given, as seen in the Opening Ceremony in the Olympic Games in Beijing, China. Governments can serve as promoters, regulators, funding agencies and purveyors of cultural performances, while also validating the cultural forms to present to tourists. Ethnic communities come to realize that their culture has economic value, and (perhaps because of this perceived 'golden egg' value) they may select certain aspects of a particular cultural tradition and establish boundaries between local customs and cultural performances for tourists that are frozen in time and space (Oakes, 1997). Tourism businesses tend to commodify the ethnic performance to serve economic interests (Xie, 2003b). The primary focus of tourism businesses is usually not protecting the host culture, but rather achieving economic gain and overall economic development through satisfying visitors.

Touristic performance, as a commodity, is viewed as an expression of a 'ritual performed to the differentiations of society' (MacCannell, 1976: 13). It may be simplistic to argue that tourism undermines ethnic culture's integrity and authenticity. As Ryan (1991: 156) has argued, 'some societies may even seek to use tourism as a means of reinforcing their uniqueness to both themselves and to the visitor'. On the surface, tourism's reproduction of ethnic arts performance has been labelled 'retrochic' (Samuel, 1996: 51), favoring style over substance, and 'playing up' by adding elements from the past and present. The ethnic community may consciously try to match tourists' expectations of what is authentic even if the results seem contrived. At a deeper level, the incorporation of tourism in the performances may be viewed as indicating a call for establishing ethnic identity and history by appropriation and changes to the art form (Taylor, 2001). The involvement of tourism may serve to strengthen ethnic identity or lead to 'a renaissance of native cultures' through the performances (Van den Berghe, 1994: 17).

Situational adaptation

In this stage, the growing commodification of an ethnic attraction results in the emergence of a new culture, which is distinct from the traditional practices of 'tourees' and is less authentic because of its qualities of being both 'staged' and used as a commodity. Greenwood (1989) engaged this assumption by asserting that commodification changes the meaning of cultural products and practices to such a degree that they eventually become culturally meaningless; that is, the instruments, repertoires and costumes for visitors may eventually differ completely from those in community use and to some extent, traditional performing instruments may be adapted to new purposes. One opinion may be that the 'staged authenticity' of commodification culture is not authentic at all. Ryan (2002), ignoring concerns for authenticity, suggested that a 'visitor culture' emerges, which is distinct from the daily cultures of either tourists or tourees; tourism can lead to the emergence of a culture different from the original one of the tourees. Cohen (1988) considered that tourism-related cultures may in due course become incorporated into and perceived as manifestations of local culture, and to some extent, are even accepted by the local community.

It is evident that the success of the tourism-focused ethnic performance relies on trade-offs between authenticity and interpretation and understanding of ethnic culture (Altman, 1989; Hollinshead, 1992). Ethnic attraction at this stage becomes a vehicle for explaining culture and translates ethnic features into those with meaning in a wider global community. Cultural differences can be aestheticized and intentionally exaggerated to create a sense of quaintness. Tourists are exposed to ethnic cultures within the context of staged portrayals of traditional life styles (Hinch & Butler, 1996). It is possible that there are no authentic tourist experiences (MacCannell, 1976; Urry, 2002). Rather, ethnic performances are staged for tourists in ways that manipulate cultural traditions and customs (Edensor, 2000). The performances have become a standardized model for proclaiming and establishing ethnic identity.

An example of this can be seen in the work of Mason (2004), who documented the situational adaptation of Native American music performances in Ottawa, Canada. His findings suggested that ethnic musical interpretation was constantly influenced by tourism businesses, changes in federal–ethnic relations in order to challenge non-native stereotypes, and most importantly, re-signification of aesthetic forms with indigenous meanings through musical interaction with visitors. Many visitors are familiar with key symbols and gestures that represent 'native authenticity', although this recognition is based on inaccurate images from the media. Tourism businesses exploited the recognizable features of traditional culture (e.g. sights, music and sounds) expected by their customers and recoded them to reflect the ethnic culture (Mason, 2004). To generalize from Mason's findings, the authenticity of arts performance often means that tourists perceive ethnic people as exotic and quaint rather than members of a dynamic and complex culture (Harron & Weiler, 1992). On the other hand, the inaccurate portrayal of information about ethnic performances and their life style can promote stereotypical images (Dyer *et al.*, 2003), which as Harron and Weiler suggested, may misrepresent the dynamism of ethnic culture by describing aborigines as 'primitive' or 'traditional'. Cultural involution (McKean, 1989) emerges, as tourism injects new meanings into current cultures; eventually, culture and tourism can become inseparable.

Revitalization

This is the stage of ethnic performance that resurrects the original form of the commodity to the extent that it is recognizable to the tourists. Forms are removed from their socio-historical context and given a new meaning by the marketplace. The revitalization can be viewed as a 'cultural revival' process shaped by ethnic communities and outside forces. Grünewald's (2002, 2006) case study explored the changing ethnic arts produced by the Pataxó natives of Southern Brazil. In order to support the communities, the Pataxó began creating handcrafted articles to sell to tourists. The traditional function of the handicrafts has gradually been lost owing to their popularity in the tourist market. The

Pataxó started producing three different categories of handicrafts catering to different markets: those reflecting indigenous traditions, those that are transitional (made by the Pataxó people infused with non-Pataxó elements) and those that are non-indigenous but recognizable as global tourist souvenirs. This segmentation can be seen as 'functional authenticity' because the handicrafts can still retain the internal significance while at the same time they acquire new meanings. As Root (1996: 86) observed, 'interestingly, because the recorded, commodified version of traditional arts retains the external look of the original, and in fact explicitly refers to ways of life presented as existing outside the market, the illusion of seamlessness sometimes breaks down, and visitors occasionally do get a glimpse of something real'.

Authenticity is viewed as an emergent quality, therefore, initially contrived programs may, over time, acquire social recognition as authentic, 'historic', cultural objects or events (Cohen, 1988). Ethnic arts performances are revived and become a new form of cultural identity consumed by large numbers of tourists. Performers may see cross-cultural interaction between themselves and tourists as a way of reducing stereotypical impressions and enhancing understanding. Even though the ethnic performers may be troubled by misrepresentation of their culture, they believe that the performances instil pride and interest in cultural revitalization. For example, the Maori in New Zealand incorporated the historical inaccuracies of early anthropologists into a contemporary understanding of their own culture (Taylor, 2001). Picard (1990, 1996) proposed that the effects of commodification have blurred the characteristics of Balinese cultural performances, because it is difficult to tell what is Balinese and what is the product of tourism's influence for everyone, even for the Balinese people. Therefore, their cultural identity is fluid, mutable, and indicative of various time periods. The ethnic arts performance is seen as remembrance of the 'imagined past' (Hanson, 1989) or as a typical example of 'inverted traditions' (Hobsbawm & Ranger, 1992).

Selwyn (1976: 21–28) proposed revitalization as a division between so-called 'cool' and 'hot' authenticity, in other words, the 'authenticity of knowledge' as opposed to the 'authenticity of feeling' (Wang, 2000: 48). Cohen (2002) further suggested that the permutations of the concept of authenticity reflect the transition of one's society: tradition and 'fixed modernity' are transformed into a kind of 'liquid modernity' (Bauman, 2000: 1). In other words, a shift occurs from the modern tourists' concern with the 'cool' authenticity (e.g. original, pristine, *genius loci*), to the postmodern visitors' quest for the experience of 'hot' authenticity (e.g.

contrived, constructed, existential). These changes may be aggravated by 'genuine fakes' (Brown, 1996: 33) since both 'cool' and 'hot' authenticities cater to tourists' gaze and expectations. Tourists may be satisfied with 'stylistic' authenticity in which the authentic elements of ethnic cultures are combined in an artificial and aesthetic way. The aestheticization of authenticity may be necessarily carried out in terms of aesthetic principle rather than in terms of historic principle, in order to make the authentic entertaining. A piece entitled *How 'They' see 'Us'* by Evans-Pritchard (1989: 97) asserted that Native American women need to 'play the native' in order to be 'accepted as authentic by tourists on whose dollars she depends'. Ethnic arts performance has evolved into a nostalgic experience where culture is molded through different images of the past so that 'either we have not lived the past and rely on the images to create it, or we relive the past through recollected images' (Markula, 1998: 80).

Management: Modernization, conservation or decline

This is a complex stage because the life cycle enters a phase where ethnic arts performance becomes managed not just by the demands of ethnic peoples and the demands of visitors, but by cultural and political commentators, and by cultural and political managers. Management can bring changes of many kinds, and the forces of management can be multifaceted. There may be cultural managers, advising on, and arranging performances; there may be cultural entrepreneurs; also, there may be grant-giving bodies, exerting influence through bestowing, or withholding, funds. Three types of impact can be envisaged:

Modernization: A new form of ethnic performance may be, for example, presented at theme parks or shopping malls where non-authenticity and fragmented cultural forms are conspicuously consumed (Ritzer & Liska, 1997). Given the ubiquity of mass media in the society, simulation becomes the most prominent source and purveyor of 'reality'. In this vein, Baudrillard (1995) argued that we are living in a 'virtual reality'. The concept of authenticity is now part of a modernization process and can no longer be seen as singular because ethnic arts performance can be endlessly copied and extended. The tourism industry tries to present the past and present as unlikely equivalents and to attract tourists through various types of folklore experience. Traditional artistic renditions may be superseded by the best-selling artefacts created in a 'diluted and westernised form' (Turner & Ash, 1976: 141) with an emphasis placed on being commercial, rather than being authentic (Medina, 2003). These renditions frequently take the form of ethnic presentation because the spectacles presented for tourists feature exotic costumes and performers who look different from the visitors themselves. The pursuit of the Other detaches the ethnic arts performance from its context in the local society and traditions and draws it out to the 'front stage' for visitors. The performance becomes part of a framework based on the exchange of cash payments. This transformation affects various aspects of the tradition, for example, dancing clothes become costumes and cultural practices are swallowed by an abstract concept of folklore (Root, 1996). Concern for authenticity gives way to a discourse on how aesthetic forms are utilized, in what context, by whom, for whom and for what purposes (Diamond *et al.*, 1994). Authenticity at this stage is defined by outside forces (e.g. Western exoticism, postcolonialism, postmodernism) and arts performance is dependent on 'the external form of the object, integrity takes into account how and where the object is used' (Root, 1996: 80). 'New' ethnic arts performance can be composed of a range of complex elements incorporated from different fields. Eventually, new forms of authenticity may be created.

A salient example reflecting the modernization stage of management is Hawaii's Hula dance. Ancient Hula dances originated from historical events, tales and the accomplishments of royal rulers. Facial expressions, hand gestures, hip swaying and dance steps all showcased the ethnic identity of Hawaiian Polynesia. Initially, the tourism industry in Hawaii heavily promoted the natural features of the islands, not the ethnic people. However, the figure of the Hula girl first appeared in advertising in 1910. By the 1920s, images of native Hawaiians and specifically Hula iconography had become an integral part of tourism promotions. Gradually, native Hawaiian culture became commodified and enacted through dance shows as a way of authenticating the destination image (Desmond, 1999). In recent decades, the original meaning of the Hula dance has evolved into a display of 'ideal' natives who present visitors with an alluring encounter with 'soft primitivism' (Smith, 1985: 5). The choreography of Hula has been influenced by contemporary or modern dance, and, in what Kaeppler (2004: 294) calls 'recycling tradition', a fusion form of the Hula dance was created. Tourists were attracted into a new folk dance – *Hapa Haole* (a performance by a person of half-white, half-Hawaiian descent). The performance has been rejuvenated into a large commercial *luau* show featuring a smorgasbord consumed by visitors encompassing native food, songs and dancing by a 'whitened' Hawaiian.

Conservation: The search for 'cool' authenticity, original, genuine and pristine, noted earlier can become a major tourist attraction for valuable niche markets. Such attractions can be linked to festivals, summer schools, and ultimately to the establishment of a carefully planned cultural heritage industry. In some sense, this could be a dream scenario of sustainable tourism in which visitation preserves and deepens a cultural resource, acting as a tool for enhancing the value given to conservation (Lane, 1994). In another sense, the intellectualization of the ethnic artistic process can move it far from authenticity: in William Wordsworth's words, 'we murder to dissect'. Examples of this type of change include the Welsh traditional performance festival at Llangollen, now the International Musical Eisteddfod, the Great Lakes Folk Festival, in Michigan, with its links to the University of Michigan and to the Center for Great Lakes Culture, and many others.

Decline: Without tourism money or grant aid, in an age where performance skills are increasingly professionalized, the ethnic performance can decline and ultimately disappear. Grant-giving organizations are a powerful management tool within the arts: failure to obtain funding can be a critical event. Withdrawal of funding is often a death blow. Examples of this type of decline can be found in the loss of music from the ethnic Hui in China (Yang, 1995). Hui music performance has been marginalized by the state government due to the vague identity of this ethnic group (the majority of Hui are identified as Muslims and do not reside in a specific location). Changes in tourists' tastes and the confusion between Hui and other ethnic music have exacerbated problems for promoting Hui arts performance, thus it is disappearing.

Whatever the path taken in this part of the cycle, authenticity has become the currency at play in the marketplace of cultural difference (Root, 1996: 78). In other words, authenticity implies consumption of self-defining symbols that are not self-produced, but instead obtained in the open market. These symbols become a series of niche markets and niche products, which in some places can co-exist, even cross-fertilize. In other places, these markets and products can be pure or can be managed to be pure. Perhaps the common factor is that none of these can be pure in the sense that they lack any commercial aspirations.

There are, however, a series of important caveats to be applied to this life cycle model. Ethnic tourism is a relatively new activity, and a provider of rapid, sometimes short-lived change. By contrast, culture and ethnic arts performance are primeval concepts. The life cycles of some ethnic arts are long, demonstrating strength, continuity and conservatism, and thus slowing the operation of the life cycle concept. These caveats make the application of a life cycle model to tourism and cultural change a debatable and even disputable idea. Within tourism itself, there are deep discussions about the suitability of linear progression as a concept. Ethnic tourism may be best understood as a complex adaptive system, with, in many cases, dynamic non-linear change. Thus, the cycle proposed here could be interrupted by unforeseen events including changes in cultural fashion, competition between destinations, rising fuel prices, terrorism, and natural disasters (Farrell & Twining-Ward, 2005). The S-shaped curve may not be followed in all cases. And even within regions, the cycle may be represented at different stages by different performances at any one time. One of the most interesting issues raised here, however, is that of the deep desire to seek the authentic, and what is presumed to be original, driven along by a belief that the original must somehow be best. That desire is not peculiar to ethnic tourism. It can be seen in the classical music field, where original instruments and the *Urtexts* of great works are now much in demand (Johnson, 2002). Another example is found in the world of food and catering: organic food and the slow food movement both strive for excellence through a return to their origins, and to a simplicity of means and ideas.

Set against the search for original authenticity is the search for living culture, capable of adapting from a secure base to meet the needs of its local society. Cultural commentators have long debated this issue. In his Wales-based essay on *Heritage as National Identity*, Pyrs Gruffudd (1995: 49) noted the problem that 'ethno-histories – encoded as "traditions" – are frequently inventions or recycled myths'. However, they apparently serve the requirements of society. Gruffudd goes on to discuss the need to see the heritage of rural Wales as a dynamic repository of identity, available for a future cultural revitalization – something labelled techno-arcadianism by Luckin (1990) – able to maintain and strengthen Welsh cultural values through change creating relevance.

It is important to realize that ethnicity – whether performing or not – has always changed to reflect the needs of society. Such changes are discussed at length in John Carey's (2005) challenging book, *What Good are the Arts?* He suggested that tourism, both its supply and demand, is now often a fundamental need in many societies and the performing arts increasingly reveal that fact. The life cycle concept helps both tourism planners and cultural commentators understand and explain those changes. Stage 5, the current end stage, is unique because it is one where a conscious – even self-conscious – management process tries to determine cultural evolution and conservation goals. Ethnic tourism can play a part in funding and guiding the determination and management of those objectives. It can be one vehicle through which ethnic communities harness their cultures and traditions to engage in and shape their developmental direction within broader global processes. In particular, the interplay between tourism development, economy and culture across settings is required (Dredge, 2004). Culture has always been driven by the market. The central difference in the 21st century is that markets that were once local are now increasingly global. Therefore, the discussion of authenticity will be more useful to understand who drives these changes and what are the goals sought. The following section will present a 'travel map', a conceptual framework of authentication, to identify the stakeholders and their tensions and paradoxes during the process of authenticating ethnic tourism.

A Conceptual Framework of Authentication

Ethnic tourism encompasses a variety of dimensions including the social, economic and political, as well as attributes of the physical environment. The proposed life cycle of authenticity provides a processual model to trace the changes in various stages. However, questions remain about who authenticates the ethnic cultures and how to balance the delicate relationships, such as economic development and cultural preservation, during the process of authentication. Answers to these questions involve the identification of key players (stakeholders) and the criteria that they employ for making their assessments of authenticity. The attribution of authenticity is important because it involves the conferring of status. The designation of something as authentic may also be associated with the assessment of what is appropriate and the exercise of power, thus an understanding of the process of authentication often has considerable significance. While the proposed conceptual framework has general applicability, it is particularly useful in China where ethnic communities have experienced drastic changes in recent years as tourism impinges on their daily life. The proposed framework is designed as an organized way of thinking about how and why authentication takes place and about how its activities can be understood. By identifying key stakeholders, this framework facilitates exploration of their perspectives on the development of ethnic tourism and, more importantly, measures their positions on the tensions that arise when these stakeholders authenticate the ethnic tourism product.

Swain (1989) proposed a conceptual model of ethnic tourism based on extensive fieldwork in China. The model includes: (a) interrelationships of the primary groups in tourism development; (b) characteristics of the process; (c) paradoxes encountered; and (d) proposed economic resolutions. Oakes (1992) has further noted that in the Chinese case, ethnic tourism interacts within three different dimensions: structures of state power, ethnic identity, and commercial development. Structures of state power determine how tourism policies can be implemented at various levels and the effectiveness of the system to deliver the economic benefits. Ethnic identity refers to the vulnerability of cultural change in the process of tourism. The major focus is on whether ethnic cultures are exploited, debased and trivialized by commercial development. Concerns have been frequently voiced about the impacts of ethnic tourism on the host communities and the complex relationships between hosts and guests. Robinson (1999) suggested that a key issue in measuring cultural changes is inclusion of a wider-ranging set of 'cultural indicators' of tourism impacts. The notion of these indicators is that the various stakeholders involved in tourism, from the local communities who judge the cultural appropriateness to the governments who exercise control of tourism development. Hitchcock *et al.* (1993) proposed that at the root of ethnic tourism are the questions 'who should be the main beneficiaries from tourism development?' and 'who should determine its pattern and pace?'. For example, tourism has functioned primarily for the benefit of *the tourist*, and its form and dynamics have principally been driven by *the industry* itself. *Governments* have taken it on themselves to act on behalf of the people by facilitating or moderating the development of tourism within their respective territories. Meanwhile, *local communities* may have a sense of powerlessness and have found themselves largely excluded from the decision-making process. Based on the above arguments, I propose that the subjects of analysis for the issue of authentication should include at least four key stakeholders (although other stakeholders could be included): (a) governments; (b) tourism businesses; (c) tourists; and (d) ethnic communities. These stakeholders relate to a wider environment of people and entities that can affect, or be affected by, ethnic tourism. The following briefly introduce these four stakeholders in relation to Chinese ethnic tourism.

Virtually all countries in the Asia-Pacific region have made 'culture' the focus of a government ministry. Ethnic labels, cultural display and tourist access are all tightly regulated by the State (Wood, 1997). Ethnic identification in China was based on the ideas of Joseph Stalin's four common characteristics: a common language, a common territory, a common economy and a common psychological nature manifested in a singular culture (Harrell, 1995). Furthermore, Chinese government ethnic policy draws on both indigenous and imported notions of ethnicity, such as the evolutionary ideas of American anthropologist, Lewis Henry Morgan (Wood, 1997). Morgan's uni-linear scheme of evolution from primitive to modern as society progresses provides a solid foundation for the Chinese government's official recognition of 55 ethnic minority 'nationalities'. Most of these nationalities reside in designated autonomous regions at the periphery of the country, which range in geographical scope from a village to a province. In China, the structures of state power vary but can be broadly divided into three main levels: national, provincial and local. Tourism policies are set by these levels and involve empowerment, which is a practice to help ethnic minorities exert control over factors that affect their lives. Whatever the impetus and control, many of the key policy decisions at national, provincial and local levels need to be made; for example, who will have ownership of the tourism resources and how can sustainability of tourism development be ensured? Ethnic autonomy is national government policy in China, but it may be difficult to implement at the local level because of possible social, cultural and economic barriers.

Tourism businesses have great potential for generating employment opportunities within both the formal and informal sectors. Employment in tourism has increased rapidly in many developing countries. Tourism studies (Bryden, 1973; Gerry, 1987; Sharpley & Telfer, 2002) estimate that as much as 50% of developing countries' labor forces may be participating in informal sector activities. In terms of investment, tourism created more jobs per dollar than manufacturing, primarily through higher multiplier effects. Cukier's (2002) research in Bali, Indonesia, suggested that tourism jobs were highly regarded with above-average incomes. Moreover, almost all employment opportunities associated with tourism were accorded a high status by the local population. Such opportunities not only paid better wages than traditional types of employment, but also offered relative physical ease compared to traditional agricultural labor. Oakes (1997), who conducted research in Guizhou, China, suggested that in most cases, the tourism business brought a substantial change to an ethnic village's economic situation. Three major factors contributed to this economic change: (a) foreign tourist demand for ethnic cultures; (b) the availability of tourist resources and returns on investments (as a rule of thumb, developing an ethnic tourist village requires less money than developing scenic sites); and (c) ethnic tourism offers locals direct benefits that scenic tourism does not. The focus of research on tourism businesses in this book will be on the managers and owners of these tourist folk villages, where business vigorously promotes and uses ethnic resources for the purpose of tourism.

Tourists are mobile, enjoying their leisure time and absorbing the experiences in different destinations, while the hosts, defined as ethnic minorities, tend to be stationary and spend a great deal of 'front stage' time catering to the tourists. Walle (1996) observed that since developing countries and rural regions of the industrialized world often benefit by showcasing indigenous societies, it is important to understand how tourists think about such ethnic experiences and to determine their perception of the authenticity of the attractions. Ideally, an ethnic tourism site should provide the tourist with a rich, accurate and entertaining understanding of cultural resources. The tourist facility within or close to the community should evoke a fascinating and memorable tourist experience while avoiding degradation of the 'real' culture. Tourists' attitudes, perceptions, motivations and comments on ethnic tourism sites provide feedback for future improvement and reflect the degree of commodification of ethnic culture. Kaplan (1996) expressed the view that tourists seek the exotic and authentic in an effort to displace the instrumental rationalism that has come to dominate their life. Contact with the ethnic Other provides such an opportunity. Kaplan (1996: 63) described this type of tourist as possessing 'a specifically Euro-American cultural myopia which marks shifting peripheralities through travel in a world of structured economic asymmetries'. Hughes (1995) proposed, from a broader perspective, that there are two possible market segments for ethnic tourism. First, members of the *postindustrial* segment are likely to be sensitive to impacts on the host population and are concerned with behaving responsibly in ethnic contact situations. Second, members of the *postmodern* segment enjoy contrived spectacles while remaining aware of their inauthenticity. The postmodern segment seems to care less for the origins of an attraction as long as the visit is an enjoyable one. Moscardo and Pearce (1999), in an empirical study at an aboriginal cultural park in Australia, identified four portfolios of ethnic tourists: the ethnic tourism connection group, the passive cultural learning group, the ethnic products and activities group and the low ethnic tourism group. The study points out that it is necessary for ethnic groups who seek to use tourism to their advantage to find out how potential markets are likely to respond to products that they develop.

In terms of the ethnic communities, both ethnic identity and the employment of ethnic people are likely to be important aspects of understanding authenticity. Cultural attractions, such as tourist folk villages, open the window to cultural exchange for the ethnic minorities who have been relatively isolated from other cultures for generations, thereby promoting national and international understanding between hosts and guests. In particular, employees, such as dance performers, play an active role in presenting ethnic cultures as well as communicating with tourists. Such cultural exchange opportunities may not only provide tourists with a chance of appreciating ethnic cultures, but may also help ethnic minority groups to build a sense of pride in their own cultures. An important aspect of authenticity, in fact, is an ethnic minority's perception of its own culture. Tourism can conceivably influence cultural changes and ethnic identity in different ways. Ethnic identity is always conditioned by a dynamic tension between exogenous forces and local traditions. It is appropriated, constructed and traded through and around the development of tourism and the material objects of touristic exchange (Doorne *et al.*, 2003). Long and Wall (1995), based on empirical research in Bali, documented that a traditional ceremony by Balinese communities seemed to be affected by the tourism industry. In addition, they found that those who work in the tourism industry often do not have enough time to participate in required traditional ceremonies. Ethnic tourism was seen to be more intrusive because it requires direct interaction with Balinese families. Furthermore, the traditional family structure was affected by tourism development.

Increased competition for tourism business inevitably causes conflicts within and between local communities. The ensuing chapters will focus on the ethnic Li communities and Chinese-Indonesians as diaspora communities on Hainan Island, China, who are actively involved with tourism and who work as employees of the tourism industry. They are distinctively different from the majority Han people, speak different languages and have different skills. My focus on the ethnic community will be on the dance performers working in the folk villages. Dance forms, as part of ethnic arts performance, are differentiated from one another in style, type and context. Until the appearance of tourism, the mixing of forms was generally judged as a violation of boundaries. Combinations of dance steps from different traditions, that is, inter-traditional mixtures, have often been judged as 'fakes', 'frauds' and certainly less than authentic. However, sometimes such mixed performances possess a creative aspect, from both emic and etic perspectives (Daniel, 1996). Frequently, touristic performance has become the category of dance in which the mixture of varied traditions and major change may take place. The tourism setting may provide the space and time for definitions to expand, for play and experimentation at the boundaries with combinations of styles and traditions that reach for innovation and creativity.

Having identified four key stakeholders as foci for the research, a central problem was encountered; that is, the process of authenticating ethnic cultures is rife with tensions among the key stakeholders because they hold different positions with respect to the authentication. Both Oakes (1992, 1997, 1998, 2006) and Swain (1989, 1993) have addressed the tension between national and local priorities and minority identity in China. For example, Oakes (1997) observed that tourism in China combines two very different processes to influence ethnic identity significantly: one is the process of commercial, economic and social integration inherent in tourism development; the other involves state policies regarding ethnic minority culture and its preservation. The primordial approach from the government inherently conflicts with economic and cultural changes. Oakes called the processes 'a paradox' in China's ethnic tourism development, which ultimately produces a false modernity. The question becomes one of degrees of change: how do ethnic communities view cultural changes that occur with tourism development? Swain (1993) drew attention to three paradoxes common to situations where ethnic minorities have become tourist attractions. These are: state regulation and ethnic rights; museumification and cultural evolution; economic development and cultural preservation. These paradoxes are not distinct, but are intertwined in intricate and changing relationships. Furthermore, the paradoxes inherent in ethnic tourism occur because of basic contradictions between cultural preservation and evolution in the process of development. Based on Swain and Oakes' work, I propose five pairs of paradoxes along with the four identified stakeholders to form a conceptual framework in order to better understand the interrelationships between culture, economics, politics and authenticity. Figure 2.2 provides the framework of the approach and the context within which this book resides.

(1) Authenticity versus commodification. The concepts of authenticity and commodification appear to be antithetical. One of the specific challenges to authenticity is the trend toward commodification of ethnic tourism experience. The spontaneous, impulsive and relatively unorganized aspects of ethnic tourism become increasingly subject to planned control, regulation and commodification. In order to satisfy demands for authenticity, tourism businesses and ethnic communities package certain or all aspects of their culture and create staged representations to make tourism more accessible to cater to tourists. Commercialization can induce the ethnic minority to alter their behaviors to suit the demands of the market and tourists' taste, resulting in a loss of spontaneity, tradition and other cultural manifestations. The worst scenario is the over-development of ethnic tourist attractions so that the community

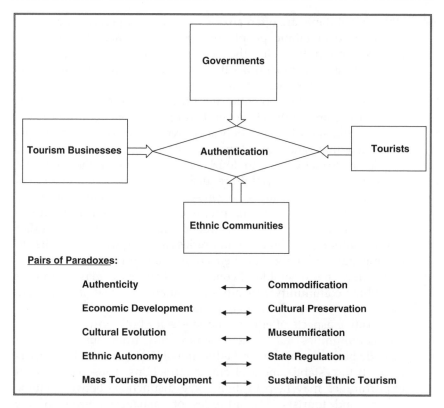

Figure 2.2 A conceptual framework of authentication

risks losing its roots and is eventually rejected by tourists as inauthentic. However, it can be countered that commercialism may actually represent a mechanism to protect cultural resources and revitalize indigenous cultures (Li & Hinch, 1998). Destinations that selectively transform cultural resources into tangible products, including folk villages, not only facilitate the exchange of cultural experiences for a financial return, but they have the potential to create a situation in which sustainable development can be promoted through the careful management of resources. An ethnic community may desire to celebrate and portray ethnicity through commodification.

(2) Economic development versus cultural preservation. Economic development is widely recognized as being an important reason for promoting ethnic tourism. Governing authorities in areas with

ethnic inhabitants are often anxious to reverse a perceived growing dependence of ethnic people on social assistance. Tourism is a favored option to foster the economic independence of ethnic minorities and to modernize the communities. Tourist attractions can generate employment and income, stimulate ethnic-owned businesses and offer potential for further economic development within the community. However, loss of traditional culture caused by modernization is commonly a source of tension. Cohen (2002) suggested that since an ethnic group's marginality is the major source of attractiveness to tourists, reservation of their cultural distinctiveness is a crucial prerequisite for sustainable tourism. On the other hand, attempts to preserve a traditional culture by denying the opportunity for progress can condemn a culture to marginalization and impoverishment (Yang *et al.*, 2008). In other words, although ethnic communities are highly vulnerable to commercial exploitation of their culture, some economic development may be desirable. Economic advantages may empower the ethnic community and build an enhanced sense of value and pride for its culture. Tourism may function as a means of preserving the positive aspects of ethnic uniqueness for both hosts and guests. The communities may benefit significantly from businesses that provide both commercial and educational opportunities for tourists through the establishment of ethnic attractions. Those educational opportunities may help to define key distinctions between ethnic groups and tourists. The attitudes of managerial levels of the villages (e.g. directors, managers) toward ethnic cultural development will be the focus of the book.

(3) Cultural evolution versus museumification (the 'freezing' of culture). Since ethnicity and identity can be viewed as processional, contested and changing in modern society (Cole, 2006), ethnic tourism often plays a key role in the cultural evolution. There is a paradoxical struggle between the ethnic communities that strive to maintain the boundary and the tourists who expect the ethnic culture to be quaintly traditional. MacCannell (1984) stressed that once an ethnic attraction becomes routine of a culture's functioning, the performers in ethnic attractions begin to think of themselves as representatives of the ethnic way of life, and come to believe that any change would have economic and political implications for the whole group. Thus, a community may be forced to be 'frozen in an image of itself or museumized' (MacCannell, 1984: 388). Kirshenblatt-Gimblett (1998) called this kind of museumification a 'genre error' in which the

exhibition of the quotidian distorts the actual ethnic life in a museum setting regardless of place and spectators. The fossilized ethnic culture is used as a form of exoticism to draw tourists, yet there are countervailing forces from the communities to promote political, economic and cultural integration of the mainstream society. The cultural evolution has pressured the communities to demand a share in the benefits of modernization.

(4) Ethnic autonomy versus state regulation. There is an asymmetrical power relation between governments and the ethnic communities. Standardization of ethnic culture controlled by state regulation can lead to staged authentic events, such as folk dance performances and costumed photo sessions. Conflicts between state priorities and power and local autonomy is characteristic of ethnic tourism. Two sets of policies and processes are at work in the development of ethnic tourism in China: the persistence of state control and the empowerment of ethnic communities. The interaction of these two forces appears to generate tension when ethnic resources are used for tourism. Governments at various levels have to be involved directly in the establishment and management of tourism infra-structures in order to jump-start economic development in the ethnic communities. However, a focus on the ethnic minority as a tourism attraction serves as a basis for negotiations between the state and minority communities (Wood, 1984). Ethnic tourism provides minority groups with a forum for making claims about themselves and their villages. The use of such a forum may contribute to ethnic autonomy in the near future (Swain, 1989, 1999). Ethnic communities may see tourism as a 'pot of gold' and be in consultation and negotiations with governments to demand a better socio-economic status. Since ethnic tourism enhances aware-ness of cultural values, recognition and protection of ethnic cultural and intellectual property have been raised. Local participation in ethnic tourism has pressed governments to loosen stringent regula-tions and provide more freedom for entrepreneurial activities to grow. Tensions flare as autonomous processes meet bureaucratic red tape, mismanagement and inefficiency. The ongoing transformation of a centrally controlled state regulation to a market-oriented one will surely necessitate more explicit recognition of the autonomous rights for the ethnic communities.

(5) Mass tourism development versus sustainable ethnic tourism. Mass tourism has been blamed for a variety of social changes (Robinson & Boniface, 1999). The optimum relationship between tourism and

ethnicity is sustainability. Mass tourism is desired in most developing countries, including China, because potential economic prosperity and job satisfaction tend to be positively associated with elevated tourist numbers. However, ethnic tourism is a fragile commodity that requires a delicate and highly vulnerable balance of factors. It is intrinsically self-destroying unless carefully planned (Van de Berghe, 1994). Mass tourism development may cause environmental degradation, or as evidenced in existing research, a potential clash of cultures. Questions about whether tourism is an appropriate means of economic development in remote ethnic communities are increasingly relevant in attempts to pursue sustainable development. However, it is argued that sometimes choosing or excluding expressions of culture for presentation may keep certain sacred or special aspects of an ethnic culture from being denigrated by the intrusion of mass tourism, such as the 'honeypot' tourism planning. Staged authenticity keeps mass tourism development in purpose-built tourist villages or other predetermined locations, rather than introducing it to the minority hinterland areas (i.e. back stages). Doing so may relieve the pressures of mass tourism on naturally and culturally sensitive places (Li & Hinch, 1998). Sustainable ethnic tourism will be ideal since it has low impact on the environment and ethnic culture while helping to generate necessary income, employment and the conservation of the local ecosystems. Sustainability is typically useful for my research setting, Hainan Island, China, where the remote island setting requires special environmental protection and the preservation of the ethnic culture.

The above paradoxes, taken together with the four identified stakeholders, are much more expansive than many conceptualizations of authenticity in the existing literature. In fact, they reach into many aspects of the cultural, social and even economic aspects of ethnic tourism. It may be noted that the five paradoxes are not distinct and, moreover, are extremely difficult to quantify. None of these continua or any particular polar position is inherently superior to another. Rather, its value will depend on circumstances and the priorities of the stakeholders. The conceptual framework presents interactions of power, legitimacy and urgency among the stakeholders in authenticating ethnic tourism. These identified interconnected paradoxes provide a basis to compare the roles of different stakeholders. They also contribute to understanding the interrelationships among politics, culture and economics within ethnic tourism. They offer a more tractable way of approaching authenticity, realizing the impacts of ethnic tourism and evaluating the extent to which experiences are authentic or contrived. Most importantly, the paradoxes can be used as a set of yardsticks to examine the degree of authentication. Identified stakeholders may exhibit different positions with respect to the various paradoxes and the tensions that exist between their positions.

The following questions, central to the issue of authentication, are raised: (a) what is the position of differing levels of governments with respect to state regulation and ethnic autonomy? (b) how do the dance performers, as part of ethnic communities, regard the tension between museumification and cultural evolution? (c) how do the directors of folk villages deal with the tension between mass tourism and sustainable ethnic tourism? and (d) how do tourists view the tension between authenticity and commodification? These questions will be answered by using a variety of research methods to gauge the levels of tension that exist on issues related to authentication. The following chapters will examine the construct of authenticity through investigation of Li minority culture on Hainan Island. Attention is given to the identified stakeholders, their roles, interactions, management and their influence on ethnic tourism development. Applying the conceptual framework to assess stakeholders' positions on the paradoxes as well as across the authentication process will help organize much of the information on, and many concepts pertaining to, ethnic tourism. The research results will not only be in regard to the Li minority culture on Hainan Island, but to other locations as well.

Chapter 3
Hainan Island and Folk Villages

Introduction

On 1 April 2001, a US surveillance aircraft collided with a Chinese fighter near the South China Sea. The Chinese fighter and its pilot were lost. The US aircraft, badly damaged, was forced to make an emergency landing on a Chinese island called Hainan. The incident came at a time when Sino-American relations were under increasing strain. Chinese officials blamed the USA for the incident, while the Americans accused China of intercepting military aircraft in an 'unsafe manner'. There was much finger pointing between the two countries until China finally released the crew and returned the surveillance aircraft to the USA. Nonetheless, the Island of Hainan had never received so much world-wide attention. Major news media in the West continually featured maps and terrains of Hainan on television and in newspapers, some of which were so detailed that the island's tourist folk villages were precisely pinpointed. The extensive coverage put Hainan on the map and with the spread of the globalized media, it became an instant international destination. Ironically, Hainan, the tourism attraction, catapulted to world fame because of a tragic military collision.

This chapter addresses the links between the past and present on Hainan Island to explore the historical and cultural development of tourism. Economic development in recent years after Hainan was established as a province is documented; in particular, the problems and prospects of its rapid urban sprawl and efforts to attract tourists with the support of the governments are discussed. The ethnic Li minority on Hainan, their heritage, identity, rituals, customs and involvement with tourism are introduced.

Additionally, the population of Hainan includes a 'forgotten' diasporic community – Chinese-Indonesians who settled on the island in the late 1960s due to anti-China suppression in Indonesia. This diaspora is composed of ethnic Chinese, born and raised in Indonesia, who left and settled on Hainan. Next, I trace the original model of the folk village, the Skansen in Sweden, and analyze various views of using folk villages as a means of promoting ethnic and national identity. Specifically,

I propose that the perception of authenticity in the folk village needs to be re-examined by tourism researchers. Finally, I use my field observations to highlight the shifting pattern of the folk village locations along the highways on Hainan, in order to demonstrate that changes in accessibility have reduced the authenticity of locations in which the ethnic tourism experiences are provided.

Tianya Haijiao

Hainan is arguably the most unique island in China. It is the only tropical province in China and is located by the South China Sea. It was described by ancient Chinese as *Tianya Haijiao* (the end of heaven and sea) because it is far from the heart of Mainland China. Geographically, Hainan has a land area of 34,087 km^2 and a coastline of 1,584.8 km, located in the central part of the Pacific Economic Circle and lying along the same latitude as Hawaii. The western coast of the island borders the Gulf of Tong Kin, with Vietnam visible in the distance. The eastern portion of the island is near Hong Kong, Taiwan is to the north and the Philippines is located to the southeast. The eastern portion of the island is near Hong Kong, Taiwan is to the north, and the Philippines is located to the southeast (Figure 3.1). It can be noted that Hainan

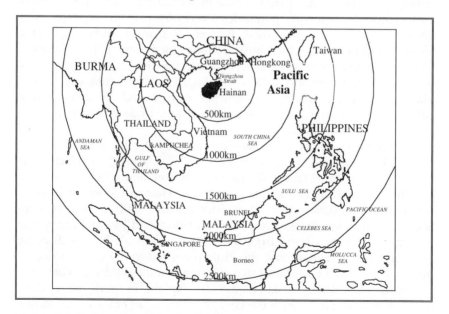

Figure 3.1 Hainan Island in the Pacific Asian area

Province includes not only Hainan Island but also Xisha, Nansha and Zhongsha islands and more than 2 million km^2 of sea space. These smaller islands, many of which are reefs and shoals, are also called the Spratly Islands. They have been controversially claimed by different Southeast Asian countries.

Historically, Hainan, whose ancient name was Qiongya, was always considered a backwater of the Chinese Empire. It was viewed a miserable place of exile and poverty, a place of banishment for criminals and political undesirables. Li Deyu, a prime minister of the Tang Dynasty, exiled to Hainan, dubbed it 'the gate of hell'. During the Song, Yuan and Ming Dynasties (about 1000 years ago), Hainan was a remote corner of China, attracting only 18 documented tourists (Storey *et al.*, 1999).

The majority of Hainan's inhabitants are Han Chinese who migrated from the mainland as early as the Han dynasty (200 BC–220 AD) when Hainan was first incorporated into China's territory. The indigenous inhabitants are the Li, Miao, Zhuang and Hui tribes, of which Li is the largest ethnic group. By 2007, the total population was about 8.19 million and the ethnic Li population about 1.26 million, which was about 15% of the total population (Statistics Bureau of Hainan, 2008). The ethnic distribution is disproportionate, with most of the Han residents concentrated along the coastal plains, while in the central-south mountainous areas, ethnic Li and other minorities are clustered in the scattered, low density, Li and Miao Autonomous Regions. Hainan Island belongs to the *Lingnan* culture circle, which includes Guangdong and part of Guangxi Province. As a sub-strand of Chinese culture, the distinctive *Lingnan* socio-cultural system is a hybrid of Han mixed with the ethnic minority culture, Mainland China's orthodox Confucian culture and Western culture obtained from a long history of industrial and trade contacts with the outside world (Gu, 2002).

After the Communist Party took power in 1949, Hainan Island, as an underdeveloped and peripheral part of Guangdong Province, was considered an important military post in containing Southeast Asia and the surrounding contentious territories. Hainan's strategic location was used as a 'buffer zone' to counter possible military attacks from Southeast Asia, but its economy was not prioritized by the Communist government. Preparedness from the 1950s for possible border disputes between China, Vietnam and the Philippines led to the construction of the naval, air and missile bases that still stand on the southwest coast (the proximity of military installations can explain in part the mid-air collision in 2001, after which the US aircraft made an emergency landing in Lingshui, a military airport in southern Hainan). Some argued that military installations resulted from the 'colonial policy' of the mainland toward the island in the pre-reform period: that is, it was viewed as an outpost of national defense and as a source of domestic rubber production, which developed after the US-led embargoes of the early 1950s (Cadario *et al.*, 1992). Lack of investment caused Hainan to lag in industry and infrastructure development and become one of the most economically backward regions in China.

Constraints on economic development were lifted with the initiation in 1978 of China's open door policy. The central government named Hainan as the site of China's biggest Special Economic Zone (SEZ) in an attempt to rejuvenate its dormant economy. Perhaps because the island's peripheral location insulated it from the mainland, Hainan was chosen as the location for an experiment in market-oriented development and was accorded greater economic freedom than any other SEZ (Xie & Wall, 2002). On 13 April 1988, the Seventh National People's Congress officially promulgated Hainan's status as an SEZ and as a province comprising two main urban prefectures, Haikou and Sanya, seven county-level cities, four counties and six ethnic autonomous regions (Gu & Wall, 2007). The SEZ status allowed Hainan to offer foreign investors an attractive package of tax exemptions, including such incentives as duty-free status for production inputs. In addition, Beijing affirmed its intention to make Hainan a special area that would go beyond the other SEZs in system reform. The intent was to have a 'small government and large society', implying minimally detailed government intervention in the economy and few state-operated enterprises (Cadario *et al.*, 1992). More specifically, the island would be allowed to offer investors land-use rights on a leasehold basis for up to 70 years, to operate a free market in foreign exchange. Broadly, the island would function primarily by free-market principles, with no discrimination among enterprises on the basis of their ownership status (Cadario *et al.*, 1992). Government promotion policies were designed to offer privileges and incentive packages, including lower taxes and lax regulation, to stimulate the infrastructure improvement. The income tax of an enterprise was slashed to 15% from the national norm of 33%. Hainan was allowed to offer foreign currency exchange business to investors abroad so that these outsiders might set up enterprises with preferences in such areas as loans, site selection and land transfer. In addition, visa authorization procedures for foreigners were somewhat easier than those in other SEZs. Hainan is the only province in China that implements 'visa issued on spot' for temporary visitors (Cadario *et al.*, 1992). This regulation significantly increases accessibility to the island and is potentially advantageous to the development of international tourism.

The significant benefits that the SEZ derived from the foreign exchange, government revenues and job creation are considered central to the provincial economy and are the reasons for gaining local government support for tourism development. Domestic tourism has received a great deal of attention from the governments at various levels. The provincial government has provided a series of preferential policies for tourism development. For example, it issued 'the Regulations of Tourist Management of Hainan Province' and 'Rule of Tourist Management of Hainan Province', protecting the rights of tourists and tourism developers in 1999 and 2002. The provincial government has capitalized on existing natural and cultural tourism resources, including a tropical climate, mangrove forests, coral reefs, beaches, spas, cuisine and ethnic cultures. The main tourism development zones are in Haikou, located on the tip of the northern coast, and Sanya, the most important resort hub on the southern coast. The beaches at Yalong Bay to the east of Sanya feature a 7-km strip of sand that is much longer than the Waikiki beach in Hawaii and has been dubbed 'the Chinese Waikiki'. In addition, Hainan has unique tropical forests in the western part of the island with great potential as an excellent ecotourism destination (Stone & Wall, 2004).

On 4 January 2010, the central government approved the construction of Hainan as 'an International Tourism Island', providing incentives and financial supports. According to a statement of the State Council, the purposes are not only to develop Hainan as an SEZ, but also to shape it into a world top class tourist destination by 2020. The government said that it would maintain the healthy development of the island's property sector and encourage developers to build premium hotels and resorts. It also supports family-run hotels and property-rental services. The aforementioned 'visa issued on spot' policy has been extended to more than 26 nations, including Scandinavian countries, Ukraine and Kazakhstan. In order to boost tourism on Hainan, the central government even allows the island to 'test the waters' of the gambling industry by building casinos and lotteries.

Despite the generous support from the governments, Hainan's designation as the largest SEZ and tourism island has been a mixed success. On the positive side, Hainan is in the throes of rapid change and modernization despite the fact that the island was primarily a rural, newly demarcated province. At the end of 2008, the gross domestic product (GDP) was RMB 145.9 billion (US$21.36 billion) compared to RMB 40.99 billion (US$4.93 billion) in 1997 (China Daily, 2009).

Agriculture has long been the mainstay of Hainan's economy with plantation rubber, smallholder rice paddies and vegetable plots as the main crops. Growth in the last decade has been concentrated in commercial crops: coffee and tea, bananas, pepper, sugar cane, and tropical medicinal herbs. Nonetheless, agriculture as the primary sector has gradually declined from 50% in 1987 to 36% by 2002, while the share of the tertiary sector, primarily from tourism, increased from 31 to 40% over the same period (Gu & Wall, 2007). Tourism plays a key role in the service sector and is the most important economic engine in Hainan's development. The island now has two international airports, with connections to most of the major cities in China and other places in Southeast Asia. Coupled with the improved tourism infrastructure, its palm-fringed beaches and warm temperatures year round have drawn tourists from Mainland China. Similar to other destinations, such as the Greek Islands and the Canary Islands in Spain, Hainan has been transformed from a remote and peripheral island to a modern tropical resort. The travel website of Condé Nast Traveler put Hainan Island on its 2008 'It' list, naming it one of the 10 must-see destinations of the year and even comparing it to Hawaii – 'without the Honolulu high-rises and crowds' (Cohane, 2008). According to the Statistics Bureau of Hainan Province, the island attracted 16.05 million overnight tourists in 2006. Of that total, 15.43 million (96%) were domestic tourists from Mainland China. The number of international visitors also grew, but more slowly by only 617,000. Of the international arrivals, the majority were overseas Chinese from Hong Kong, Macau and Taiwan. Travel patterns of international tourists to Hainan are spatially uneven. Overseas Chinese mainly use the highways to travel from Haikou to Sanya, while Sanya has become a popular destination for Russians who fly in to enjoy sandy beaches and warm weather. The total number of star-grade hotels increased from 223 to 263 during 2006, of which 13, 50 and 117 were rated 5-, 4- and 3-star, respectively, at the end of 2006.

Despite the positive developments, Hainan is largely perceived as the 'wild west' and has undergone a series of boom-bust spirals since its establishment as a province. Often, Hainan's economy was developed as an enclave of free-market bedlam, operating on the periphery of the law. Reflecting the Chinese phenomenon *tiangao huangdiyuan* (so far from Emperor and so far from the Heaven), local government officials deliberately kept the central government in the dark in order to avoid interference. The local business mentality has long been described as daredevil and receptive to any extra legal activities. For example, instead of establishing a solid economic foundation in the 1990s,

Hainan became a place for auto smuggling, real estate speculation and corruption. One of the most famous fiascos occurred in 1993 when the provincial government imported 90,000 duty-free Japanese cars and resold them on the mainland at a 150% profit (Storey *et al.*, 1999). The chain of involvement, which even involved the army and navy was traced to the Governor of Hainan. Also in 1993, the island opened a stock market without authorization in order to attract external investment and was forced to close it two years later after being accused of casino-style stock transactions.

Gu and Wall (2007) have summarized the major obstacles in developing Hainan's economy and urban planning: the property bubble, development zones, over-urbanization; and chaotic land use. With regard to the property bubble, land prices on Hainan tripled in value between January and June 1992, spurred by a flexible and subsidized land-leasing policy (Lu & Xu, 1998). While Hainan's population accounted for about 0.6% of the national total, its vacant floor space constituted 10% of the national total. After experiencing the most prosperous growth in the early 1990s, the bubble burst and a fragile economy has since seen a much-reduced annual growth rate. The legacy of real estate speculation left numerous shells of abandoned, unfinished construction in the center of the business districts from Haikou to Sanya. The effects of the bubble economy have lingered and the downturn has eviscerated Hainan's economy and business confidence in the 2000s.

The growth of a burgeoning tourism sector has quickly become the major revenue source after the real estate bubble. The founding of the development zones is widely seen as strong government support for seeking out an alternative economy. Designated zones, managed by local government or by joint ventures, provided the physical infrastructure for investors' needs. Since 1996, in addition to 25 national and provincial urban development zones (about 301 km^2), 6 industrial developments, 14 tourism developments and five comprehensive developments have been established by the government in China. In 1992, Hainan received approval to build Yalong Bay State Tourist and Holiday Resort Zone about 20 km west of the central business district of Sanya. It was one of the biggest development zones in the nation. The resort zone was designated as an 'international standard tourism resort with characteristics of tropical ocean and ethnic minority and Chinese traditional cultures' (CAUPD, 1997: 5), offering a full range of accommodation and leisure activities. The detailed development control plan for Yalong Bay in 1997 identified a 146 km^2 area as a tourism development zone, in which 18.2 km^2 was earmarked for resorts and related hospitality services (Gu & Wall, 2007). Encompassing a 10-km recreational beach and well-conserved tropical ecological environment, the development zone was made up of three parts: golf courses, public recreation facilities and luxury resorts (CAUPD, 1999: 13–15).

In 2009, Hainan government has positioned the island as a destination for wealthy vacationers, expanding the size of resorts to real estate for luxury villas and manors. These new government-backed development projects engendered controversies over land control and the public participation. Li (2004) analyzed the social impacts of development on the Nanshan cultural tourism zone, a privately-owned tourist attraction located within the designated resort zone. He found that tremendous barriers existed due to lack of community involvement. The increasing antagonism from the ethnic Li, who have resided in Yalong Bay for centuries, was evident when their land was identified as a tourism resource. The reality of the powerlessness of the ethnic communities was apparent following the provincial government's land appropriation for Yalong Bay development. The controversy centered primarily on the amounts of compensation ethnic Li received and the impacts of tourism on minority traditions and culture (Wang & Wall, 2005).

The establishment of the development zone on Hainan has also proved vulnerable to changes in fashion and economic fluctuations. Income disparity and labor shortage surfaced as Hainan tourism industry experienced a vast expansion. In recent years, while the number of domestic visitors has increased, occupancy rates in hotels located in the resort zone have declined and many, if not most hotels, operate at a loss. There is difficulty in finding skilled labor on Hainan. Except for some involvement in the informal sector, migrants from the mainland take the majority of the tourism positions even though ethnic minorities make important and distinctive contributions to tourism. Thus, while Hainan has great tourism potential, it has yet to be realized. I will detail the ethnic communities' reaction toward tourism development in Chapter 5, particularly the struggles between the displacement of the existing Li minority villages and the location of the new settlements built for them.

It is often pointed out that many urbanization problems are the direct result of mismanagement, poor planning and absence of coherent urban policies. Hainan's development trajectory has brought about over-urbanization and chaotic land use, causing particularly acute problems in the cities of Haikou and Sanya. The promise of economic prosperity has attracted thousands of migrant workers from Mainland China to fill a wide range of jobs, though mainly in the construction industry.

Meanwhile, in-migration peasant workers congregate in sprawling urban peripheries that lack the basic amenities, giving rise to such serious social problems as crime and prostitution. These difficulties have been exacerbated by inappropriate regulation, lack of tenure security, inadequate taxation, and poorly coordinated control of the land market. Unbridled expansion in the region has caused severe environmental damage, leading to the destruction of sensitive ecosystems and altering the hydrology of coasts and affiliated natural features, such as mangrove swamps, reefs and beaches.

Macleod (2004) has suggested that an island's salient elements, such as its remoteness, insularity, cultural traditions, its 'Otherness', unique environment and character, present an ideal context for tourism development. However, islands often face structural handicaps owing to their peripheral locations and a high degree of dependency on such external forces as an over-reliance on tourism as a major source of income. The finite resources on islands hinder the sustainability of a tourism economy. In the case of Hainan, when widespread economic benefits were expected after building the resort zone and the ensuing tourism initiatives, various socio-cultural and environmental problems occurred, posing challenges for the sustainable development. Tourism on Hainan has reached a stage where both its potential and competitiveness have become questionable. The boom-and-bust spiral has led to Hainan repeating past errors of other settings. The social and economic impacts are profound on small, closely knit communities, such as those of the Li ethnic minority. These communities are faced with a stark choice of tourism or living off welfare (Gu & Wall, 2007). It is evident that the tourism issues facing Hainan are similar to those in other peripheral regions and islands, but Hainan is distinctively characterized as the 'last untouched' island in China based on its strong natural and ethnic environments. Therefore, the long-term prosperity of both tourism destinations and the residents should be the major priorities for tourism planning.

Ethnic Li Minority

There is a paucity of literature about ethnic minorities on Hainan, home to the Li ethnic group, one of 55 classified minority peoples of China. Hainan is also home to other smaller ethnic groups, including Miao and Hui, each with a population of approximately 60,000 and 10,000, respectively (Hainan Statistical Yearbook, 2007). Figure 3.2 shows the composition and proportion of the population on Hainan Island in

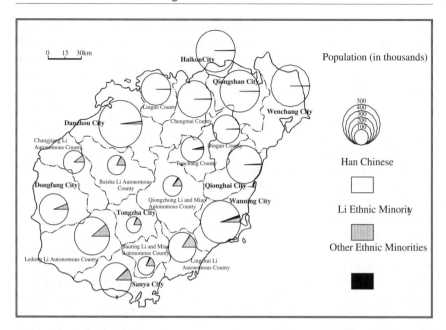

Figure 3.2 Composition and proportion of the minority population on Hainan Island

2000. The pattern of population and city distribution is imbalanced, most of the Han people being concentrated along coastal plains, while in the central-south mountain area there are counties with low population densities. Minority populations are concentrated along the south-central part of the island in the designated Li and Miao Autonomous Regions. These regions cover an area of 1169 km^2 with a majority population of Li (Hainan Tour Atlas, 1997). In addition, there are locations on Hainan populated by Hui (Muslim or 'Utsat') and the Indonesian-Chinese diaspora (Pang, 1996).

According to historical records, the term 'Li' first appeared in the Tang Dynasty (AD 618–907). They are believed to be descendants of the ancient Yue ethnic group, with especially close relations to the Luoyues – a branch of the Yues – who migrated from Guangdong and Guangxi on the mainland to Hainan long before the Qin Dynasty (221–206 BC) (Su *et al.*, 1994). Archaeological finds on the island show that Li ancestors settled there some 3000 years ago during the late Shang Dynasty or early Zhou Dynasty. In that era, they led a primitive, communal life that was matriarchal in organization. Ethnically, the Li are closely related to the

Zhuang, Bouyei, Shui, Dong and Dai ethnic groups on the mainland, and their languages bear resemblance to those groups in pronunciation, grammar and vocabulary (Su *et al.*, 1994). The Han majority group began to settle on the island in the 15th century as farmers, fishermen and merchants. Massive immigration began driving the Li into the southern mountains and forests, forcing them to abandon their traditional settlements on the coastal plains of Hainan Island. There has been a long history of rebellion by the Li against the Han majority (Su *et al.*, 1994). Eventually, the Han controlled the entire periphery of the island, but the 'steep terrain, thick forest, wild animals, and tropical diseases' (Netting, 1997: 4) kept them away from the Li in the interior.

The Li minority had no written script. Its spoken language belongs to the Chinese-Tibetan language family (Wu, 1991). A new Romanized script was created for the Li ethnic group in 1957 with the government's help. The central government has long seen education, in particular the teaching of Mandarin Chinese (*Putonghua*), as a key component of its ethnic policy in the region. Bilingual schools where courses are taught in Li are non-existent on Hainan. Over at least 60 years, the Li language has gradually been abandoned in favor of Mandarin Chinese as it becomes necessary to find jobs. The Li communities on the island are still very poor. Over 90% of the population work as cultivators in their villages, earning about 700 yuan (US$102) per year (Jiang, 1999). Illiteracy rates are over 50% for young Li and over 90% for Li over 40 years old (Netting, 1997).

In modern history, the Japanese invaded Hainan Island in 1939. The Li minority aided the Communist guerrillas on the island and formed an anti-Japanese guerrilla force. Perhaps partially for this reason, the island was granted the status of an ethnic autonomous region after the Communists came to power. The dramatic changes in Li's culture and customs began with the establishment of the People's Republic of China in 1949. The Hainan Li and Miao Autonomous Regions were founded in July 1952 and the initial policies offered the Li an enclave to support their self-sufficiency. The government provided seeds, farm tools, cattle and grain to support the autonomous regions in developing agriculture.

Land reform, starting in the 1960s, brought tremendous upheavals to the Li communities. The policy basically appropriated the land owned by the Li and nationalized the farming business. Among the Li, land provides a framework for organizing social bonds and belief systems that incorporate divining the unknown, myths and rituals. Cessation of land ownership disrupted the Li's socio-cultural existence. A sharp decline of the Li economy ensued, accompanied by a Communist atheistic ideology that imposed the infamous policies of *pochu mixin* (eradicating superstitions) and *yifengyisu* (changing prevailing cultures and altering social traditions) in the 1960s and 1970s. Under this pressure, the animistic religion of the Li, which included worshipping ancestors and shamans, as well as their traditional arts and crafts were overwhelmed (Krutak, 2007).

Typically, there are two levels of local government in Li and Miao Autonomous Regions: the formal structure of local governance often imposed and supported by the Han majority and a traditional form of government associated with ethnic Li cultures. The informal governance is characterized by: (a) reliance on the village council of elders, (b) highly valued communal and kinship bonds, and (c) decision making through consensus building (Wang *et al.*, 1992). Li communities are highly influenced by the traditional forms of government. For example, the Li are organized in a social unit called *kom*, which differ in size and have strict territorial boundaries. A big *kom* made up of several small ones is called a *Hemus*. These larger units fall into two major categories: communal farms based on maternal or paternal blood relations and larger farms that admit 'outsiders' who have no blood ties with the original member families. Each commune has a headman who is in charge of production and distribution and officiates at religious ceremonies with his wife's assistance. The headman is also a social leader who mediates disputes and is empowered to admit 'outsiders' as communal members. While cattle remain common property, farm tools, hunting and fishing gear and work tools are privately owned by families. The Li dwell in boat-shaped thatched bamboo houses with woven bamboo or rattan floors. The houses are raised half a meter above the ground and have mud-plastered walls (Wang *et al.*, 1992). Most disputes among the *Hemus* concern the infringement of each other's territory for hunting, fishing or wood-cutting purposes.

Each *Hemus* also includes shamans who guide the spiritual affairs through their communication with spirits, deities and ancestors. The shamans function as mediators between the physical and supernatural realms. They harness supernatural power to ensure success in hunting and curing the sick. Before 1949, animism and ancestor worship were common among the Li, who also believed in witchcraft. The worship of ancestors is reflected in Li's dance performances, such as the bamboo-beating dance, and songs to praise the family or to mourn the dead.

Outsiders tend to view the ethnic Li minority as exotic for its unique culture and heritage. They are widely viewed as 'mystical beings' by people in Mainland China. In particular, the Han majority population is fascinated by the traditional Li marriage ceremony and their tattooing customs. The former remains a relic of a maternal clan society, in which women were in charge of selecting the men and rearing the children. The Li wedding ceremony is different from the Han Chinese practice in which the woman leaves her family to move to her husband's natal village or to live with her husband's family. When a Li girl reaches puberty at around 12 or 13 years old, a single room, called a *Liao*, is built beside the family house. The girl can start to see any man she likes. Shortly after the wedding (marriages are arranged by the parents when their children are still young), the bride goes back to live with her own parents. She can have relationships with other men until she becomes pregnant. This marriage custom, prohibited by the Communist government as a corrupt practice, had virtually disappeared; however, the onset of tourism has rejuvenated 'staged' ethnic wedding ceremonies in recent years. Tourists from China, mostly Han men, view non-Han minority women as feminized, exotic Others, so that the re-enactment of the wedding ceremony provides an instant, voyeuristic opportunity to view 'sexually promiscuous, erotically titillating, and available' ethnic women (Schein, 2000:70–71). The mock wedding ceremony with the participation of the tourists is typically used for entertainment in which expressions of sexuality are highlighted. Bruner (2005: 215), jokingly recounting his participation in a mock wedding with an ethnic woman in a tourist folk village in China, reported that 'after the ceremony, as I was carrying my "bride" into the bedroom, my wife, seated in the audience and getting into the spirit of the event, called out, "Don't close that bedroom door!" Someone provided an immediate translation, and everyone laughed'.

Tattooing is a vanishing tradition in the Li communities. Traditionally, Li tattoos signified that a woman was eligible to be married and the ritual was accompanied by an elaborate puberty ceremony in the village center. Li women, tattooed on such bodily surfaces as the face, neck and legs, believed their tattoos not only made them beautiful, but allowed them to be recognized by their ancestors after death. It was a practice handed down from the ancestors to connect with the myths and heritage of the Li. Krutak (2007) documented the history of Li culture and found that all Li groups tattooed and the practice was more common among women, although men tattooed three blue rings around their wrists for medicinal purposes. Furthermore, tattoo designs and motifs differed between each tribe, and sometimes they differed within families. Tattooing served as an important cultural marker among Li communities, providing an identity differentiating each village. However, currently, it is rarely practiced given Hainan's close integration into the Chinese state. On my fieldworks to

Hainan from 1999 to 2009, I found facial tattooing was extremely rare and I only observed tattoos on the arms and legs of persons in isolated villages in the western part of Hainan. The Li who had tattoos were all old women who have been used as a promotion in the folk villages, such as the Baoting Areca Manor. The tattooed faces have even been published in the leaflets and tourism brochures to emphasize the uniqueness of Li culture.

Although the Li minority populations are not heavily involved in tourism, their existence is widely publicized in the tourism brochures. The tourism industry capitalizes on ethnic culture in a way that brings members of the Li minority into mainstream development. Ethnicity on Hainan has become a popular and marketable resource. The Li minority generally participates in the informal tourism sector by selling craft souvenirs and local fruit. However, a small proportion of the population works in the hotel and hospitality industry. Since there is a growing interest from Mainland China in the aboriginal island cultures, the most visible manifestation for ethnic employment is in the tourist folk villages where Li work as dance performers and staff. A number of folk villages have been established on Hainan, where song and dance shows, the enactment of ceremonies and the availability of ethnic foods and souvenirs provide opportunities for visitors to become acquainted with ethnic cultures.

It can be noted that the situation of the Hainan folk villages is very different from those in North American and Australian contexts. The primary difference is that the issue of aboriginal land claims by ethnic minorities does not exist on Hainan. All lands belong to the national government and the Li minority has no control of the territory where the village is located. The central government has set up a number of autonomous regions populated primarily by an ethnic minority. However, the state's definitions of ethnic space were seldom in keeping with the perceptions of the ethnic groups themselves. Ironically, the creation of an autonomous region was not designed to foster independence for ethnic peoples, but rather to initiate the process of socialist transformation and to establish spatial relations between the centralized cultural, political and economic power of the Han Chinese and the disenfranchised ethnic minorities on the periphery. The Li believe that they are joined inseparably with nature and see the Earth as their 'root' rather than viewing it as a resource to be used only for their short-term advantage. However, since the government controls all land, the population has to relocate their homes if development occurs in their communities. Many of the attempts by the local government to integrate ethnic minorities into prevailing wage economies have led to the alienation of these groups from the land with resulting negative impacts.

Indonesian-Chinese Diaspora

The Chinese-Indonesians who settled on the island in the late 1960s, have seldom been mentioned in the tourist brochures or used for tourism marketing on Hainan. The population is composed of ethnic Chinese, born and raised in Indonesia. Using the word 'ethnicity' to describe this diasporic community has been challenged. Hague (2001) suggested that a diaspora largely possesses a duality of ethnicity and citizenship whose ambiguity forms a so-called 'hyphenated community'. Historically, ethnic 'Chinese' have lived in Indonesia for generations and it is virtually impossible to distinguish the *pribumi* (indigenous Indonesian) and *non-asli* (not original) (Chua, 2004). However, considering the ethnic Chinese to be 'Others' has long been a convenient policy for the Indonesian government, because doing so creates a scapegoat to blame for its economic malaise and social tensions. Heryanto (1998) analyzed the reasons for classifying Indonesian-Chinese as a problematic Other into four broad categories: (a) the geographical argument that the ethnic Chinese were perceived to have originated from some discrete geographical location far from the boundaries of Indonesia, and thus the ethnic Chinese appeared to pose a threat to the nationalist project of seeking native roots and authentic origins; (b) the cultural explanation, which held that due to their segregation from the majority of the population, the ethnic Chinese were not Muslim and had been seen as the least integrated ethnic group in Indonesia; (c) the economic rationale based on the view that the ethnic Chinese controlled a large proportion of the nation's wealth as business middlemen and investors, who were generally well-off financially compared to the average Indonesian (the widespread belief was that the Chinese constituted only 3.5% of the population but controlled 70% of Indonesia's economy); and (d) the suspicion that the ethnic Chinese are Communist sympathizers deeply attached to the People's Republic of China.

By providing ethnicity as an answer to problems, or *Masalah Cina* (the Chinese problem), the Suharto administration forcefully marginalized the community and denounced 'Chineseness' after a military coup overthrew President Sukarno in 1965. Stimulated by the mass media of the government, the public decided that economic disparities and social conflicts were caused by the presence of the ethnic Chinese. During the anti-Communist insurrection, which occurred from 1965 to 1967, a large proportion of ethnic Chinese were killed in an extensive purge of communists and their alleged sympathizers (Heryanto, 1998). The ensuing New Order decreed by the Suharto administration officially endorsed the assimilation and integration policies toward ethnic Chinese, leading to draconian laws. These included the closure of Chinese language schools, public ban against speaking Chinese, compulsory changing name from Chinese to Indonesian and identification cards specifically designed for the ethnic Chinese (Chua, 2004). Consequently, the erasure of everything that was traditionally seen as indicative of Chinese heritage and culture and the concurrent violent ethnic cleansing, resulted in an exodus of thousands of ethnic Chinese to China.

The majority of these *non-asli* refugees were resettled on Hainan Island, arranged by the Communist government with the assistance of local communities. Their resettlement on Hainan served a dual purpose; on the one hand, the Chinese government believed that since the geographic location of Hainan is closest to Southeast Asia where many of the early emigrants originated, it was much easier to assimilate the population into Hainan. Another reason for settling these refugees on Hainan was based on an unwritten policy of keeping them at a distance from Mainland China. Godley (1989) found that the government has a deep distrust of the returned overseas Chinese (*guiguo huaqiao*) owing to their previous foreign connections. Hainan, as a remote island with a backward economy in the 1960s, was considered an ideal place to segregate these exiles from contact with the 'real' Chinese.

Subsequently, the Indonesian-Chinese worked in tropical agriculture on the island, e.g. on rubber and coffee plantations. They built the Overseas Chinese Farm in the County of Xinglong on the eastern coast of the island. Although these exiles came to Hainan possessing a culture that was deeply shaped by their centuries-long residence in Indonesia, the local government refused to recognize their cultural difference, rather, simply calling them *huaqiao* (overseas Chinese). Owing to the lack of recognition of the group by the government, it is extremely difficult to know exactly how many Chinese-Indonesians were resettled on Hainan since the 1960s because the census mixed them with Chinese. Godley (1989) estimated that the total of Chinese-Indonesians who fled to China exceeded a quarter of a million. The provincial documents showed that the number was about 20,000 for the first generation of the diaspora living in Xinglong. The second generation, who were raised on Hainan, speaks virtually no Indonesian, nor keeps the traditional practices. However, the ambiguity of diasporic identity relegates these people with an existence on the fringe of two cultural worlds, but full members of neither. The neglect of the uniqueness of the Indonesian-Chinese on Hainan caused a growing conflict among the diasporic communities, the Han majority and the ethnic Li.

Tourism development in the 1990s was not only one of the more instrumental tools for enhancing ethnic social status, but was also expected to become even more important for the forgotten community of Indonesian-Chinese on Hainan. It was brought to the attention of local governments in the County of Xinglong and tourism businesses that Indonesian-Chinese culture could be a gold mine for attracting tourists. In 1996, an Indonesian village was founded in Xinglong, in response to increased demand by tourists to experience Indonesian cultures during trips along the eastern highway. This tourist village, located in diaspora community, provided a liminal experience for tourists to appreciate ethnic differences. Such performances as Indonesian folk dances, songs and rituals were conducted by the first generation of the diaspora. The performances were colored by nostalgic memories of their homeland. It was estimated that about 60% of tour buses on Hainan visited the village with attendance averaging about 2300 persons per day in 2000 (Xie & Wall, 2008).

Although the Indonesian Village was born out of a desire to portray Indonesian culture, this tourist attraction has faced stiff resistance from the Chinese-Indonesian communities. The village provided an opportunity to revive the memorable rituals and dances that Chinese-Indonesians grew up with, but performance in the village was largely perceived as 'entertainment' rather than 'culture'. Cultural performances in the village were commonly commodified for tourism purposes and several were rejected by the community. The local government supported the establishment of the village as a way of replacing the agriculture industry and economically revitalizing the Chinese-Indonesian communities. Nonetheless, the village was a business enterprise whose 'success' was largely decided on by its level of popularity among tourists. Catering to tourists with entertainment and a certain degree of excitement was, therefore, a crucial element of the performance. Tourists lacked reverence or interest in Indonesian performances and had little knowledge that would allow them to appreciate the programs, especially when commentary or interpretation was not provided. Diasporic Indonesians were seen as a marketable resource, yet little attention was paid to the quality of the performance. Tension between economic development and cultural preservation was evident in the village. I will discuss and compare the Indonesian Village with the Li folk villages in Chapter 7 to demonstrate conflicts that often arise in the process of authenticating diasporic and ethnic identities.

Tourist Folk Villages

The forerunner of the folk village made its appearance at the turn of the 20th century, though there is some dispute regarding its origins. Skansen near Stockholm is widely regarded as the first of its kind (Hitchcock, 1998). Arthur Hazelius, the founder of Skansen, traveled in Sweden's rural hinterland in the 1850s and 1860s, and noticed that the traditional forms of village life were disappearing as a result of the growth of industries and modern communications. Hazelius started acquiring objects in the 1870s and eventually established a small exhibition of these artifacts in Stockholm. Later, he arranged for the purchase of the site known as Skansen in 1891. Here, he displayed such traditional artifacts of Sweden as houses, farms, workshops and mills. Hazelius was convinced that if future generations were to be able to understand what Sweden had been, then collections of traditional objects had to be formed before the material disappeared. The original purpose of the open air folk village was to bring together the surviving remnants of Swedish folk culture and to create an imagined 'intact' farm landscape unchanged by the industrial revolution. Emphasis was placed on creating exhibitions to produce an ideal national community and a distinctive heritage. The Skansen displays are what anthropologists call 'timeless primitives', where an enduring and unchanging folk culture is presented (Crang, 1999). Hazelius' approach implied that the locus of Swedish identity is a palpable entity supported by a particular narration of the past and its myths. The representational milieu can be transformed into a re-created environment and the imagined cultural landscape help preserve the memories of former old days.

The goal of a folk village, as conceptualized by Hazelius, is to create and recreate a representation of life before technological advances, which caused the disappearance of various traditions (Hitchcock, 1998). Most importantly, the folk cultures on display can be fixed and insulated from contemporary life. Exhibitions in a folk village reflect a static cameo of the past where time is frozen, tradition is fossilized and heritage is codified to become the property of history. Hazelius' vision was to encapsulate Swedishness as a holistic and bounded entity by showcasing selected artifacts. The fragmented and complicated character of the history is replaced by an organic and self-contained folklore in the folk village setting – a Sweden in miniature inviting tourists to go back in time.

Hazelius' beliefs have spread rapidly and aroused enormous interest worldwide. The 20th century saw the introduction of Skansen-type museums across the length and breadth of Europe and North America. For example, open air, museum-like villages opened in the Netherlands (Arnhem) in 1911, the USA (Colonial Williamsburg) in 1926 and Canada (Louisbourg) in 1961. On their establishment, these folk villages focused on the history and heritage of the nation and endeavored to accurately portray the societal context of the region. However, in recent decades, the concept has gradually shifted from an emphasis on education to a focus on recreation. Folk villages have morphed to a dynamic and fluid theme park, capable of moving around rather than being confined to their original location. The line between the folk village as a living history and as theme park entertainment has become blurred. Mobility and techno-logical improvement have facilitated the establishment of folk villages to other settings. The surge of new villages, such as Huis Ten Bosch in Nagasaki, Japan, and Taman Mini in Indonesia, successfully blended history, museum and folklore with travel and tourism.

The establishment of Huis Ten Bosch is rooted in the historical relationship between Japan and the Netherlands, reflected in the trading post in Japan by the Dutch in 1609. The folk village was built as an accurate replica of Dutch landscapes in memory of the history of trade between the nations. The meaning of Huis Ten Bosch, according to its website, is to present a theme 'rich in history and romance'. It also employs Dutch staff, who bring Dutch traditions to life and act as a walking advertisement for the 'authentic' Netherlands.

The Taman Mini in Indonesia was established as an Indonesian's self-imagining, initiated by ex-President Suharto. Errington (1998: 201) has called the Taman Mini, 'a political text of nationalist self-representation', whose purpose is to 'construct nationhood'. The replica of Indonesian archipelagic territory and the ethnic pavilions emblematize the tradi-tional cultures of the 27 provinces of the nation, with people dressed in costume on behalf of each province. Ironically, there is nothing to represent the lives of fellow-nationals of Chinese, Arab or Indian ethnicity, nor is there anything representing modern Indonesian culture. On the other hand, East Timor is included and Bali, owing to its cultural significance, was given disproportionate prominence in the exhibition (Hitchcock, 1998). The Taman Mini is a setting where stereotypes have been institutionalized and national identity has been consolidated by the selected themes from the government.

Despite the complexity of folk villages, Gunn (1972, 1994) has proposed that the optimal approach for ethnic communities is to develop an ethnic interpretative center. The aim would be to give tourists descriptive information and interpretation by means of ethnic performance, guidance, exhibits and demonstrations. The success of the Mennonite and Amish communities in using museum-like folk villages for tourists is well documented as an effective method to maintain the boundary between tourists and the 'authentic' communities. Tourists may gain rich experiences by visiting the center without destroying the setting and the carrying capacity of the 'back stage' of the communities. These villages are based on a selective representation of the indigenous culture that presents those characteristics most accessible to tourists. To some extent, the Mennonite and Amish centers offer an opportunity for the ethnic minorities to interact with the outsiders without markedly challenging the integrity of the cultures.

Tourist folk villages have been marketed as a sort of 'salvage anthropology', allowing outsiders to enter a disappearing setting for a transitory moment. The village setting tends to presuppose and freeze a conceptualization of holistic ethnic identity prior to Westernization, industrialization and globalization. The milieu of tourist folk villages provides a glimpse of a bounded space and the recaptured era of a lost culture. For example, the popularity of the Tamaki Maori Village in Rotorua, New Zealand, showcases 'the journey back in time to a Pre-European lifestyle experience of customs and traditions'. Similarly, the Tjapukai Aboriginal Cultural Park in Cairns, Australia, offers a wide array of ethnic performances day and night by posing the catchy question 'have you ever thrown a boomerang?' For both Australia and New Zealand, ethnic cultures make up an idiosyncratic national heritage that masks tense relations between colonialists and aboriginals. These villages present an open space where different stories, histories and memories are romanticized and brought together as the past interacts with the present. Because of their ability to stimulate the imagination of tourists, these villages have become an integral part of cultural tourism.

The advent of the folk villages inevitably raises an intellectual debate on the issue of authenticity. *Prima facie*, authenticity in these folk villages is defined as purity with an ethnic identity immune from either foreign or domestic contamination. Nonetheless, the founding of Skansen museum has long been questioned regarding the selected representation of traditional Swedish life: the reconstructed farmhouse tended to have a strong Danish influence and the thematic displays are not uncommon in Nordic countries. The mélange of various artifacts in the village raises the possibility of creating a mixture of local cultures and heritage that has no basis in any particular setting. Furthermore, the Swedish farmhouses *in situ* can be transported, re-erected or removed from their original sites to create a new tourist destination. The commodification of Swedish culture can even be exported in the Ikea furniture stores worldwide, where the folk dances and songs can be performed from Tokyo to Tel Aviv. Similar ambiguities relate to the restoration, preservation and renewal of the folk village, in which the original meaning can be altered to suit current business needs. To some extent, the part of hybrid peasant culture in the Skansen folk village is fraught with ambivalence, contradiction and contestation, difficult to interpret and explain to the public. Graham *et al.* (2000: 93) pointed out that 'the complexities of dissonance are further exacerbated by the contemporary expansion in the meanings and scope of heritage, and the concomitant multiplication of conflicts between its uses'. The Skansen-type folk village is historically grounded but 'fictively' reinterpreted and reconstructed to cater to the tourists' needs.

My argument here is that authenticity in the context of folk villages needs to be carefully re-examined. Folk villages are purpose-built tourist attractions that provide tourists with access to expressions of folk culture for a fee. Essentially, they are small theme parks centered on ethnicity. On the surface, folk village displays fit what French philosopher Michel de Certeau's (1984) termed *L'invention du quotidien* (the practice of everyday life) so that facets of social forms, such as traditions, heritage and art, make up a culture. However, culture is constantly being appropriated and consumed by people in everyday situations. Certeau's approach to 'quotidian' as the system and discipline of the status quo is discernible in modern society. The premise that the folk village can reflect the daily life of Other or Self for tourist consumption stands in contrast to the view that cultural appropriation could be a galvanizing force to revitalize the marginalized communities or a disappearing heritage. The success of the folk villages rests on the capability of the 'the infinite quotidian reproducibility' (Anderson, 1991: 183) and 'ways of operating' (Certeau, 1984: xviii). Folk villages generally erase the chaos of everyday life and replace it with recognizable markers. A tourist folk village alludes to the spectacular creations of heritage sites in size, scope, architectural detail and meaning. However, the representations typically are not exclusively from a particular community's history because the founders of the folk village formulate a version of ethnic culture by selecting various images and symbols, by rejecting some and by creating new components. The folk village necessarily falsifies place and time by inventing an ideal setting where 'space [is] practiced place' (Certeau, 1984: 117). Ethnic culture has largely been replaced by an array of tourism *practiques*: the aestheticization of space, the construction and production of nostalgia and the idealization of ethnicity (Gotham, 2007). The value attached to ethnic authenticity motivates tourists to seek out distinct cultural elements, such as rituals, myths, customs, dress, beliefs and food. Callero (1994: 232) coined the term 'performance image', suggesting that the key to authenticity is the way people play other roles – an existence of Otherness leads the performers to behave or to act as the ethnic minority. Tourism in the folk villages highlights ethnic differences and uniqueness while ignoring social divisions, inequality and conflicts. Therefore, whether ethnic displays and cultural differences are authentic or not is irrelevant, the issues remain as to who decontextualizes the symbols of ethnicity and who authenticates ethnic cultures for tourist consumption.

At a deeper level, folk villages are essentially 'Disneyfied' to cater to tourists' need. They are not a strictly museum-like setting, but provide easy access allowing tourists to appreciate ethnic cultures in a transitory period of time. Judd (1999: 39) labeled the folk village as a 'tourist bubble', which is 'like a theme park, in that it provides entertainment and excitement, with reassuringly clean and attractive surroundings'. This stands in contrast to Urry's (2002) view that tourists are often looking for a potentially life-changing experience and an escape from everydayness to spaces and times that are 'out of ordinary'. Bruner (2005: 227) offered a different view, namely, that tourists do not go to the folk village seeking authenticity, but rather for 'a reaffirmation of an authenticity already known and experienced... they do not discover the Other but rather witness a performance of themselves in a different context'. The meaning of authenticity has been constantly influenced by tourists' tastes, cultural authorities and the demands of running the village as a business. McIntosh *et al.* (2002) conducted a study in the folk villages of New Zealand and showed that even with good intentions of being represen- tative and authentic, there is a predisposition to create a so-called attraction-based Maori identity that eventually slips into a commercia- lized version of cultural display. In a folk villages, authenticity is not the 'real history' of a place since their physical elements can be moved or remodeled, instead, authenticity should be viewed as the 'opposite of generic' (Florida, 2002: 228) or a *genius loci* – the spirit of place – since various contested representations are juxtaposed.

Discussing the cycle of authenticity in Chapter 2, I suggested that the origins of cultural forms have eventually faded and vanished, while others have emerged as 'authentic' ethnic cultures. In addition, cultural forms that were initially viewed as inauthentic by the ethnic communities have, over time, become redefined and recognized as an authentic expression. A good example of this process is the *pendet*, a welcoming dance for the gods in Bali, Indonesia. The dance was initially performed to welcome tourists in the villages. Troubled by the change in the purpose of this dance, Balinese religious authorities objected. A well-known choreographer was commissioned to create a secular version of the *pendet*. Ironically, this 'secular' version of the dance proved so popular that it soon migrated back to the temples, and 'in a curious reversal that the religious authorities did not anticipate, the tourist "welcome dance" became a sacred dance for welcoming the gods' (Picard, 1996: 151). Therefore, the impurity of the change should be viewed as an authentic form of heritage over time, or a form of 'creative destruction' (Fan *et al.*, 2008), providing a series of tensions and contestations in the development process.

The success of the folk villages highlights diversity rather than the universality of the value of 'subjectivity and dependence upon history, cultural inheritance and idealized conceptions of the world' (Jacques, 1995: 91). The purpose-built folk village should be a driving force for the preservation of national and ethnic identities with a re-interpretation of heritage dissonance. The following section demonstrates how changes in the locations of the Hainan folk villages has (a) raised problems highlighting the intricacy of authenticity and (b) affected accessibility to the villages because the building of the highways shifted the supply-demand relationship in the folk villages and their presentations.

Accessibility, Commodification and Authenticity

The rapid change in traffic patterns has laid a solid foundation for the tourism business on Hainan. The majority of tourists fly there, but coach is the most common mode of transportation for travel within Hainan. There is only one railway, built in WWII during the Japanese occupation, but it has been abandoned for years. Three routes traverse Hainan from north to south: the eastern, central and western. All routes run from Haikou, the capital city on the northern tip of the island, to Sanya, a major beach resort in the south. The central highway was the first one built in the early 1990s, traversing the Li Autonomous Region where the majority of Li live. The cities of Wuzishan (formerly known as Tongzha) and Qiongzhong have the largest Li ethnic communities with 60 and 45%, respectively, of the population of Li ethnicity (Statistics Bureau of Hainan, 2007).

Although conditions are extremely rough on the central route due to the ruggedly mountainous topography, the road was a huge success because it improved access to the natural resources in the center of the island. The direct user benefits accruing to commuters and travelers include time saving and vehicle operating cost reduction. In the late 1990s, the construction of the eastern route spurred economic development in cities and townships along the freeway. Because of its modern infrastructure, it is by far the fastest route, requiring about three and half hours to go from Haikou to Sanya by the central route, but only an hour and a half by the eastern route. The western route was built at the same time but it crosses the least developed part of Hainan. The degree of discrepancy in the allocation of resources for improving transportation and communication can also be seen in the limited extent of construction of roads, rest areas and telecommunication facilities here. Overall, three routes have stimulated the local economy and mitigated income disparity, including opportunities for tourist attractions and tourism development. Tourist attractions encompass the impacts of business investment on the types and quantity of new economic activities that develop in the affected regions as a result of the highway; for example, resort villages, golf courses or residential villas built along the eastern highway. Expenditures resulting from new travel patterns provide convenience and incentives for travel, either for the purpose of sightseeing or investment.

The locations of tourist-oriented folk villages have been greatly influenced by the evolving transportation network. There was a warm reception from the Li communities when the central highway was established because it enhanced the convenience of transporting agricultural products grown in the area to Haikou and Sanya for sale. Orders could now be placed directly with the communities, and the local specialties such as bamboo shoots and teas are readily available on the shelves in the grocery stores. However, the original purpose of the central route has shifted to tourism. Tourists began to take the coaches from Haikou to Sanya in 1990 and a growing number of tourists found the route was extremely scenic and breathtaking even though the trip took longer than three hours. A rest stop in Wuzhishan was recommended, since the drivers needed to get gas and the passengers had to eat late lunch before arriving in Sanya by dusk. By coincidence, Wuzhishan has one of the largest concentrations of the ethnic Li minority, who work in the majority of positions in the service sector, such as selling tropical fruit, snacks and crafts on the streets when the tour buses stop in the rest area.

In the summer of 1992, a tour bus had to have a flat tire repaired and its tourist passengers were stranded in the area on a very hot day. Several curious tourists asked the tour guide if they could see the nearby Li village or watch an ethnic dance during the break. The tour guide contacted the village head to see if the tourists would be able to wander freely for an hour and take some pictures. The request was instantly approved and the tourists from Mainland China could enter the 'back stage' of the Li village. Initial reaction to the unplanned visit was mixed, because the village was unprepared for the swarm of tourists 'intruding' in every corner. There was no live performance or entertainment. At the end of the tour, the village head agreed that he would organize a Li dance performance should these tourists plan to visit again (obviously they would not).

The departure of the tourists left the community with interesting questions: (a) is it possible to build a primitive tourist attraction along the highway to accommodate those who are interested in touring the village? and (b) would it be possible to arrange a Li dance performance to showcase the ethnic culture to these tourists? The community's opinions were divided. For some of the Li, the tourist folk village would be an excellent opportunity to present the Li in front of tourists who come from Mainland China and to have a share of the tourism benefits on Hainan. Others saw as it as a challenge that none of the community members knew how to start a tourism business, nor was there an understanding of what kind of programs they could offer. The residents of the village eventually decided, with the support of the village head, to 'test the waters' by building a thatched hut adjacent to the village with an open stage for Li dance performances. Instead of aimlessly wandering through the village, tourists would spend about 30 minutes in the hut, watching the bamboo-beating dance and listening to the Li folk songs, both generally performed on 3 March, the traditional Li festival.

The village leaders presented the plan to the rest area personnel, who agreed to post a schedule on the entrance door to inform tourists about the times and dates of the performances. The quickly developed project worked almost seamlessly: tourists expressed interest and a willingness to spend a short period of time at the hut, and bus drivers and tour guides were also pleased because they now had an additional tourist program that allowed them to take more break time during the performance. The thatched hut was named *Fan Mao*, meaning a 'humble hut' in the Li language. Dance performers and staff who had no formal training were all from the village. The programs offered depended on the availability of the performers. The tourists were permitted to tour the village after the performance, allowing them to buy the local products at a cheaper price than in the rest area. Owing to the hot and humid weather at midday, the performances were scheduled four times a day: two in the morning and two in the late afternoon. No fee was charged for watching the performance, but a bucket was left near the exit door with a note, 'the Ethnic Li thanks you for your help', soliciting donations.

The success of the Fan Mao instantly changed business in Wuzhishan. The region was extremely poor and received little economic benefit from tourism on Hainan because, previously, tourists had passed through the city and had nothing to do with the villages. Besides selling the fruits and crafts in the rest area, tourist-related activities were virtually non-existent and the infrastructure was too backward to attract any investment. The bold idea of the Fan Mao was not commercially oriented, but was designed to satisfy the tourists' curiosity about the Li minority. However, the attraction had significant impact on the region: street vendors started moving back to the village because business was better next to the Fan Mao; the bucket left at the exit was quickly filled with money donated by the tourists, surprising the village and performers. It became routine from 1992 to 1994 that tour buses along the central freeway to Sanya included a short stop at the Fan Mao to watch 'exotic' Li performances and to purchase 'authentic' Li crafts and souvenirs. The original schedule of four times per day was increased in order to accommodate the influx of tourists. By 1994, the Fan Mao was the only Li attraction on the central freeway offering 10 to 15 performances per day.

The establishment of the Fan Mao on the central highway created problems and conflicts between the village and the rest area. With the popularity of the folk village, the employees in the rest area felt strongly that though they had helped promote the Fan Mao, they did not receive a fair share of the economic benefit. The business near the rest area was down due to the return of street vendors to the village. When the tour buses chose not to stop in the area, and instead parked directly near the Fan Mao, employees of the rest area feared it could be abandoned. The employees complained to the village that if the rest area was to close, the Fan Mao would go under. A revenue sharing plan was proposed as a necessary step to keep the rest area operating. However, the plan received a cold reception from the village. Many of the residents argued that its business had nothing to do with the rest area, though the presence of the rest area had helped set the stage for the development of the village's tourist attractions. Performers in the Fan Mao accused the employees of the rest area of having 'red-eye syndrome' (a Chinese idiom meaning jealousy and fury). Given the steady flow of tourists, the village decided that the *status quo* (that is, no revenue sharing) was in their best interests.

The news of the success of the Fan Mao spread fast. By the end of 1994, another tourist folk village was built about five miles from the Fan Mao, with a much better dance hall and planned programs. By 1997, three folk villages mushroomed along the central highway and each offered identical programs. They were located near the city of Sanya further away from the Li communities and were opened swiftly in a sponta-neous process with new entrepreneurs attempting to emulate the success of the Fan Mao. Commercial activities were dominant in these villages. Instead of using a bucket to collect donations, the new businesses charged every tourist a fee to watch the performance. The Li commu-nities were not widely involved in these folk villages; however, some members were employed to work as dance performers for meager pay.

These newly established folk villages actively recruited tour buses to make stops so that tourists could stay as long as they could afford. Such incentives as cigarettes and free meals were provided to bus drivers in order to maintain their loyalty. As a result, the original location of the Fan Mao experienced a sharp decline in tourists and revenue because of intense competition from the newly established folk villages. Tour buses passed by the Fan Mao simply because the village did not provide incentives to the drivers. In addition, it was thought that the Fan Mao setting was too primitive to attract tourists to stay for the performance. In retaliation for not getting a share of the Fan Mao profits, the employees of the rest area told tourists who used its facility that Li tourist attractions lacked improved sanitation and had chaotic management and, therefore, did not merit a visit. The fierce competition with the other folk villages ultimately caused the closure of the Fan Mao in 1998. The community decided to go back to traditional farming. The thatched hut remains adjacent to the village, but has deteriorated rapidly and is barely noticeable whenever the buses pass through the area.

The demise of the Fan Mao did not ensure the success of other folk villages. Those along the central highway received a severe blow when the eastern highway was completed in 1996. Construction of this new route changed the tourism traffic dramatically and provided the fastest and most direct connection between Haikou and Sanya. Although the central route had a wealth of authentic ethnic culture and rugged scenery, poor road conditions discouraged travel through the center of the island. Tour operators preferred the eastern highway because it allowed tourists a longer stay in Sanya and more time for shopping. Because of this shift of traffic, new folk villages were opened along the eastern route, which now carries most of the tourism traffic. The number of folk villages built along the eastern route has increased to six, while the folk villages on the central route experienced a sharp decline in tourist arrivals. In order to counter that decline, villages along the central route aggressively cut prices and increased incentives to lure tourist traffic. Tour bus drivers were given commissions for bringing tourists to the villages. However, such efforts were in vain because the business had moved to the eastern route to the detriment of folk villages on the central route. A downward spiral with fewer tourists leading to further declines ensured all folk villages eventually ceased operation along the central route by 2009.

Figure 3.3 illustrates the changing distribution of folk villages on Hainan in 10 years. The map on the left was plotted in 1999 when the development of folk villages was in full swing and both eastern and central routes were clustered with purpose-built ethnic villages. As a result, there has been a slow shift to the east as transportation has improved significantly and the majority of tour buses use the eastern highway. The map on the right, plotted in 2009, shows that all folk villages disappeared, except the Areca Manor. To make matters worse, the number of folk villages along the eastern highway decreased to only one, i.e. Longgun folk village built in 2008. The continuing downward trend of folk villages can be viewed from the following perspectives.

One can attribute the eventual failure of the folk villages to shoddy imitation and intense price competition among these villages. Nonetheless, construction of the eastern highway should also be seen as an

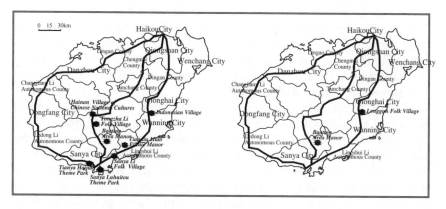

Figure 3.3 Changing distribution of folk villages on Hainan from 1999 to 2009

important catalyst for change. The most recent folk village, Longgun, has been constructed in areas that were not previously occupied by Li people. Although the village now employs some Li people for dance performance, its offer is very similar to those formerly available on the central route. Longgun is outside the Li Autonomous Region in a location that is deemed inauthentic. With the change in the location of folk villages in the past 10 years, a series of social changes have gradually occurred. Many of those changes involve a reduction in the authenticity of the cultural content of the performances and handicrafts offered to tourists. For example, most of the employees and dancers in the original tourist folk village were Li; however, newer folk villages were located adjacent to the eastern route where the Li minority was largely absent rather than a majority. Tour operators, who largely determine where tourists will travel and stop, have little concern about presenting authentic aspects of Li culture. Some employees in the new villages who wore Li ethnic clothing were not of Li origin. Ethnic clothing has become a business uniform and the 'traditional' dance performances have become 'manufactured' routines.

Another factor that has had an important impact on folk villages, along both the central and eastern routes, stems from the reality that the number of villages surged in a short period of time, allowing tour planners to become increasingly selective. Instead of touring two or three folk villages, tour guides select only one village on the tour route. Thus, opportunities for interaction between tourists and ethnic minorities have been influenced by transport planners and tour operators as well as the managers of the folk villages. The decline of folk villages along the eastern route by 2009 reflected a diminishing interest from tour operators to promote ethnic tourism. Fierce competition forced tourism businesses to change their marketing strategies by emphasizing beaches, golfing and other sporting events, rather than the folk villages. A general phenomenon was that the promotion of folk villages dwindled significantly in the mass media. The number of advertisements from the village business was almost zero from 2005 to 2009.

A third factor that can be identified as having had an important impact on the folk villages on Hainan, is that since the inception of the Fan Mao, the folk villages have been regarded as major employers in the surrounding ethnic communities. However, those that remained along the central route declined, they offered lower wages and less security of employment than those in the east. The redevelopment of folk villages in the eastern periphery of Hainan led some ethnic Li people who formerly lived in the center of the island to migrate eastward. In particular, the establishment of Nanshan cultural tourism zone near Sanya attracted young members of ethnic families, who left the traditional Li communities to seek employment opportunities. Thus, the development of ethnic tourism is gradually changing the social structure of the Li minority, as well as causing a decline in the authenticity of the presentations of Li culture to tourists.

Summary

Since ethnic tourism tends to be more interested in economic success than concerned about the authenticity of its attractions, the content of performances, the location of those performances, as well as the accuracy of the handicrafts offered can become ludicrously inappropriate. A concern for *genius loci* is inconsistent with an inappropriate relocation of material and non-material culture. A salient example of such incongruity is the Elgin marbles, which are from Athens, Greece, and are now exhibited in the British Museum in London. There is heated debate about the appropriateness of that location (should they be returned to Greece?) as well as of cultural expression (is the heritage of the Parthenon lost in the museum?). Both points were emphasized by Harrison (2005: 3), who stressed that 'it is highly unlikely that most visitors to the British Museum – including Greek visitors – could distinguish the genuine Elgin/Parthenon marbles from plaster casts' and yet, 'certainly, much store is set on something being "the real thing"'.

Like the Elgin marbles put on view in the British Museum, the purpose-built folk villages on Hainan reflect a misplaced authenticity in the context of ethnic tourism. With the enhanced accessibility of the eastern route, tourists who once traveled to Li villages to access the ethnic culture, no longer need to do so because the villages have moved to the tourists: a supply orientation has been replaced by a pattern dominated by demand. Consequently, the commodification of culture has increased and the authenticity of experience, especially with respect to location, has diminished. The changing distribution of folk villages has further marginalized the Li minority population whose ethnic culture is being commodified by others and displayed in inauthentic locations.

The question of authenticity of the folk villages on Hainan can be summarized by a variation of what Boniface and Fowler (1993: 121) have termed 'the moving object story'. In their original view, this relates to artifacts such as paintings and statues that have been removed from their original geographical and cultural milieu to an alien context. The object remains authentic but its context and significance are not, which raises the question of authenticity. Boniface and Fowler (1993: 142) have argued that the 'moving object' represents a problem because the pursuit of authenticity by the mass of tourists directly causes 'the clash of public and private interests, of money and culture, of ownership and location, physical and interpretive mobility in cultural property'. In a similar vein, Urry utilized the metaphor of a sandcastle to describe the role of place in relation to mobility. He noted that:

> A particular physical environment does not itself produce a tourist place. A pile of appropriately textured sand is nothing until there is embodied activity, sociality especially around family life, memory especially as recorded photographically, and image of places. Indeed places only emerge as "tourist places" when they are appropriated, used and made part of the memories, narratives, and images of people engaged in embodied social practice. (Urry, 2006: ix)

The folk villages on Hainan are tantamount to sandcastles, which are not permanent but fluid and varying. The conventional wisdom that tourists travel to the folk villages in order to experience ethnic culture has shifted to a strategy of folk villages being 'on the move' in search of tourists. In my view, the shift of the major transportation pattern from the central to eastern route should be seen as resulting in the creation and interaction of human and non-human factors that place the convenience of tourists and tourist agents, over a concern for the authenticity of culture. Given the increasing ease of transportation, a sharp awareness of the relationship between location and authenticity is vital. In this case, constructing authenticity is a mode of resistance against the mobility of the folk villages. The Fan Mao, as the first folk village on Hainan, is illustrative of authenticity because the Li community was the genuine owner of its culture. Its dance performers and staff were all ethnic Li from the village. Their dance performances were unassuming but deeply rooted with primitive cultural presentation. It is evident that ethnic tourism is a double-edge sword, which can have positive economic effects while at the same time causing damage to the authenticity of a culture. When the factor of *place* is not of importance, inauthenticity becomes the norm in the new folk villages and, thus, ethnic tourism becomes a process of Disneyization that transforms an authentic place into an ageographical and ahistorical theme park bereft of real authenticity.

Chapter 4
Governments

Introduction

The Southern Metropolis Magazine (*Nan du Zhoukan*) in China published an investigative report on the Qiang ethnic minority after the massive earthquake in Sichuan Province in May 2008. The earthquake was catastrophic for this ancient ethnic group, killing 30,000 of their population, or about one-tenth of the Qiang. Among the dead were 40 people who were officially designated as cultural masters by the local and national governments, including all six Qiang music and dance experts. The national government has vowed to invest $1.5 billion to salvage Qiang culture, including building Jina Qiang Village. However, there is just one hitch: many residents of the Jina Qiang Village are not actually Qiang. National public radio (NPR) in the USA interviewed village residents who openly admitted that they actually belonged to the Han majority, but were following orders from the local government to change their ethnic group to Qiang (Lim, 2008). One of the villagers told NPR that 'it was a government decision; we only did what we were told', including the alteration of their identification cards to Qiang ethnicity. At refugee camps for earthquake survivors, there were actually classes on how to become Qiang. Rows of shy, smiling Han women learned the distinctive Qiang embroidery in a large Qiang cultural center. For these residents, learning the Qiang culture will help develop tourism here in the future and being an 'authentic' Qiang is a necessary step for the village to become a sanctioned tourist site. However, the NPR staff observed that many of the women attending the class had only the sketchiest idea about Qiang culture. When asked what the difference is between Han and Qiang, these women answered warily that 'there are so many differences. We don't really know what they are; that's why we're studying them'. All those interviewed agreed that before the earthquake, only some of villages' residents were of Qiang ethnicity, but after the earthquake, officials made everybody change their ethnicity to Qiang. At the end of the interview, NPR raised a seemingly simple question 'Could the government be fabricating a culture to attract tourists?' This was denied by Lin Chuan, the tourism and culture director for the county, who is himself Qiang. He emphasized that many Qiang have become thoroughly sinicized and have forgotten their own customs. Further, Lin explained that 'in the past, there was discrimination against minority groups, now we are restoring the Qiang. If people have Qiang lineage, they can recover their Qiang ethnicity. That is national policy. It is not fake'.

The NPR's report on creating 'fake' ethnic identity after the earthquake reminded me of Bigenho's (2002) book entitled *Sounding Indigenous*, on authenticity in Bolivian ethnic cultural performance. Bigenho has described government intervention and policies as constituting an 'authenticity police'. She asserted that

> while the Weberian state may refer to bureaucratic institutions and a monopoly over the legitimate use of force, the hyphenated nation-state pretends to place this authority and organization over a hypothetical single common community whose members reside in a single common territory. (Bigenho, 2002: 4)

Furthermore, Bigenho believed that the 'mythic isomorphism of one state-one nation-one culture-one community' is derived from a position of relative power that governments use to impose some politically determined criteria of what is ethnic or authentic on Other. Kaup (2000) documented the ethnic politics in China's classification process after the Communists took power in 1949. It was estimated that more than 400 groups registered as separate ethnicities in the 1953 census; however, following an 'objective' assessment by officials and anthropologists to determine the 'unique ethnicities', this number was reduced to 55 groups. The classification system was one of the most controversial policies in Chinese modern history, yet it supported the power of the government to decide who is qualified as 'ethnic' and who should be 'ethnic'. Ethnic identities were lifted out of their cultural context and were selected to dovetail with the expectations of government policies. In the case of the Qiang minority in China, the concept of ethnicity was altered or manipulated to make the group more appealing, accessible or sensational for tourists. Ethnicity, it seems from this perspective, is not a fixed characteristic built on lineage, but a commodity whose value is set by the governments. Being an ethnic minority is a prism through which the assertion of authenticity often results in contradictory and competing consequences: the women of the Han majority learn to be Qiang with financial support from the governments; official identification cards can be altered to include another ethnicity; consequently, tourist attractions can be sanctioned as 'authentic' by various levels of government agencies. It is evident that the manipulation of the Qiang identity has tangible economic value with huge tourism potentials. However, it is also clear that various governments have controlled ethnic identity and exerted a profound influence during the process of its development. The system resonates with what Clifford (1988: 14) called 'matters of power and rhetoric', meaning that the politicization of ethnicity reflects a shift from the culturally and historically authentic to its reflecting a set of bureaucratic practices.

This chapter compares perspectives from three types of government involvement in ethnic tourism, namely, the nature of national, provincial and local involvement. This examination uses as a framework the five dichotomous measures proposed in Chapter 2. These measures provide a means of comparing government involvement at various levels when authenticating ethnic Li culture and identity. Different tiers have different objectives for ethnic culture and for tourism uses of that culture. Ethnic tourism is commonly seen as a set of discrete economic activities and a mode of tourist consumption in a spatially bounded locale. In this instance, the process reflects the relation of 'internal Orientalism' between 'imaging and cultural/political domination that takes place inter-ethnically within China' (Schein, 1997: 73).

I have constructed my arguments on the basis of a highly complex set of institutional and political relations that involves government interventions, policies and sanctioned tourist enterprises. There is a need to address the interrelationship between the various roles played by the governments (Hall, 1996). A false impression exists that these roles are independent of each other. In fact, the roles played by governments are collaborative and interconnected. It is essential to examine how interactions among the national, provincial and local governments shape outcomes for individuals, communities and regions. The study of Hainan's Li minority reflects the extent to which governments' roles in tourism vary but are interrelated according to the conditions and circumstances in different regions. Ethnic tourism is a transaction process driven by the macro and micro political levels. These political levels often hold divergent views on managing ethnic resources, in particular, the reification of ethnic markers and cultural identity. I examine how, historically, the meaning of ethnic authenticity has been constructed, specifically in terms of theme parks and folk villages in China. In addition, I analyze how tourism-related tensions have changed over time. I also address wider issues that arise when governments at three levels authenticate ethnic culture and transform cultural experiences for tourist consumption.

Authenticity versus Commodification

National level

'Why are you interested in the Li minority?' 'What are the purposes of researching the Li?' and 'Are they worth your time?' These were the most frequent questions I encountered when interviewing government officials and cadres at various levels on Hainan. They elucidated the different ways ethnic Li are perceived and how policy making is developed by the governments that are tightly controlled by the Han majority. The undertone of the officials' comments communicated their view that the ethnic minority is 'backward', 'uneducated' and 'inferior'. Historically, the Li have faced prejudice from the Han for being 'lazy, dirty, violent, and drunken, and incorrigibly inept at study and business' (Netting, 1997: 14). Perhaps like no other nation, modern China has persistently attempted to eradicate 'backward' (*Luohou*) as a means of modernizing and civilizing ethnic minorities. However, this policy did not come into existence overnight. For many decades since the establishment of Marxist dogma became dominant, a policy of ethnic groups' being placed into two broad categories – 'revolutionary' or 'counter-revolutionary' – has been followed. No matter the level of economic development achieved by ethnic groups, the ultimate perfection of Communism was the only way to erase all boundaries among all the ethnicities (Sofield & Li, 1998). It was not until December 1978, a watershed moment, when the Third Plenum of the Eleventh Central Committee of the Chinese Communist Party concluded that economic reform should be the top priority. The paramount leader, Deng Xiaoping, prevailed and the Open Door policy was born. In the following three decades, the archetype of modernity, largely driven by the mentality of a rags-to-riches narrative, has become widely accepted in Chinese society.

As an integral part of economic revitalization, tourism became a viable form of development. Zhang *et al.* (1999) examined three periods of political changes in China: the first period was from 1978 to 1985, when government regarded the nature of tourism as both politics and economics, as opposed to tourism used solely as propaganda prior to 1978; the second period was from 1986 to 1991, when the view of tourism shifted to economics from politics; and the third period was from 1992 to 1999, when the government regulated tourism as part of a 'market economy' model and offered greater freedom and flexibility. Following Zhang *et al.*, I propose a fourth period, from 2000 to present, which revisits the first period when tourism was viewed as having both political and economic significance by the various governments.

At first glance, the combination of authoritarian politics, state capitalism and a frenetic private sector has been a potent wealth creator. The 20th century *fin de siècle* witnessed vast improvements in information technology and mobility in China. The result is that travel and tourism have become possible for ordinary Chinese. The liberalization of tourism to foreign countries because of successful economic reforms, disposable income and time, has reshaped Chinese attitudes toward the world (Zhang, 2003). However, China's meteoric rise is facing mounting challenges as the development of modernity results in a series of socio-economic consequences; for example, the centrally planned economy and egalitarian society created by the state government has gradually become characterized by a widening gap between rich and poor, also, a crumbling social safety net and a new hierarchy of social classes are apparent. Conflicts in the development of modernity in the new millennium reinforce public perception that the Communist-led government is quickly losing moral control and is powerless to resolve these tensions.

Tourism has once again become a political tool, albeit a somewhat ineffective one, to balance the demands of power and freedom. Governments at various levels have been more actively involved and played key developmental and operational roles in tourism as an element in their efforts to remain in power. Those multiple roles include: an operator who provides tourism infrastructure to stimulate the economy; a regulator who formulates business practices; an investment stimulator who grants financial incentives; a promoter who advertises tourism activities worldwide; a coordinator who synchronizes different government departments; and an educator who offers training programs for tourism and hospitality (Zhang *et al.*, 1999). Governments have attempted to assert their cultural and moral authority by regarding tourism as socio-economic activities designed to reach various goals. For example, the Beijing (central) government has encouraged more Mainland Chinese tourists to visit Hong Kong, a former British Colony, as a means of stimulating its economy. By contrast, the government called for boycotts on tourism to France after the Olympic torch relay protests in Paris in June 2008. Although these measures to harness tourism as a hegemonic instrument are not always effective, both policy changes clearly reflect the governments' important role in shaping tourism demand and tourists' behaviors. As noted by Henderson (2007: 250), the value attached to tourism as a propaganda channel is especially high within a communist context 'where the fundamental insecurity of authoritarianism gives rise to a compulsion to trumpet the superiority of the doctrine and the benefits of life in a socialist utopia'.

Ethnic culture (*minzhu wenhua*) is viewed as an exotic and primitive source of vitality for modern China. The national government has begun to move cautiously to include *minzhu wenhua* as an acceptable component of tourism since the 1980s. Ethnic tourism emerged as part of a state-led marketing campaign and a broad-based service sector modeled after the consumerism in the West (Nyiri, 2006). The objective is to alleviate poverty and to expedite the process of modernity. For example, the national government launched the 'Open Up the West' project in 2000, a large-scale economic stimulus package to revive the economy in the western part of China, including Tibet, Xinjiang and Yunnan provinces, where a large number of ethnic minorities live (Sofield & Li, 2007). A new guideline called the 'Outline Program for Poverty Alleviation and Development in the Rural Areas of China' was proposed in 2001, to identify the ethnic minorities who need immediate assistance (Mackerras, 2003). Tourism has naturally become a viable path for the ethnic minority to 'get rich by culture'.

According to Culler (1981: 137) 'to be fully satisfying the sight needs to be certified as authentic, it must have markers of authenticity attached to it'. By choosing the representatives of the ethnic markers for tourism and commodifying them for public consumption, the national government anticipates that *minzhu wenhua* will be fully integrated into the economic orbit of the state system, and, concomitantly, to fill a symbolic and commercial niche in modern China (Oakes, 1992). Ethnicity has increasingly become a useful political instrument for the government to appropriate, select or ignore the elements of *minzhu wenhua*.

Tensions between authenticity and commodification stem from the physical and psychological distance between the Han majority and the ethnic minority when the tourist gaze occurs, as I proposed with the term 'ethnic panopticon' in Chapter 1. The relative power and function of the 'authenticity police' direct China's gaze toward minority cultures and standardize them into a set of markers easily recognizable for tourism marketing and campaigns. Liu (1997) called the power relations 'spatial hierarchy', where the ethnic minority is categorized in varying degrees of civilization, such as 'advanced' or 'uncivilized', depending on the economic status of the communities. The backwardness (*luohou*), the feminization, and the infantilization of ethnic minorities are a polemic of 'flexible positional superiority' (Saïd, 2003: 7). This process allows their cultures to be pigeonholed into a Han-centric gaze. Schein (2000), through extensive fieldwork in Guizhou, China, discovered that the Chinese government purposely classified the ethnic Miao into a pejorative taxonomy of 'raw' and 'cooked'. The 'cooked' Miao referred to those who lived closer to Han settlements and assimilated into Chinese culture, while the 'raw' Miao were defined as unruly, living in terrain that was more rugged and isolated, or without the influence of the majority culture. Disparaging socio-economic status produces what I call 'modernity dissonance' and raises the problem of what to do with existing ethnic cultures that no longer conform to the present goals of the policies. By conveniently assigning an ethnic minority to a state of permanent infancy or exotic feminized status, the national government selectively discards, revives and reinvents ethnic materials, performed cultures and traditions to fit new conceptualizations of Chinese modernity and political economy (Doorne *et al.*, 2003). The concept of backward (*luohou*) can be seen as having positive and negative implications. On the one hand, it assigns ethnic minorities to the bottom of the economic continuum. On the other hand, cultural features identified as *luohou* can be favorably marketed as 'untainted', 'uncorrupted' and 'unspoiled' attractions developed and sanctioned by the government for the purpose of ethnic tourism. The vision and presentation of ethnic cultures in China are typically conducted solely within the dominant mainstream discourse (Chinese Han majority) and various levels of the dominant hegemony. The modernizing Other enables the governments to have a tight grip on the interpretation of ethnicity.

Although the national government is taking an active role in tourism planning and policy making, in managing commodification of tourism, it tends to be cumbersome and bureaucratic. According to the interviews with the National Tourism Administration staff, the national government runs two parallel paths for authenticating ethnic cultural resources: one is the active pursuit of modernity, including commercial, economic and social integration inherent in tourism development; the other involves top-down administrative policies to formulate ethnic culture and to monitor heritage preservation. Regarding the first path, ethnic tourism is closely associated with alleviating the financial burden of the state and eventually reducing high unemployment rates in ethnic communities. The second path mandates policies to certify ethnic tradition as *zhen* (authentic) or *jia* (inauthentic).

There is a labyrinthine structure for managing ethnic tourism from the national level. Its simplified elements are: the Nationalities Affairs Commission (*minwei*), the Religious Division of the State Cultural Bureau (*zhonjiaoshuo*) and China National Tourism Administration (*lvyouju*). These three political agencies determine which ethnic cultures are authentic and authorize which elements should be preserved. Whereas the administrative duties of *minwei* is concerned with all aspects of nationality affairs and provides funding for ethnic preservation, the *zhongjiashuo* is more specifically responsible for choosing and preserving cultural artifacts and the *lvyouju* is in charge of the marketing and promotion. For example, while *minwei* sanctions the traditional ethnic Li festival on Hainan, on the Third of March of the lunar year as authentic and representative of Li folklore, *zhongjiashuo* approves the folk songs and the musical instruments used during the festival and *lvyouju* recommends the festival as a 'healthy' ethnic tourism program for travel agencies. It goes without saying that the 'spontaneous' Third of March festival would not happen without the approval of the three agencies. The agencies' sanctioning and promoting of an ethnic cultural revival has had a significant impact on the identity of ethnic groups.

Ethnic attractions in the era of commercialized tourism are often required to have a 'canon' for it developed by the governments. A canon of the site, as noted by Nyiri (2006), represents a process of 'indexing' and 'indoctritainment' (Sun, 2002: 191) to produce specific and delimited cultural markers used in creating and selling images of ethnic destinations. Nyiri (2006: 48–57) summarized five stages of the Chinese government's intervention to 'enshrine' tourist attractions. The first stage centers on delineation and development of the culture. This stage is designed to create a tourist product supported by a multitude of performance and interactive features that will be 'tourable'. Tourism is viewed as a means of modernization of selected delineated destinations. Nyiri identified the second stage of developing a canon for an attraction as focused on classification and endorsement. Tourist attractions have to be classified and approved by the governments, cultural authority and overseas agencies. Rankings of the tourist destinations are initiated and controlled by the government to reflect the tradition and the mixture between tourism and politics. The third stage proposed by Nyiri is 'serialization'. In this stage, the original tourist attraction is reproduced and expanded with different meanings by government agencies. Tourist narratives, brochures and guidebooks are made uniform and located under the cultural authority. Ethnic traits are selected for performance or display for tourists. In the fourth stage, 'standardization and commodification', a process of branding and commercialization is undertaken to make the public believe that the destination is 'pristine' and 'popular'. Commodification in the ethic attractions is not only rapid but also standardized; however, as Nyiri (2006: 54) pointed out, 'unlike tourism development in the West, no attempts [in China] are made to disguise commercialization through clever design, use of materials, or sales behavior'. The final stage, the establishment of 'enclaves', centers on the development of 'enclavic tourist spaces' (Edensor, 1998: 45) that cater to the specific domestic tourists or tourists from the West.

The national government's institutionalization of ethnic identities determines which aspects of culture are deemed marketable for tourism. Among the most successful ethnic attractions with the backup of the national policies are the theme parks and tourist folk villages. Exactly like those in Taman Mini Indonesia, theme parks in China provide an encapsulation of the identities of the different cultures found in a region. Most importantly, the valorization of cultures and heritage were undertaken with the support of the various levels of governments. These open air 'village museums' were promoted to inculcate national pride in a 'harmonious' multi-ethnic society. The 'theme park fever' (Bao, 1995) in the 1990s was attributed to several influences: (a) a growing popular fascination with ethnic minority culture as an exotic and primitive source of vitality in a modern China facing global capitalism and massive changes; ethnic tourism provided a convenient gaze to take a glimpse at ethnic cultures and life; (b) theme parks encompassed a set of 'authentic' markers easily recognizable for public consumption; (c) theme parks provided amusement, entertainment and a museum-like function that could be applied to widely different contexts; and (d) the need for lucrative profit flowing from high admission fees.

The best example of how these four factors operated can be found in the popularity of Shenzhen's Splendid China, a theme park showcasing Chinese cultures located near the border of Hong Kong. It comprises over 30 ha of miniaturized national landmarks, ranging from the Great Wall to the Terra Cotta Warriors. The establishment of Splendid China in 1989 created a nostalgic platform for national identity. The project also combined tourism and commercialism (Oakes, 1997). Following the instant success of Splendid China, folk culture villages were built in 1991 and Windows of the World (a miniature display of world famous architecture) in 1995. The folk villages cover 180,000 m² and are situated next to Splendid China. Featuring 'authentic replicas' of 'typical' dwellings for 21 of China's 56 officially recognized ethnic groups, the village seeks to authentically represent Chinese ethnic minorities. However, the displays were carefully selected and the politically incorrect items were removed to ensure the unity of the nation. The images are carefully crafted, like Disneyland, so that the touristic vision is that of a poetic and colorful mosaic, a distinctive tapestry woven by the happy and servile minorities (Oakes, 1997).

The 1990s witnessed the apogee of theme parks in China followed by their decline. False expectations for the parks led to a glut of construction in new settings to replicate the more successful ones. Ap (2003), critiquing the failures of the theme parks since the 2000s from planning, development and management perspectives, described the development of the parks as 'a roller coaster ride'. One of the most important issues in this decline has been political interference by government officials at varying levels attempting to exert strong influence over the development process. The assessment of the feasibility tended to be opaque with governments focusing more on the pursuit of foreign investment than the viability of the attraction. Government involvement has spurred the fever of these attractions nationwide and the case can be made that the parks are the most visible manifestation of central government's cultural policy – success or failure. Nonetheless, the multiple roles played by the government have detrimental effects on the prosperity of the theme parks in the long run.

Provincial level

From the provincial perspective, Hainan Island does not have nationally sanctioned theme parks, but it has numerous grassroots folk villages established by private entrepreneurs with the support of the provincial government. The establishment of Hainan Province in 1988 was the first new provincial-level unit to be created in China since the Communists took power in 1949. There has been increasing decentralization involving delegation of decision making and resource allocation (Xu, 1999). The establishment of Hainan Province was the fulfillment of a local desire for greater economic freedom that, in turn, aroused great enthusiasm for the development of Hainanese culture and identity. Hainan Island is one of the few areas of China with ongoing entrenched social and political conflicts between local and national interests (Feng & Goodman, 1997). Geographically, Hainan is far away from the national government and psychologically separated from Mainland China whose national policies have little effect on the provincial economy and culture. Hainan's political culture reflects not only its quasi-colonial experience, but also various ethnic communities and the differences among them. Historically, ethnic hostility against Han Chinese has long existed on Hainan and there were numerous rebellions from the Li against the dominant Han settlement (Wang, 1992). Other factors, such as land alienation, onerous taxation and administrative abuses, have caused serious problems during the massive economic development that has taken place in recent history. Politically, the majority of the administrative positions are occupied by Han people dispatched directly from Mainland

China. My observations during fieldwork were that Han officials generally had little knowledge, understanding or appreciation of ethnic cultures; rather, they held distrust and prejudice toward ethnic minorities. The current provincial government is controlled by mainlanders who have tended to deny the existence of a Hainanese culture different from that of the mainland, arguing that the Li have already been assimilated into Han culture.

Ethnic tourism is seen as an integral part of tourism development on Hainan. In particular, tourist attractions are located in remote areas and are viewed as helping to improve local economic conditions. The provincial government has a dominant role in determining what is most authentic. Often, the villages portraying the cultural traditions of various ethnic groups are located far from the urban centers. The government also sanctions historical preservation in the remote places where local architecture and ethnic customs have served as the model for folk villages.

Commodification is strongly encouraged by the provincial government for the purpose of economic development. The Hainan Ethnicity and Religion Bureau (HERB), a provincial branch of the Nationalities Affairs Commission (*minwei*), serves as an authoritarian agency to authenticate ethnic cultures. The HERB controls and monitors any social event related to ethnic events and religion. If the selected ethnic tourist villages are granted 'Preserved Cultural Relics' status under the HERB, the villages are assumed to be 'more authentic'. Travel agencies on Hainan are thus more likely to take tour groups to these sanctioned ethnic villages. The most important tourism administrative body on Hainan is the Provincial Tourism Bureau, which provides strategic guidelines for local development. It also serves as a coordinator between the national government and local tourism businesses. Tourism has come to be seen as a 'panacea' for many economic and social needs on Hainan. The perceived value of tourism development for employment and economic growth has substantial implications for the allocation of provincial resources at the local level. Ethnic displays at folk villages are seen as a good way to commodify culture into a marketable tourism product. The provincial government, in fact, shows considerable enthusiasm for authenticating ethnic cultural resources for tourism.

Local level

Local governments have an essential, but often overlooked impact on the establishment of tourism policy (Hall, 1996). Hainan has a number of Li and Miao Autonomous Regions concentrated along the central highway. Tourism development was an unfamiliar activity for autonomous local governments because agriculture had long been seen as the leading economic sector and had made important contributions to several autonomous regions. The local collectives are characterized as based on *guanxi* (trust/connections/social relationships) and *renqing* (human feelings and touches) (Jackson, 2006). Both are viewed as essential when dealing with community business and administration. Li *et al.* (2007) examined how *guanxi* as a social reality in China, poses a stumbling block to local communities' participation in the development of tourism. The roots of *guanxi* are in family and business. However, when applied to entrepreneurial ventures, it creates a barrier to cultural change. In particular, a 'circle of *guanxi* elites' (Li *et al.*, 2007: 132), including the local government, private developers and village authorities, often control the necessary ingredients for socio-economic development. Local officials emphasize that allocations of the resources and social structure should strongly rest on *guanxi*, *renqing* and inter-regional cooperation. In other words, there should be teamwork and everyone in the community should be treated as a close associate.

After Hainan became a province, tourism was introduced as an alternative to agriculture. This new endeavor challenged the traditional social fabric of *guanxi*. With a large proportion of the ethnic population having only completed primary education, working in tourism can be both accessible and appealing, especially for members of the younger generation, who clearly prefer such employment to the rigors of agriculture employment. Although salaries for employees in tourist folk villages were found to be well below the salaries paid by international hotel chains on Hainan, they were higher than those of local agricultural workers (Ouyang, 2000). Tourism development has gradually displaced *guanxi* and *renqing*, since the younger generation is willing to relocate to the locations where tourism business thrives and jobs are easily found. Increased mobility promotes a shift of perception in communities that have begun to understand their cultures' economic worth. However, they lack strategies for turning their authentic cultural assets into tangible financial resources.

The local government has been much more active than the provincial government in commodifying Li culture and to achieving its vision of modernity. One local official told me in private that the dominant factor in the evaluation of an official's performance is the status of the local economy. An official's job promotion and pay raise virtually hinge on the economic betterment of the local community. The popular phrase 'backwards will be beaten (*luohou jiuya aida*)' translates 'officials will be sacked for being backwards'. Pursuit of modernity is the primary goal for local governments, while the concept of authenticity was barely mentioned in my conversation with them.

When I asked local officials about the difference between authenticity and commodification, their perspective indicated that it centered on issues of 'location'. That is, my interviews in the Li Autonomous Regions revealed that local officers firmly believed that '*zhen*' (authenticity) and '*jia*' (inauthenticity) of tourist attractions rests simply on their distance from the core of the ethnic county. 'This is the only criterion in my mind' said one local official in Qiongzhong, 'it is impossible to believe the folk village is real if it is not located in our [Li] community. No matter what the degree of *shangyehua* (commercialization) is of the village, if it is here, it always represents Li culture in this region'.

Cultural Evolution versus Museumification

National level

The political implications of cultural evolution brought about by tourism are problematic: they involve the values of the viewer and the viewed, the gazer and the gazee, the tourist and the touree. Richards and Wilson (2006: 1211) used the term 'heritage mining' to describe the process of revalorization of cultural heritage that the governments promote in the 'serial reproduction' of culture. It has been noted that cultural evolution driven by tourism is not determined by ethnic communities; rather, very often, it is a part of policies set by the governments. Such evolution is not internal (i.e. based on historical or contextual authenticity), but external with governments and tourists determining how the 'genuineness' and 'realness' of the performed culture presented in the folk villages is defined.

MacCannell (1984: 368) commented that 'touristified ethnic groups are often weakened by a history of exploitation, limited in resources and power'. However, Greenwood (1989: 183) has asserted that 'the objectification of local culture via tourism does not always destroy it; on occasion it transforms and even stimulates its further proliferation'. Cultural evolution can be viewed as a matter of creativity and a process of commodification mingled with globalization and localization (or glocalization). However, the national government in China was relatively slow to recognize the potential of ethnic tourism. In part, this delayed response reflected the government's assumptions about tourism in general; that is, natural and historical landscapes, not exotic customs, are the most highly valued tourist resources (Nyiri, 2006). The approach of policy makers toward ethnic cultures is to fossilize ethnicity through its cultural representations. National policies for cultural evolution focus on the 'uniqueness' and 'distinctiveness' of ethnicity while ignoring the impact of assimilation and acculturation policies that have been operative for decades. This has resulted in the reconstruction of the ethnic identity and the manipulation of cultural difference. Bhabha (2004: 72) called such identity reconstruction as 'the uncanny of cultural difference', which 'becomes a problem not when you can point to the Hottentot Venus, or to the punk whose hair is six feet up in the air; it does not have that kind of fixable visibility. It is as the strangeness of the familiar that it becomes more problematic, both politically and con-ceptually...when the problem of cultural difference is ourselves-as-others, others-as-ourselves, that borderline'.

The extreme expression of the cultural evolution is museumification, which freezes the culture for display. From an anthropological perspec-tive, museumification plays a significant role in shaping a local discourse of place identity and ethnic markers under the auspices of the governments. Museumification offers a metanarrative of 'real things' in a sealed environment. Artifacts and material objects must be classified, labeled and displayed in order to distinguish them from those of other institutions. Museumification lends credence to the authenticity of culturally bound discourse (Scott, 2005), however, it also narrows the tourists' interpretations of featured artifacts, including the ethnic arts performance. The contradiction embedded in museumification is that ethnicity is regarded as 'primitive' and 'pre-modern'. Negotiated identities and hybridity are excluded because they are viewed as impure. Most importantly, the museumizing of minority identities tends to endorse particular markers of differences, and, concomitantly, hide the state's suppression of cultural practices that previously led to social difference (Jonsson, 2000).

When critiquing Said's *Orientalism*, Clifford (1988: 275) posed several questions regarding the consequences of cultural evolution: 'what processes rather than essences are involved in present experiences of cultural identity?' 'are traditional cultures destined to be lost?' 'who has the authority to define a culture, to identify and authenticate the current transformations of traditional cultures?' These questions are not easily answered. From the national government's perspective, ethnic culture is characterized by difference, or is a different society compared to the majority of the population. The Chinese government is a firm believer in the Darwinian idea that survival of the fittest is the key way to distinguish those *luohou* people with non-*luohou* people. According to Lewis Henry Morgan's evolutionary ecology, cultural evolution is a part of biological processes that have been recognized as complex and multi-layered. Morgan delineated a uni-linear evolution, postulating that all societies pass through similar developmental stages. The uni-linear approach is widely accepted and utilized in Chinese society and is entrenched in policy making. A 'primitive' ethnic minority in China is presumed to represent stages in the development of a more advanced Han society. Thus, the presence of matriarchal patterns of the Other categorizes ethnic social behavior as 'savagery' and 'barbarism' since its identity is arrested in the past. The underlying assumption of the Han majority who enjoy a higher economic status and social advancement can be summarized as 'thinking your own group's ways as being superior to others' and 'judging other groups as inferior to your own' (Burns & Novelli, 2006: 2). Ethnocentric policies assume that distinctive ethnic culture, traditions and local variations can be diffused and reconstructed through the process of acculturation and assimilation. Modernity is a yardstick to measure the relative success of the acculturation among all ethnic groups. Ethnic cultural evolution is generally seen as a step toward 'sinicization' or 'hanification', in which culture can be 'ex-plained', 'adapted' and 'advanced'. Although seemingly paradoxical, the advent of ethnic tourism demonstrates that uni-linear evolution is counterproductive, or at least inadequate, since the acculturation process would diminish the tourists' interest to visit other 'cultures'. The progressive model does not work well in tourism marketing and promotion. In recent years, government policies cautiously use the term 'constructive development' (*jianshexing fazhan*) to illustrate the dilemma inherent to the process of authenticating ethnic culture and traditions while keeping a delicate balance between acculturation and museumification.

Provincial level

From the provincial government perspective, ethnic cultural markers have become the primary determinants of ethnic status on Hainan. Ethnic tourism gives locals an opportunity to identify their cultural markers and to realize their cultural values. This process is an ongoing redefinition of place in new terms under the influence of tourism. Some cultural elements disappear, while new elements emerge. Cultural evolution has, in fact, weakened the distinctiveness of ethnic Li culture. In particular, so many cultural assimilations have occurred in the past decades that ethnic markers have become less prevalent. The establishment of Li folk villages sanctioned by the provincial government strengthens the Li markers. The distinctiveness of Li cultural display leads to the creation of folk villages as 'open air museum'. Through sanctioned tourist folk villages, many Li communities have become aware of their traditional past by visiting the villages. From the perspective of the provincial government, the function of folk villages may be related primarily to economic development, however, the establishment of the villages serve to redefine ethnic culture.

One of the mechanisms for regulating cultural markers is a rating program. All tourist sites on Hainan are eligible to participate in a rating evaluation since 2003. Through inspections by the national and provincial tourism bureaus, the sites are rated from A to AAAA based on a set of criteria; for example, resources, landscapes, quality of the environment and tourist arrivals. Li (2004) has detailed how the process of the rating program in China functions. He pointed out that the significance of being ranked highly is that government recognition is linked to the augmented commercial value of the site in the tourism market. In other word, the higher the rating, the better the financial benefit for the site. Although China's National Tourism Administration (CNTA) has the ultimate power to authorize the rating, the evaluation is often done by the provincial tourism bureau.

The intention of the provincial tourism bureau was that the rating process would greatly increase tourist arrival and enhance the 'authenticity' of the villages. Since the rating process also regulates how ethnic culture is presented to tourists, it was anticipated that ethnic groups would come to have a clear understanding of their strengths and weaknesses. However, the rating program did not work well on Hainan. The process takes time and money that many folk villages found unattractive. The hotel industry has its own ranking, therefore it does not help increase the financial value. Most importantly, the rating program had difficulty in determining the quality of folk villages since the majority of them are privately owned small enterprises. The mobility of the village and their changing ownership complicated the rating process. Several folk villages declined to participate and suggested the program would do little for business. Some villages even believed that the rating would make it difficult for the village to change its theme or programs, causing the village to be in a state of museumification, thus lowering the rating it would earn.

Local level

Li scholars and others, sympathetic to ethnic groups, have made efforts to reconstruct an 'objective' history of the Li (Feng, 1999). In their opinion, the Li are the founders of Hainan civilization. They had achieved fairly high levels of development in animal husbandry, agriculture and the handicraft textile industry before the Han Chinese came to the island. However, the dominant Han-centric vision has important implications for the manner in which ethnic peoples are perceived. There is a fear among many senior Li people on Hainan that contact with tourists may devalue traditional Li culture and lead to further social breakdown in some communities, and that 'boosterizing' tourism by the provincial government could exacerbate the loss of an intrinsic part of Li culture. In response, the local government argued that while tourism might influence Li cultural identity, it often does so in a positive way; for example, improving living standards and eradicating the 'unhealthy' elements of the communities. One local official has pointed out the motto of 'change is constant and the only constant is change' to explain the inevitability of the cultural evolution.

The ethnic museum of Hainan is widely viewed as local government's effort to showcase 'museumified' Li culture. Although the museum was built with generous financial support from the province, it is located in Wuzhishan, the central part of Hainan where the majority of Li reside. The museum displays Li cultural relics, pictures, costumes, folk arts and various aspects of the minorities living on Hainan. The main attraction is the replication of a Li residential village presenting a Li kitchen, living rooms and bedrooms. The purpose of the replication, according to the museum's brochure, is to 'appreciate the Li customs, watch dances and shows of the Li minority, appreciate tropical flowers and plants, taste special Li cuisine and buy some crafts work of the minorities'. Unfortunately, the museum does not attract as many visitors as had been anticipated. Transportation is the major reason that few tourist buses stop in Wuzhishan. The museum visit is not included in the travel itinerary, thus few travel agencies knew of the replication of the folk village. The second reason is the irony of replication – the village has too many artifacts, too little entertainment. The museum's tour guide told me that the replication of the village was based on the Li in the 19th century. It is virtually a fossilized village that cannot be found anymore. In reality, the Li residential villages are much more 'modern' and 'advanced' than the displays in the museum. It has become increasingly difficult to portray authentic Li to the public.

Economic Development versus Cultural Preservation

National level

The concept of tourism development for governments is almost synonymous with economic development (Hall, 1996). Ethnic tourism is widely viewed as a shortcut to increasing the economic viability of marginalized areas, for improving the living conditions of communities and stimulating social regeneration. Government policies and practices have promoted tourism as a mechanism for restructuring the traditional agricultural sector and alleviating ethnic dependence on welfare. However, tourism can have both positive and negative outcomes for ethnic communities; that is, sharing their culture through tourism and preserving it could be seen as conflicting goals. The search for economic benefit by means of marketing ethnic cultures becomes increasingly problematic when government responses to ethnic tourism development are based on a top-down approach with little input from the ethnic groups. Crang and Malbon (1996) proposed two ways of differentiating between culture and economy: the 'cultural regulation of the economic', in which governments exercise control of economic development based on limited cultural capacity; and 'cultural materialization of the economic', in which governments choose the meaningful and representative cultural markers for economic consumption. In the latter situation, tensions have occurred when ethnic culture is used as a tool for economic development. Governments may attempt to utilize tourism to shape national identity and standardize ethnic identities, but activate 'push-back' from the affected groups that can include ethnic communities, tourism businesses and even tourists who dispute the process of authenticating ethnic cultures.

Robinson (1999) has articulated the view that ethnic culture is not a sacred cow but just another tradable commodity. Ethnic societies en masse are often showcased by developing nations for economic purposes. He suggested that the interrelationship between cultural preservation and economic development may be fragile, but there is a need to view living culture as 'tradable, substitutable and separate from the natural environment' (Robinson, 1999: 383). Robinson further asserted that culture is difficult to articulate in policy terms. A paternalistic approach of the government policies is largely inadequate to deal with issues relating to community values and the variance between value systems and traditions developed over centuries. In other words, the notion of cultural preservation is more about protection and sustainability for the benefits of the tourism industry. Economic development depends on the policy-making processes and the effectiveness with which stakeholders are able to influence cultural preservation.

Ethnic minorities in China, afflicted by debilitating rural poverty, continue to be economically backward despite a marked improvement in recent decades. Chinese President Hu Jintao noted in the 'Opening Speech to the Ethnic Affairs Work National Conference' in 2005 that the per capita GDP in minority areas is only 67.4% of the national average. He also stated that rural per capita income is only 71.4% of the national average (State Ethnic Affairs Commission, 27 May 2005). This figure, however, was misleading since it did not take into account the severity of the economic discrepancies between the higher incomes of the Han Chinese in minority areas and those of the minorities. It can be noted that statistics concerning ethnic minorities are difficult to verify, and thus the accuracy of the data is often questionable. The government tightly controls statistics on Han-minority economic discrepancies, and published statistics report figures based on regional differences rather than providing breakdowns by ethnic groups. Mackerras (2003) claimed that although the number of officially impoverished ethnic minority people reportedly fell from 45 million to 14 million in the period from 1994 to 1999, minority people still make up 36.5% of those remaining in absolute poverty as of 2000. Officials in the national government cited a variety of factors contributing to minority poverty; for example, that the minority population is often located in harsh geographical terrains in peripheral regions; the lack of capital needed to extract natural resources in their territories; poor infrastructure and low educational levels, etc. Chinese authorities have argued that tensions between the Han and the minorities result primarily from 'uneven levels of economic development' (buping heng jinji fazhan). These authorities asserted that the economic consequences of being left behind makes tourism the preferred development option. National tourism policies emphasize the generation of economic growth as the only avenue for improving the living standards of minorities. As Westerners increasingly express a strong interest in experiencing ethnic cultures in China, ethnic tourism becomes a viable path for the communities to prosper. Given that the unemployment rate of ethnic communities is high, government policies place the greatest emphasis on job creation and the view that tourism could provide job opportunities for the increased number of minorities wanting to join the workforce.

However, the national government has tended to underestimate the reality that ethnic development also depends on a broad range of economic, social and political factors, including the degree of linkage among the various sectors within the local economy. Very often, government policies have aggravated discrepancies in wealth between the minorities and the Han Chinese, because decision making and wealth allocation have concentrated on the Han majority. Research on Chinese ethnic groups (e.g. Harrell, 2001; Mackerras, 2003; Gustafsson & Li, 2003) suggested that ethnic peoples have not received much direct economic benefit from tourism development. Furthermore, tourism is not the panacea for reducing ethnic disadvantage and that ethnic communities do not appear to experience substantial socio-cultural benefits. For example, many ethnic folk villages are controlled by the governments and the minorities work mainly in low-level operational positions (Li & Hinch, 1998).

In 2005, Chinese President Jintao Hu explained that 'all minority problems' can be resolved by promoting socialist development and increasing 'propaganda' on the interdependence of the country's nationalities and most importantly, on the 'correct interpretation of ethnic histories'. Only ethnic minorities that are willing to accept state controls and the official depiction of their ethnicity and histories have been able to receive funding from the government to preserve their culture. The national government imposes strict controls over how minority culture traits, histories and religions are portrayed in the mass media as well as in academic research. The news media is required to emphasize the melding of ethnicities into a 'harmonious' family. Cultural preservation is not given but government constructs the way it should be preserved. Ethnic identities have been constructed through borderline encounters, from Mainland Chinese tourists to the regulations from government policies. For example, hundreds of 'folk cultural festivals' organized by the national government have been established in China as a means of fostering the revival of ethnic cultures (Zhu, 1999). The initial motivation was to attract capital to help local economies and to promote ethnic culture and heritage; however, the themes of the festivals were required to be in alignment with the leitmotif of national unity, and the leadership of the Communist Party. Through such influence, governments have regulated cultural 'alienation' to guarantee the 'purity' of ethnic culture (Li, 2004).

Cultural preservation poses a dilemma for the national government. Contemporary tourism utilizes the cultural resources to achieve financial success, while cultural preservation has the objective of leaving something intact. Tourism as a means of economic development, seeks to create a number of opportunities for improving minorities' standard of living and, hence, their culture. To provide guidance for the process of cultural preservation, the national government has established ethnic 'cultural enterprise centers', where minorities conduct officially sanctioned research and attend approved cultural festivals and performances. These centers are the mouthpiece of the government and are generally managed by the Nationalities Affairs Commission (*minwei*). This commission provides funding for minority language publications, museums, artistic troupes and libraries. The official approach to cultural preservation stresses the role of the national government in the process of selecting 'good' practices and abandoning the 'bad' habits of the ethnic communities.

Provincial level

On Hainan, the major weakness of the local economy is its continuous dependence on the mainland, especially for capital investment. The establishment of the Special Economic Zone (SEZ) was an attempt to change the current dependent status by attracting overseas investment. Although the general consensus within the provincial government on the broad fundamentals of the provincial development strategy is 'small government, big society' (Cadario *et al.*, 1992: 5), there has been considerable disagreement within Hainan as to which sector of the economy represents the province's strength. The provincial economic development strategy has changed direction several times as evidenced by the shifting between various leading sectors, ranging from the military to agriculture from 1950 to 1980. Not until the early 1990s did the provincial government officially identify tourism as Hainan's leading sector. This identification was neither a question of understanding nor a simple economic decision; rather it was the result of a politically charged process to recognize tourism as a crucial link among various communities in different sectors of the economy.

Advocacy of tourism as a potential lead sector for the economy is widely accepted on Hainan. Provincial tourism marketing promotes Hainan as the 'Chinese Hawaii' or the 'last pollution-free province in China' to draw tourists from the mainland. Because Hainan is an island, it also boasts of being 'Chinese Las Vegas', implying that freedom is without judgment for anyone who is willing to travel. While these terms are used interchangeably in a wider context, tourism has become the provincial scheme for economic development. My interviews with provincial government officials in Haikou repeatedly centered on four major points for economic development. (a) Money brought in by the tourists is the best chance for revenue given that much of Hainan's agriculture and industry are both relatively backward. Provincial officials told me that the pristine natural resources should not be 'squandered' and they represent sources of 'money'. The government has the mandate to turn these resources into a business. (b) The development of tourism will be a strong stimulus for improving the infrastructure of Hainan, particularly for transportation, communications and other parts of the service sector. (c) Tourism will create a market for local produce and opportunities for employment in the labor-intensive sectors related to agriculture and hospitality. The officials joked that the sales of coconuts are closely related to tourist arrivals. The higher the number of tourists visiting the island, the more coconuts consumed, thus benefiting the farmers in the agricultural industry. (d) Tourism offers the prospect of substantial benefits to residents of tourist spots and those involved in the emerging service industries, including tourist agents, traders, hotel and restaurant enterprises and their workers and transport workers of all kinds.

Local level

Economic development from a provincial perspective is rooted in stimulating the recognition of ethnic cultures. Local officials interviewed pointed out that economic development in fact preserves the cultures because tourism has put ethnic resource on the map. The prevalent thinking from the provincial government is that without tourism, Li culture would have already disappeared or have been assimilated. When asked about the concerns that economic policies have disproportionately favored the Han Chinese and that the ethnic Li do not have a direct financial benefit, the officials rejected the validity of that view. They argued that the minority group has been in a state of *luohou* for centuries and it would be impossible to change without the intervention from the Han Chinese. The managerial positions occupied by the Han Chinese reflect the reality that they are better able to reformulate ethnic cultures and communities to make them accessible to economic development.

In recent years, tourism has brought significant economic improvement to the local Li communities. Many of Hainan's ethnic folk villages are located near the Li and Miao Autonomous Regions, such as Sanya and Wuzhishan, where tens of thousands of tourists come to visit every year. Although the average size of a village is small and relatively few Li people are hired, the ripple effect is marked. An estimate based on a survey of three selected folk villages (Xie & Wall, 2002) showed that tourists would likely spend the equivalent of US$700,000 annually at each village. An informal sector that grows and sells tropical fruits, manufacturing and marketing handicrafts and provides other services was typically active. Many neighboring ethnic people had moved to the area surrounding the villages to form a larger market specializing in tropical fruit and ethnic souvenirs.

My observations documented a gradual shift from selling tropical fruits to marketing ethnic souvenirs in recent years. In particular, the latter product has become a major component of retailing in the informal sector. These ethnic souvenirs range from primitive handicrafts to mass-manufactured items made in non-ethnic communities. The increasing sales of the ethnic souvenirs show that the Li have begun to value and share their cultures, instead of tropical fruits that can be found every-where on Hainan. Li clothing, such as the handmade, uniquely colored and styled skirts, is popular among the tourists. There was a growing consensus among the informal sector that Li culture was worth preserving since it was marketable and acceptable to the tourists who knew little about it. Souvenirs sold on the streets were generally viewed as 'authentic' since they were produced by the local people. Sales were greater if the souvenirs were labeled as '100% Li' or 'totally hand made' because tourists believe they are authentic and unique.

The Li Autonomous Regions have traditionally been Hainan's most economically depressed, and the Li minority a latecomer to the economic boom. Many local officers viewed tourism as an investment and the only way to preserve the vanishing ethnic cultures. One of the directors in Wuzhishan city commented that 'many young Li cannot even speak the Li language now, it is time for them to work in the [folk] villages to regain the language'. The local government encouraged so-called 'start-up business' in the autonomous region and fostered an entrepreneurial attitude toward the tourism market. The prominent change I observe is the linguistic adaptation from Li. Their higher level of internationaliza-tion is shown by the fact that they speak not only their own languages, but also Hainanese, Mandarin, Cantonese and, very occasionally, some English. Even though the direct economic impact remains low at present, tourism development is certainly a promising economic avenue for the ethnic communities. Economic development has evidently affected Li cultural preservation and its traits, such as language and handicraft.

Ethnic Autonomy versus State Regulation

National level

The Chinese Constitution, the Regional Ethnic Autonomy Law (REAL) enacted in May 1984 and a number of related laws and regulations stipulate minority rights. The establishment of the minority law entitles minorities to establish autonomous governments in territories where they are concentrated; however, like all Chinese citizens, minorities must accept the leadership of the Communist Party, 'safeguard the security, honor, and interests of the motherland', and place the interests of the state 'above anything else' (REAL, 1984). The REAL entrenches the rights of ethnic minorities to substantial self-government as long as they do not directly break central policy. In practice, the dominance of the Communist Party negates their autonomy. Ethnic law allows autonomous governments to alter, defer or annul national legislation that conflicts with local minority practices, but the next higher level of government (e.g. provincial government) must approve such changes, and autonomous governments may not contradict the basic spirit of national policies. In practice, autonomous governments have little power to change the course of the decisions made by national and provincial governments. Additionally, the operation of autonomy in China is contingent on various factors, such as religion, the size of the territories and the number of communities.

Chinese autonomy policy has explicitly declared minority areas to be an inseparable part of the People's Republic (Conner, 1984). Policies concerning minority nationalities are primarily shaped by a desire to establish Chinese national unity and, ultimately, the goal of establishing socialism. Control is an important issue in the presentation of ethnic culture. Ethnic minorities are encouraged to revive their culture and to display distinctive characteristics (*minzu tese*), but not all aspects of ethnic culture are permitted in the process (Li, 2004). The Chinese government prohibits all Chinese citizens from expressing sentiments that 'incite splittism' or 'separate nationality unity' (REAL, 1984). The terms are usually too vague to define, but they have been used to give government the authority to monitor minorities more closely than the Han Chinese. The government grants a degree of local autonomy to ethnic groups that accept the central government's authority, but silences those who attempt to advocate their rights under Chinese law. Ethnic people seeking to assert their rights, particularly land rights, are typically stereotyped as 'troublemakers'. Thus, the national government plays a double role in controlling the ethnic cultural resources. On the one hand, it supports cultural distinctiveness as a contributor to economic development, particularly tourism development. On the other hand, it suppresses any 'true' autonomous rights. Government officials perceive ethnic differentiation as a constant source of problems. One of the major concerns is that the ethnic minorities not only compete for scarce resources, but also demand autonomy. In summary, cultural diversity can be both a boon and a bane from the perspective of the national government. Where the national government remains overly sensitive to 'ethnic nationalism' or to any challenges to cultural evolution in the direction of the Han majority, commercial activities, such as tourism, provide minority groups with a forum for making claims about themselves and their communities.

China, as an authoritarian state, is often found to be at variance with the Western discourse on human rights of minority peoples. Ethnic law, such as the REAL, appears to be inadequate to grant the range of minority rights that the national government claims. Sautman (2002) contended that some autonomous rights are being eroded not by the authoritarian rules, but by what he called the 'marketization' of China's political economy. Governments at various levels have increasingly lost hegemonic power as economic liberalization proceeds. The most notable weaknesses in the government ethnic policies include: a failure to enlarge the scope of ethnic regional autonomy; a lack of preferential policies sufficient to offset the economic gap between the Han and minority areas; and a lack of programs for overcoming anti-minority bias. Tourism has been a useful propaganda channel in China; ethnic identification and local autonomy are not about self-determination but about defining regions and inhabitants according to their backwardness and need for economic, cultural and social development (Solinger, 1977).

Provincial level

Hainan Island was part of Guangdong Province before 1988 and served primarily as a naval base to contain Southeast Asian countries. Its distant geographical location from Beijing provided relative freedom of political expression. Following the establishment of the SEZ, Hainan built a distinct political and economic system based on new principles such as the 'socialist market economy' (Cadario *et al.*, 1992), which encouraged small collective or private enterprises outside state plans. To that end, the provincial government was also given leeway to follow any international regulations and practices useful for economic development. For example, in 1999, a collection of international regulations and practices was published in Hainan, to educate and guide the government and public. Many of the rights granted by the national government are given to provincial and local area governments, rather than to individual ethnic groups. The provincial government carefully controls the appointment and training of all officials, a majority of whom are dispatched from Mainland China. The underlying policy coming from the provincial

Plate 4.1 The photo display inside Baoting Areca Manor

government has been that modernity is a potent contributor to ethnicity, and autonomy is a device to exercise direct control over economic development.

Another strategy to promote state regulation is through the work with local tourism businesses (Xie, 2003b). Folk villages are required to publicize ethnic and religious policies during group tours. Exhibitions, such as political support from the provincial and local governments, are necessary in each village. At the first glance, the exhibitions are displayed by villages voluntarily. But provincial government explicitly suggested including certain degrees of propaganda to 'distinguish ethnic folk villages from other tourist destinations'. Plate 4.1 shows a photograph I took during a field trip to Baoting Areca Manor in September 2009. The passage of the hall is decorated with photographs of provincial officials visiting the village. The title states 'the [Communist] Party's Concerns', which emphasizes the significance of political support from the government. The officials' visits, to some extent, sanction the village as a state-sponsored tourist attraction.

Local level

The Li on Hainan, by contrast, have had more freedom to exercise their autonomy because they rarely challenge local authority. Religious practices of the Li minority have been so weakened by assimilation policies over decades that they seldom pose a threat to the Han Chinese. The Li language does not have a written script, therefore it has been regarded as an unintelligible dialect and no language policy has been enforced. Many Li communities welcome the opportunity to develop their Mandarin skills as a means of furthering their economic viability. Local government does not view autonomy as a threat; rather, it sees it as a good marketing tool for attracting tourists. When traveling to the western part of Hainan where agriculture is the only means of living, I was told by local residents that the government even allows a few Li communities to grow poppy seeds. Hainan is probably viewed as the most open province in China – a good place to experience business innovation.

However, after half a century of poverty-stricken life in Li communities, the bargaining power of the ethnic people vis-à-vis with governments appears to be feeble. The Li are seen as a marginalized people both economically and politically. The struggles between the displacement of existing Li villages and resettlement in new locations where farmland is scant caused ethnic protests and riots. Between 9 and 13 April 2008, local police on Hainan reportedly clashed with 6000 residents in Longqiao Township, where the local population is majority Li. The residents were protesting the local government for its confiscation of more than 100,000 m^2 of farmland (about 7000 hectares) for the construction of golf courses. The ethnic Li complained that they were offered insufficient compensation for their land. In the standoff, the police allegedly launched tear gas canisters into the crowd, wounding at least 300 farmers – some police were also wounded in the incident (Chinese Human Rights Defender, 21 April 2008). The ethnic Li detested that local officials embezzled the resettlement fees and the resort developers never addressed the loss of farmland.

There is lingering animosity toward local government officials, mainly from the Han, that they have cooperated with real estate developers to sell state-owned farmland, where the majority of the Li reside. Tourism development does not appear to bring significant benefits to the locals as forced relocation by the developers frequently occurs. Because the ethnic Li do not have true autonomous rights in terms of land use, their concerns are generally ignored by local government.

Mass Tourism versus Sustainable Ethnic Tourism

National level

Worldwide, the issue of sustainability has gained the attention of many governments, especially in developing nations, because it can contribute to long-term growth. Considerations of culture in the context of sustainable tourism have tended to treat ethnic communities as vulnerable, marginal and 'developing' peoples (Robinson, 1999). The consensus is that massification of tourism will produce more negative results than sustainable tourism does, however, the hard evidence in ethnic tourism is scant. Invariably problematic, there is no agreed-on definition to characterize and define the meaning of sustainable tourism. For years, scholars have assailed mass tourism as a force that effaces the rich texture and distinctiveness of ethnic heritage, thereby corrupting authentic cultural spaces.

Teo (2002: 469) raised a series of issues regarding the complicated relationship between mass tourism and sustainable development: how might destinations ensure the integrity of authenticity when faced with large increases in the number of visitor arrivals? She asked whether all attractions and destinations inundated by mass tourism would suffer the fate of authenticity and degenerate into the final stages of Butler's (1980) product life cycle. Moreover, she speculated as to whether there would always be demonstrated effects on cultures exposed to tourism. And, if so, should measures be designed to 'protect' cultures from negative externalities? These legitimate concerns reflect tensions at various levels of governments as they try to keep a balance between socio-economic development and sustainable ethnic tourism.

Tao and Wall (2009: 91) proposed that instead of talking about sustainability in generalities, it would be more useful to develop a differentiated understanding of how communities and individuals are sustained by various livelihood strategies. They suggested that 'livelihood' is a more concrete concept than 'development' and easier to observe, describe and even quantify. Their research in an aboriginal community in Taiwan showed at least three practices that yielded immediate livelihood benefits for ethnic communities involved in tourism: (1) flexible hours, where the aboriginal dancers perform on a regular basis with a stable income; (2) creation of cash-earning opportunities besides the traditional agriculture; and (3) provision of backup employment opportunity that offers an alternative for those unable to engage in agriculture. Many aboriginal individuals are sustained by combinations of livelihood strategies, both subsistence (agriculture) and market-oriented (tourism) activities, rather than specific jobs.

Efforts in the developed countries to make tourism a more sustainable option have focused on a community involvement approach. It is worth noting that tourism planning in China is highly centralized within state agencies. According to Hall (1991: 50), 'the administration of tourism under socialism... has implicitly acted both to contain and to concentrate tourism – and especially foreign tourism – within very specific spatial parameters'. In contrast to a community-driven approach, the tourism industry in China believes that without government involvement in tourism planning, development will lack cohesion and direction. Also, there is the fear that short-term initiatives might well jeopardize long-term potential. Government tourism planning therefore serves as an arbiter between competing interests. However, an increasing number of Chinese tourism scholars and government officials (Zhang, 2003; Liu, 2006) have asserted that tourism growth cannot be sustained by over-exploiting the resources and sacrificing the environment. Planning strategies are required to connect tourism with community for a sustainable development. Li (2006) suggested that a 'stable' tourism–community relationship is also in line with the Chinese government's top concern of maintaining social stability and power control. The difference between the Western and Chinese perspectives about community-based tourism relates to its ultimate goal. The former regards community tourism as a democratic process to enrich the community, while community tourism is viewed as a planning strategy to sustain the economy in China.

China has borrowed Western planning principles since the Open Door policy in 1978. Popular issues, such as land-use zoning and development planning, can be found in proposals and documentations in recent years. The concept of sustainable development is readily accepted by various levels of governments. Site development, accommodation and building regulations, the density of tourism development, and the presentation of cultural, historical and natural tourist features have been taken into consideration for tourism development. In recent years, some Chinese officials have raised concerns over the social impacts of tourism, particularly issues relating to the negative effects from mass tourism development. Although national government still exerts a huge influence over tourism development plans, many local officials have voiced the demand for 'smaller government'. This trend has led to the national government's shift from being an arbiter to its playing an entrepreneurial role in its involvement with tourism.

China has shifted to a concern for ecosystem preservation and has regulated both family planning and environmental protection as basic national policies since the 2000s. It is working toward sustainable development and is implementing 'A Proposal for the 21st Century of China' and 'A Basic Proposal for Environmental Protection in China'.

The national government encourages incremental changes under the framework of mass tourism. The term 'sustainability' from a national perspective appears to focus on the environment. In developed countries, both socio-cultural and environmental issues have been given greater priority. In terms of ethnic tourism development, Chinese national policies lag behind those in the West. So far, no single national-level tourism policy refers to ethnic cultural preservation. 'Sustainable tourism', by and large, is a kind of 'window dressing' in the majority of government reports. In reality, mass tourism development is the main source of revenue generation, as evidenced on Hainan where 96% of tourists are domestic. National government monitors very crude tourism indices like arrivals, bed-nights, surveys of tourist expenditures and gross receipts. It also farms out the work to research institutions located at various universities to undertake social impact studies or make systematic independent appraisals of market trends.

Provincial level

Provincial policies tend to lean toward active marketing and promotion for the island's economy. The concept of sustainable tourism is novel and foreign as mass tourism is the only avenue to generate revenue. Policy making is also dependent on the ebb and flow of the local economy. However, the provincial government has gradually realized the importance of sustainability, since Hainan's natural environment has deteriorated drastically in recent years. Tourism, as the number one income generator, has been blamed for the depletion and overexploitation of the island's unique natural resources, such as forests and wild animals. These negative environmental impacts have resulted in perceptual and behavioral responses of the minority communities who are affected by the deterioration. These communities are against the provincial government's policies dealing with environmental stresses, specifically as those policies influence socio-economic change and the functioning of various institutions (Wall, 2007). The former includes such phenomena as forced displacement of minority communities for hotel zone development, regional economic imbalances (urban versus rural) and differential opportunities by ethnicity and gender. The functioning of various institutions includes lack of integration of policies and programs and deficiencies in human resources training.

The provincial government has put forward two separate proposals regarding sustainable economic development, including tourism: the creation of an eco-province in 1999; and the branding and repositioning of Hainan as a luxury tourist destination in 2009. The former recognized the pressing need for planning on the island as a whole as it experienced an economic downturn after the bursting of the housing bubble in the late 1990s; while the latter reflected policy change due to an expanding economy and massive infrastructure development in the late 2000s. Policy changes from 1999 to 2009 showed progress in tackling socio-economic and environmental issues; however, there continues to be problems with long-term strategies and interrelationships between tourism and other sectors.

A proposal entitled 'The Creation of An Eco-Province in Hainan' was created in 1999 in response to China's Agenda 21 (the vision for the 21st century). It presented an alternative way to pursue sustainable development. As Xie and Wall have noted, the core purpose of the proposed eco-province was that of encouraging economically productive and ecologically efficient industries on the island:

> The purposes of establishing an eco-province are to use ecological theories and systems engineering, to follow the rules of economic development, to preserve natural resources in Hainan, and to work towards sustainable development. The result will be to combine environmental conservation, resource usage and high-efficiency ecological agriculture to reach the goals of healthy economic development, social civilization and rising living standards, leading eventually to harmony between economy, population, society, resources and the ecological environment. (Xie & Wall, 2000: 3)

The guidelines were initiated by the Department of Land, Environment and Resources of the provincial government, which included (a) standardizing the regulations for ecotourism development by creating a few high-class eco-destinations as models; (b) encouraging private enterprise to invest in ecotourism destinations; (c) planning the natural reserves rationally; and (d) enforcing the regulations for the ecological environment in tourist destinations. Ecotourism, a combination of natural and ethnic resources, was set as a priority by the provincial government; however, concrete plans have not been presented. The provincial government has committed itself to sustainable development, which requires the integration of social, environmental and economic factors in decision making. In particular, the government believes that ecotourism would promote positive economic changes in the western part of Hainan, which is the least developed region in the province. Ecotourism is viewed as an excellent strategy for mobilizing these regions' involvement in economic development and cultural changes.

The proposal also mentioned using Nanshan, Wenchang and Qionghai as model destinations to cultivate 'eco-culture', a term combining Confucianism, Taoism and Buddhism. However, ethnic Li and Miao cultures were not included as part of the eco-culture in the proposal.

While it put forth Hainan as the first eco-province in China, the proposal overlooked the equally important social component of pursuing a sustainability in which social needs and values are key considerations (Davies & Wismer, 2007). Ten years after the implementation of Hainan as an eco-province, the results appear to be mixed. Mounting evidence indicated that the ecological environment on Hainan has continued to deteriorate year after year, mass tourism has remained the dominant travel phenomenon on Hainan and this trend is unlikely to change in the short term. Hainan is stereotypically viewed as a sightseeing destination, rather than being a serious eco-culture or ethnic tourism destination. Initially, the minority community wholeheartedly supported environmental conservation and they were optimistic that tourism growth would yield economic benefits for individuals. However, the inclusion of the Li minority as a real partner in working on the eco-province projects was neglected (Stone & Wall, 2004). The relationship between tourism and community is strained and socio-economic benefits for the Li communities have been limited under government control of resource allocation. Policy implementation has tended to be top-down with virtually no public consultation or community involvement. Davies and Wismer (2007) suggested that the government of Hainan has not yet been able to manage social welfare, environmental and economic issues, resulting in a range of difficulties in implementing the ambitious ecological plan and in balancing short- and long-term goals. The eco-province designation neglected social sustainability. This has limited the genuine involvement of the Li people in socio-economic development and has resulted in an imbalance between the needs of the Li and the broader needs of Hainan Island.

The stereotypical image of Hainan as a 'sun-sea-sand-sex' destination for Mainland China tourists remains strong. The provincial government views domestic tourism as the 'poor cousin' compared to international tourism. Provincial officials told me openly that domestic tourism cannot bring enough revenue since the majority of such tourists visit the island on package tours with an extremely low economic multiplier. They also expressed concern that tourist-related infrastructure cannot accommodate the influx of domestic tourists during peak seasons. The function of sustainable tourism, according to provincial officials, should promote international tourism and attract wealthy Westerners. 'To be an authentic

Chinese Hawaii', said the manager of Hainan Tourism Bureau, 'first thing we need to do is to attract the same quality of tourists as Hawaii'. As an example of the sort of tourist that Hainan should be attracting, I was shown pictures of the Boao Asia Forum (BAF), which was held in the resort town of Boao on Hainan. The annual forum gathers leaders from the Asian-Pacific region, entrepreneurs, government officials and experts from China and abroad, including Colin Powell, former US Secretary of State. The manager of Hainan Tourism Bureau said that the forum raised the profile of Hainan as an island destination, and reinforced the perception that sustainability lies in the arrival of 'quality' and 'elite' tourists.

In April 2009, during the Boao Forum, the Governor of Hainan proposed the establishment of Hainan as an 'International Tourism Island'. The designation was meant to signal the development of 'a green island, an open island, prosperous island, civilized island and harmonious island'. More broadly identifying Hainan as an International Tourism Island would serve to prompt the island to become a world-class tourist destination, instead of being a cheap destination for domestic tourists. The proposal used 'One Sea, Two Cities, and Three Regions' as the blueprint for sustainable development. One Sea referred to the South China Sea in which Hainan is situated. Given this location, the island would be able to attract luxury cruise lines, establishing the island as the center of the South China Sea. Two cities referred to Haikou in the north and Sanya in the south as the two major hubs that would be branded as urban tourism destination. Three regions referred to the eastern, central and western regions of Hainan. According to the provincial tourism bureau, the western part, the least developed region, would be marketed as the Chinese 'Gold Coast', 'Costa del Sol' or 'Riviera', while the western region would be developed as a romantic gateway, featuring coconut trees and pristine sandy beaches.

Local level

The provincial government seems to ignore the reality that, for most tourist areas in China, the promotion of domestic tourism is a more practical way of achieving local economic development (Xu, 1999). Bowden's (2005) research in China showed that it is the rapid growth in domestic tourism, not international tourism, which has supported employment in both formal and informal sectors. Domestic tourism is particularly important for ethnic tourism because of its labor-intensive and small-scale characters. There is little impact from the implementation of the eco-province and international tourism for the local government. Mass tourism is still the most popular development mode, and planning has been non-existent at the local level. In the case of the Li folk villages, sustainable tourism development is translated as 'sustainable tourist arrivals'. The establishment of folk villages was largely a spontaneous phenomenon featuring entrepreneurs at the grassroots level. In general, the development of the Li folk villages has occurred without substantial financial or political support from local governments. Moreover, it is likely that business irregularities as kickbacks, commissions and bribes, have been prevalent in some folk villages in the competition for tourists. Local government has usually turned a blind eye as long as economic development is occurring. Therefore, ethnic cultural resources have not yet gained the serious attention of local government. Ethnic tourism is still an unclear (or unpopular) concept for many local officials. Although there is an awareness that ethnic culture resources can be a resource for sustainable ethnic tourism, the number of tourist arrivals remains the major focus for local government with the result that environmental and cultural preservation is overshadowed in the pursuit of economic benefits. At times, mass ethnic tourism is still an important revenue source to foster economic development.

Summary

Gotham (2007) conceptualized two distinctive political approaches to tourism development: 'tourism from above' and 'tourism from below'. The former regards tourism policy as a matter of top-down management through government intervention and business involvement. It can be held that this top-down strategy tends to result in commodification, rationalization, disneyization and branding of tourist sites and activities. The latter strategy derives from the grassroots ethnic communities, and is characterized by a linking of heritage and media. The result of this approach is likely to be localization, hybridization and creolization of culture resources. In the Chinese context, people-centered and community-responsive approaches in tourism planning and policy formulations have been absent (Xu, 1999). The top-down approach is a fait accompli through which national, regional and local governments directly influence tourism development. Each of these tiers has different objectives for tourism use of cultural heritage resources. My fieldwork suggests that during the development of ethnic tourism, various government levels exhibited different positions on the five dichotomous measures, and that this difference causes tension when each tier authenticates ethnic Li culture and transforms cultural experiences into a tourism product. Ghai (2000: 5) commented that 'the emotive power of ethnic distinctions inevitably leads to political conflict and demands. On the contrary, the ebb and flow of ethnicity, its assertiveness or decline, are explicable on a variety of social and economic factors, of which a particular concern of ours is the effect of the design and orientation of the state itself'. From the national perspective, ethnic tourism is highly centralized, featuring strong state regulation to discourage local nationalism. Although the Li are given flexible policies for developing the economy, administrative power is under the firm control of officials from Mainland China. The national government places great emphasis on job creation. Economic functions have been given precedence and cultural preservation has not received much attention.

The promotion of ethnic tourism by the provincial government has caused a series of cultural changes that can be seen in the modification of such Li cultural markers as the bamboo-beating dance. Hainan's tropical location is a major advantage for the development of mass tourism to attract mainland tourists. Ethnic attractions, such as the Li folk villages, have been built along highways in response to increased interest from tourists. However, most administrative positions are occupied by Han people sent directly from Mainland China. These administrators generally have little knowledge of ethnic cultures. The provincial government pays little attention to the negative effect of commodification and museumification on ethnic culture. Although sustainable development plans have been proposed, little work has been implemented to date.

Economic development has become a primary concern of the local government. The primary criterion of cultural authenticity centers on the distance between the locational core of the ethnic community and the tourist attractions. Tourism has become an important revenue source for economic development. Unfortunately, development of tourism can gradually erode cultural preservation activities. Local government has played a passive role in finding a balance between power, policy and place.

The five measures proposed in this investigation provide a fuller understanding of the differences among the governments with regard to ethnic tourism development. Perhaps the most fundamental political question surrounding ethnic tourism and government administration is that of the control and structure of power relationships (Hall & Jenkins, 1995). Li communities on Hainan have had little control over tourism development. The participation of the ethnic people in decision making is currently non-existent on Hainan. Although governments encourage the Li to get involved in tourism development, the issues of 'who gets what, where, how and why of tourism' are still issues on which Hainan ethnic communities have little influence. The five dichotomous measures represent the problems and prospects in the development of ethnic tourism as they involve governments of various levels. Future development in ethnic tourism ought to devote more attention toward ensuring a greater degree of ethnic participation. The needs and liabilities of different government levels must be taken into account when strategies are formulated. Government policies and tourism strategies should focus on fine tuning these imbalances to ensure optimal results.

Chapter 5
Ethnic Minorities

Introduction

On 10 January 2009, China Central Television (CCTV) broadcast headline news on 'United Nation Sponsors Plan to Promote Cultural Preservation in China'. It reported a two-year joint program called 'Culture-Based Development Goodwill Action for Ethnic Minorities in China'. The project was designed to work with government agencies dealing with ethnic minority issues and relevant partners, including ethnic artists, cultural enterprises and the media, in an effort to protect and revitalize minority cultures and arts performances. The focus of the project will be on ethnic music and handicrafts. Tourism is set to be a pillar for the project since it showcases 'cultural richness of ethnic minorities in the midst of development and enhance communication between ethnic minority regions and the world' (Beijing Review, 2009). Ethnic artists, dancers and singers from Yunnan, Xinjiang, Tibet and Inner Mongolia were carefully chosen and convened in Beijing to celebrate this program. During the celebration, a singer named Zhu Zheqin was nominated as National Goodwill Ambassador to promote ethnic music and culture. Zhu is a Han Chinese, and is famous for her best-selling album 'Sister Drum', which borrowed heavily from traditional Tibetan music. In many musical videos, Zhu Zheqin dressed in a *Chuba*, a Tibetan long coat made of thick wool, is pictured standing on the top of the rugged mountains, surrounded by herds of yak and tents. In order to be an 'authentic' Tibetan musician, she even gave herself a Tibetan name, 'Dadawa'. According to officials, the main reason for Zhu being chosen as the Ambassador was that she has traveled and lived with the minorities over the past 10 years and she won the BBC World Music Award in 2007. She is sometimes referred as the 'Chinese Enya' owing to her style and music exoticism. At the end of the broadcast, the CCTV news hinted that 'globalization' has severely endangered the preservation of traditional ethnic arts and culture, but that the Chinese government is taking serious responsibility for salvaging lost cultures.

The joint program to preserve ethnic arts performance demonstrated the urgency and fragility of ethnic culture. Ethnic minorities are coping with the broad changes taking place in Chinese society. The communities have become a hotbed of ethnic tensions fuelled by the vast socio-economic gap between minorities and Han Chinese. The central question is whether ethnic minorities are interested in assimilating into dominant Han society or whether they have rejected Han societal goals (Kaltman, 2007). Ethnic arts performances thus have become an important vehicle to distinguish their cultures from that of the Han majority. However, the chosen National Goodwill Ambassador also illuminated problems in defining ethnic identity and authenticity. After living with ethnic minorities for several years, mimicking the traditional Tibetan music, taking a Tibetan name and winning an international award, Zhu Zheqin has received the stamp of approval from the government that she authentically represents ethnic Tibetan culture. In other words, authentic arts performance need not be created by minority members; rather it seems that performance can be copied and re-enacted by artists and performers having no actual membership in the ethnic group. While the majority of Han Chinese realizes that Zhu is not a Tibetan, they still enjoy her music and mistakenly believe that her performance is authentic. Authenticity, from this perspective, is produced through the process of taking the original out of one context and placing it in another (Clifford, 1988). Although this kind of authenticity raises questions about owner-ship, it becomes 'alienable objects, where a potential exchange-value of a performance assumes priority over any use-value of a performance' (Clifford, 1988: 4).

This view seems to be based on the assumption that ethnic arts performances are authentic if they are performed by the ethnic minorities. In reality, even if ethnicity (e.g. the employees, dancers) is right, its performance can be altered or even misused to cater to an audience. For example, Cable (2008) participated in a tour of the ethnic Dai Village in Southwestern China and discovered that conflicting displays of identity in ethnic tourism was widespread, and, to some extent, offensive. She documented that in addition to the mock Dai wedding ceremony, the last dance show was *peng pigu* (bump butts) in which the 'brides' hold hands with their new 'husbands' and all the participants swing their hips wildly to knock hips and butts with others on the dance floor. The 'bump butts' was invented and performed by the ethnic Dai to entertain the tourists. Nonetheless, the physical contact between the sexes was offensive to traditional Dai culture and many Dai dance performers were 'reduced to tears' and dismayed that their culture was being 'represented in such an alien and insulting way to the tourists, and fearing that the tourists, too, would be shocked at Dai customs and not return to the area' (Cable, 2008: 273). The misrepresentation of ethnic arts and culture has not been uncommon in tourism, but as suggested by Cable (2008: 273) that 'commoditizing and packaging ethnic culture for tourist consumption have become the callous manipulation of cultural traits by outsiders and created dire situations anathema to ethnic tradition'.

Ethnic arts performance has increasingly become *mise-en-scène*, a French film phrase that literally means 'what is put onto the stage'. The issue of ethnic performance on stage is heatedly debated in the fields of anthropology, sociology, psychology and linguistics (Tulloch, 1999). Jordan (2008) posited that aspects of performance can be examined using the following framework: performativity, identities and roles. Ethnic arts performance is spatiotemporally and socially specific, relying on the characteristics of the performers on the stage (Edensor, 2000). Once on stage, the ethnic customs, décor, setting and behavior of figures are divorced from the reality regardless of the characteristics of the performers or the content of the presentation. Any performance is a cluster of theatrical and created practices in which performers, usually females, acquire a mystique to separate them from the ordinary lives of the audience (Tivers, 2002). To a great extent, the performance reinforces stereotyped images of ethnic culture. Although tourists have a desire for an authentic performance, such presentations tend to have limited realism. Performances are less accurate presentations than re-enactments created for commercial purposes. *Mise-en-scène* permits the roles of the performers to unfurl on stage and dramatizes the relationship between performers and audience in a circumscribed space. Tourism businesses and tourists often demand that ethnic arts presentations be modified into a simpler, shorter, colorful and photogenic form than is true of the original (Cohen, 1993). Eventually such performances turn into 'restored behavior' and ritualized interactions (Daniel, 1996; Taylor, 2001) that 'can be repeated, rehearsed, and above all recreated... [engage] bodily knowledge, habit, custom' (Parker & Sedgwick, 1995: 46–47).

My understanding of *mise-en-scène* is, in part, an aspect of the concept 'ethnic panopticon' in that the performances are closely watched/gazed by tourists who know little about ethnic culture but possess an 'eye-of-power'. Touristic performance is designed mainly for entertainment with less emphasis on education. Tourist experience is associated with the performance and the 'living history' of ethnic peoples. Their perception focuses on the origin of ethnicity, rather than the quality of the performance. In other words, a performance's atmosphere and arrangement, rather than the performance itself matters. Handler and Saxton

(1988: 242) suggested that perception of authenticity rests on whether or not tourists 'feel themselves to be in touch with a "real" world and with their "real" selves'. For instance, 'black' music, such as blues, played by black musicians is often considered more 'authentic' than that of white musicians playing a similar style (Grazian, 2003). Exactly like 'staged authenticity', *mise-en-scène* blurs the boundaries between front and back stages. Spectatorship is imbued with tourists' desire to get a glimpse into the experience of an ethnic group. Ethnic arts performance becomes a sensory experience that evokes affinity with the Other. However, in many cases, authenticity is relative, but the performers serve to authenticate the presentation as a genuine ethnic experience. Errington (1998: 149) concluded that ethnic arts performance tends to turn primitivism into performance whose 'look is authentic' because such pseudo-authenticity can be exhibited anywhere and be performed by anyone. Ethnicity can be infused with inauthentic elements as long as it entertains the tourists. The success of the performance thus rests on transforming ephemeral ritual media into durable forms that can be customized. Contrived ethnic displays may actually be incompatible with the cultures they are designed to mimic. In fact, authenticity in ethnic performance becomes an imperfection except from cultural-historical perspectives.

The specific purpose of this chapter is to present the opinions of Li dancers regarding Hainan's folk villages. The most common features of ethnic tourism are songs and dances, and presentations of the minority's rituals and festivals. Using Li dance performers and performance as a construct, I examine Li attitudes toward tourism, describe how they cope with their minority status, and identify how they view being actors and actresses on the stage. As members of an ethnic minority who are employed to represent their culture to tourists, Li performers are in a particularly good position to make informed comments on aspects of the interface between the desire for enhanced economic opportunities, and concerns about cultural preservation. Empirical observations from Hainan are examined from a perspective of authenticity of experience. Rather than attempting to determine whether something is or is not authentic, I suggest that it may be more pertinent to determine how Li dancers view the issue of authenticity as it relates to the presentation of their culture to tourists.

There are many people and organizations involved in ethnic tourism – all have positions concerning tourism on the island and the place of the Li minority within it. These include governments, from national to local, tourists, tourism entrepreneurs and members of the Li minority. My interviews with Li dancers included discussions centered on dance programs, educational opportunities, employment and economic development, and relationships with the tourists. To supplement these interviews, I carefully observed dance performances in each village and sought to understand the essence of Li dance performance. The data from the interviews were structured according to the five polar constructs relating to authenticity described in Chapter 2. Prior to presenting these results, the characteristics of dance performances and dancers are described. Particularly, I emphasize the feminized images characterizing the dance performance and the impact of the performance on female dancers. Descriptive data relating to the five continua are presented, followed by qualitative analyses of the interviews with the dancers, illustrated by quotes of their statements (translated directly from Mandarin by me and the Li language by the research assistant, a native of Li) as appropriate.

Li Dance Performers

Whether viewed as an expression of high or low culture, dance has long been a tourist attraction. Traditional ethnographic and historical studies have characterized ethnic dance as reflecting (post)colonial/ (post)modern cultures, including the constitution of gender, ethnic and national identities, the discourses of exoticization and the production of social bodies (Reed, 1998). In recent years, there has been substantial examination in the Western world, concerning attendance rates of arts presentations. Data concerning popularity of the areas have been gained from both household surveys and those attending performances. Such investigations are frequently undertaken for marketing purposes or to bolster requests for public subsidies. Of more pertinence to this chapter are observations made concerning dance as an ethnic expression and the manner in which dance performance is shaped to cater to a tourist clientele. Observation that changes in audience, timing, duration, complexity, location of performances and the attributes of dancers have caused some to suggest that dances change in form and when offered in tourism settings. At the same time, dances originally developed and staged for tourists have also been incorporated and performed in more traditional settings (Gibson & Connell, 2005). Such phenomena, while common, are usually noted by external observers: the meaning and significance of such changes to the culture in which the dance is embedded, let alone the dancers themselves, have seldom been ascertained.

Artistic forms in tourism are often represented by products that are commonly used, and thus more 'authentic' or 'genuine', outside the tourism setting. For an ethnic dance, authenticity generally revolves around anonymous authorship and skill or accuracy in the replication of something used by members of a given society (Daniel, 1996; Grazian, 2003). It also centers on functional items of a society that are used or viewed as ornamentation, entertainment or for contemplation by members of another society (Cohen, 1988). A boundary between differing sets of conventions, rules or regulations is implied (Kasfir, 1992). Handler and Saxton (1988) argued that there are two kinds of authenticity in arts: that applied to visual arts is generally an external judgment by the spectator; and the one applied to performing arts. In the visual arts, authenticity is most often based on collectors' tastes and organized by collectors' naming and categorization of genres and styles (Kasfir, 1992: 44–45). For example, the Western ballet can be viewed as having tourism art dimensions (Daniel, 1996). Although ballet is not commonly regarded as tourism art, it is actually a European-American cultural (or ethnic) dance form and, as such, it has often been staged, prepared and packaged to frame European-American cultures. Experiential authenticity is concerned with 'perfect simulation', replication of a past, an isomorphism or similarity of structural form between a living history activity or event, and that piece of the past it is meant to re-create (Handler & Saxton, 1988: 242). Touristic dance performance has similarities to living history projects in that it relies heavily on the desire for non-commercial experiences to satisfy the tourists' desire for the authentic (Daniel, 1996).

From the performers' and their community's points of view, 'authentic' dance forms are differentiated from one another by means of style, type and context and, until the appearance of tourism, the mixing of forms was generally judged as a violation of the boundaries. Combinations of dance steps from different traditions, that is, inter-traditional mixtures, have been judged as 'fakes', 'frauds' and certainly less than authentic by tourism researchers. Phillips and Steiner (1999: 9) explained that 'stylistic hybridity' in arts performance conflicts with essentialist notions of the relationship between style and culture. Both arts historians and anthropologists regard performance for an external market as inauthentic. However, sometimes such mixed performances possess a creative aspect, both from emic and etic perspectives. Frequently, touristic performance has become a category of dance in which the mixture of varied traditions and major change may take place. The tourism setting may provide the space and time for definitions to expand, for play and experimentation at the boundaries with combinations of styles and traditions that search for innovation and creativity.

Xie *et al.* (2007) proposed that the combination of tourism and ethnic arts can be viewed through three technologies of gazes: initial gaze, mass gaze and authentic gaze. Initial gaze involves voyeurism, mimesis and appropriation of the original culture. Ethnic arts begin with the initial gaze by tourists attracted by their curiosity about the Other. Initial gaze is spontaneous and the original culture has not been used for the commercial purpose. Mass gaze is characterized by commodification and glocalization. Ethnic arts have evolved from 'folk culture' to 'popular culture', and eventually to 'mass culture' consumed in a variety of manners. Authentic gaze is centered on a clear desire by tourists for authenticity and is eventually sought by them as special interest tourism.

Although, as indicated above, research on authenticity in tourism dance performances has appeared in some scholarly journals and books (e.g. Silver, 1993; Daniel, 1996; Desmond, 1999; Gibson & Connell, 2005), little academic attention has been given to the ethnic dance performers themselves and, especially, to their views on their employment as dancers, as representatives of their ethnic group and on their participation in tourism. This chapter is centered on the belief that through research on ethnic dance performers on Hainan, one can ascertain an important insight into the process of cultural authentication by Li people.

Dance performers in folk villages were selected as an accessible group to represent Li perspectives on cultural tourism. They are generally recruited from regions of Hainan with a majority Li population, to enact ethnic dances and ceremonies for tourists. Dance performers were chosen as a focus for this chapter for several reasons. First, they are familiar with Li culture and the majority comes from Li communities. Also, their performances are one of the most visible manifestations of Li culture to tourists. Moreover, they gain financially from tourism. Finally, they interact with tourists both on and off stages. Thus, as a group they are generally well informed about cultural performance and at least some aspects of tourism. However, they are not truly representative of their culture because, unlike most members of their cultural group, they are employed in tourism. They are also disproportionately young adults and female.

As part of a larger investigation of the authentication of Li ethnic tourism on Hainan, 102 dancers at eight folk villages were contacted and interviewed (Wall & Xie, 2005). Interviews were conducted in villages along both the central and eastern routes on Hainan. While some interviews were conducted with individuals, semi-structured and unstructured interviews lasting two to three hours were also undertaken with groups of dancers. Furthermore, I spent two weeks in Baoting Areca

Manor and in the Indonesian Village and the surrounding ethnic communities in order to acquire an insight into the lives of dance performers. All villages showed predominantly Li culture (although some also included Miao). None showed expressions of Hui culture, a Muslim minority living predominantly in the south of the island. Additionally, the Indonesian Village that portrays the culture of diasporic Indonesians who migrated to Hainan following the anti-Communist riots in Indonesia in the 1960s, was included in this research to provide a point of contrast.

Although the physical scales and themes of folk villages varied slightly between locations, the characteristics of dance performances and dancers were consistent. Ethnic dance shows were generally performed in a large dance hall (a thatched hut) that can accommodate between 300 and 500 tourists at one time. The total number of dance performers in a show was usually between 30 and 50. The dance programs, creations of exotic, colorful elements of ethnic folklore, were staged for tourists and presented selected aspects of Li culture. For example, the most widely performed Li dance on Hainan is the bamboo-beating dance that can be seen in every Li folk village. The performances apparently were viewed as authentic from the tourists' perspective. The dance performances are spectacles. They keep alive (even revive) traditional art forms and practices, giving the tourists a chance to view some limited aspects of a bygone lifestyle.

The dance performers do not constitute a cross-section of Li society: most were young (30% of performers were under 20 and 65% were between 20 and 29 years of age), single (70%) and female (70%). The gender imbalance can be explained by the nature of the dance performances that require more female dancers. Nagel (2003) demonstrated that ethnosexuality plays a critical role in ethnic tourism, in that sexual images help form racial, ethnic and national stereotypes, differences and conflicts. Ethnicity and sexuality join hands to fashion new and hybrid identities while ethnosexual encounters between tourists and female performers can simultaneously resist and reinforce racial, ethnic and national boundaries. Since the dance programs have been designed as an exotic and feminine performing art, male dancers generally play a minor role during the show. Among the 30% of dance performers who were married, the majority of their spouses also worked in the same folk village. In terms of income, dance performers received a higher salary than other employees in the villages. The reasons for this are the higher workload, their visibility in the villages and the skill required. However, dancers in the folk villages were not required to be professional performers.

In terms of educational levels of dancers with those of tourism employees on Hainan (i.e. those who work in the hospitality industry sanctioned by governments, hotels, restaurants, travel agencies, guides), dance performers in the folk villages generally had a much lower education, with a majority (80%) holding only a junior high school diploma. Only 4% had a senior high school diploma. Comparatively, 60% of employees in the tourism sector on Hainan were found to have a senior high school diploma and 17% had a college degree. No dance performers interviewed had a college degree. In addition, a small proportion of performers were junior high school dropouts and most of these were female.

Authenticity versus Commodification

Dance performers are a distinctive group in the village. Although a number of folk villages used part-time dancers in order to reduce costs, full-time dancers are paid relatively well. As the folk village managers strive to make a profit, dancers are required to perform as long as there are tourists in the village. However, charging for entry to a dance performance does not necessarily mean that it has become a commodified activity. In fact, many tourists do not pay a fee directly to enter the folk village, it being included in the price of the tour package. Furthermore, even if they do pay an entry fee, they are usually not charged specifically for viewing a dance performance – once having entered the village, the performance is free.

One telling example of the struggle between authenticity and commodification is that the Li dances originated as spontaneous improvisation in the communities. The Li people developed different dances to celebrate the harvest or to mourn the dead. The bamboo-beating dance, the most famous Li dance, originated from the funeral ceremony (Plate 5.1). However, given the huge success of its debut performance in Beijing after the Communist Party took power in 1949, the bamboo-beating dance acquired a new meaning. The Communist Party proposed that the dance theme be changed to reflect the joy of a 'new society'. Instead of being performed only as part of the funeral ceremony, it is now viewed as a festival celebration and has been completely integrated into the contemporary tourism offerings. Other aspects of the traditional dance have evolved. Previously, the bamboo selected for a performance was red in color. The selection of the bamboo

Plate 5.1 Li-Style bamboo-beating dance

is a long process in order to find that which was 'light and clapping' for the ceremony. The Li believe that the color red is a 'good omen' and can drive away evil (Su *et al.*, 1994). However, since the bamboo-beating dance has been turned into a touristic dance, the importance of the bamboo's color has disappeared and its religious meaning has been forgotten. Instead, the dance emphasizes the bamboo-beating rhythms, intimate team play and smiling faces. The 'new' (restructured or reinterpreted) form and style of the dance has become 'authentic' for the Li community. Nowadays, the bamboo-beating dance has become the primary symbol of Li performed culture and can be seen in major hotels and restaurants. The dance performance has moved to Mainland China, where the music and tradition are of less importance for tourists, and the rhythm and style are considered most important. The tour of the bamboo-beating dance means that ethnic Li identity, if not wholly detached from its original geographic and cultural setting, is becoming significantly so.

The discussion of the authenticity of the bamboo-beating dance revealed a dilemma inherently a part of the process of commodification (Xie, 2003a). Government involvement in ethnic arts performance has reshaped the original meanings of the dance culture. While symbolic aspects of the bamboo-beating dance remain intact, the original meaning has been lost. Chinese Communist ideology restrained the public showcasing of Li cultures and treated them as religions to be avoided.

However, recent tourism development has revived these vanishing cultures and Li dance performance is viewed as a source of pride and identity. There is more than a little irony in the recognition that the meaning of the bamboo-beating dance has changed from an expression of mourning to become a celebration of the harvest. Nonetheless, it should be recognized that the bamboo-beating dance has not become an object of museum display, but rather it has become a vibrant marketable commodity to promote Li culture and heritage. The popularity of the bamboo-beating dance has resulted in a change in who performs the dance. Now anyone who puts on a Li ethnic costume may claim to be presenting an authentic Li performance. Thus, the ownership of the dance has been lost since the performance can be presented by dancers who are not Li, and performed in places other than the traditional Li home territory.

The communities have redefined their cultural identities by tourism development and government influences. On 27 September 2009, *Hainan Daily* published an article tracing the evolution of Li dance performance. It was suggested that ethnic arts and performance needs 'assistance and helps from the majority Han and local government', since they know how to promote and market ethnic arts and performance to the wider audience. Commodification is not possible to avoid and is a positive process to publicize ethnic cultures. The process of cultural evolution associated with tourism does not necessarily break down a place-based sense of identity nor render it inauthentic. Instead, it may become an important factor in the ongoing construction of ethnic identity. Reflecting this perspective, Gotham (2007: 158) has suggested that constructing a repertoire of authenticity is 'neither a process of adaptation to changing social conditions nor a mode of resistance against tourism expansion'.

Tourism has also led to a variety of other modifications in Li dance. In order to fit tourists' schedules and tastes, villages have reorganized a broader range of traditional dances in addition to the bamboo-beating dance. Generally, the 30–40 minute shows presented to tourists by Li performers have five different segments: (a) a harvest celebration; (b) love songs by Li youth; (c) a religious ceremony for curing disease; (d) the bamboo-beating dance; and (e) a visitor participation program. Tourists are encouraged to participate in the dance performance in the final part of the show. Shepherd (2002) has suggested that the direct outcome of tourists' participation in ethnic performance is the objectification and commodification of both the culture and ethnicity of the performers. Tourist outsiders and local insiders interacting on the stage in a short time span reshape the tourist gaze in several ways. First of all, since tourists do not usually know the forms and rhythms of the dance, they are often indulged when they mistakenly cross boundaries, by dancing their own versions or imitations of dance. Also, tourist participation often results in persons entering a dance from which they, on the basis of such characteristics as age or gender, would traditionally be excluded. Thus, the pitfalls in tourists 'becoming other', and the responding behavior of performers in attempting to make the guest feel safe and free from embarrassment, encourages spontaneity and improvisation facilitating innovation. Therefore, Li dance performers are freed to experiment with variations, to indulge in mixtures among dance traditions and to be creative.

It seems a paradox that the commodification of Li dance can be viewed as a positive mechanism in the pursuit of some proscribed spontaneity. The experience of performing, especially the experience of dancing can, in the best of circumstances, be a route toward genuineness: to a space and time where the energy of a dance performance moves beyond a routine presentation to a more intensely experienced performance by both the performer and the viewer. This experiential authenticity, as clarified by Errington (1998), lends greater depth to the concepts of 'authenticity' and 'reinvention' of the dance performance for tourists. Definitions of authenticity and commodification are relative terms, reflecting the judgments of both performers and tourists. Evolving Li dance performance represents a reborn cultural identity that is built according to a broader set of political, economic and cultural processes rather than an evolution taking place in relative isolation from those processes.

Economic Development versus Cultural Preservation

Gustafsson and Shi (2003) suggested that the income gap between the ethnic minority–majority in rural China has in fact widened in recent years. Although different spatial distribution and physically unfavorable conditions might explain income inequality, government policies at the provincial and local level seem to have been unsuccessful in bringing the income of minorities up to and even above the level of the majority of persons living in the same area. Governing authorities in destinations where indigenous people are in the minority have been anxious to reverse what is perceived as a growing dependence on social assistance. Increasingly, economic development through tourism is one of the strategies being chosen to foster the economic independence of ethnic minorities. Frideres (1988) proposed that there are structural inequities built into this capitalist approach to economic development, inequalities that run counter to the interest of ethnic people. He argued that the economic mechanisms most likely to lead to success must be based on community control rather than those conducted as an individual enterprise. From this perspective, considerable effort is required to provide effective protection to ethnic community interests as they increase their participation in the capitalist framework of tourism development.

Maurer-Fazio *et al.* (2004) suggested a correlation exists between economic growth and labor force participation rate (LFPR). According to their data, the overall LFPR for the ethnic Li is 74%, more specifically, 76.92% for males and 71.11% for females. Although the Li's LFPR rates were slightly below the Han majority (76.57%), they represented only Li working in urban areas, such as Haikou and Sanya, and excluded a vast majority in rural areas. The proportion of Li aged 15 and above with educational attainment above junior middle school was only 9.96% compared with 17.04% of the Han majority. The illiterate and semi-literate Li aged 15 and above were 15.88% compared with 12% of the Han in 2000. It should be noted that the definition of the illiterate in Chinese statistics is a person who has never stepped into a classroom. If a person attends only a day of the class, he/she will be loosely classified as semi-literate. Therefore, the income gap between Li and Han could be significantly widened if disproportionate semi-literates were identified as illiterates. In 2007, the Chinese Education Bureau reported that the number of people deemed illiterate in China grew by 30 million to 116 million in the five years before 2005. The majority of the increases occurred among migrant workers and ethnic minorities clustered in urban centers and not having access to public education, health care and other basic social services. In terms of percentage of the labor force in professional, technical and administrative occupations, in 2000 only, 3.57% of Li were identified as such compared to 7.25% of Han. These figures undoubtedly show that few Li people hold administrative positions on Hainan, and that these positions were taken by the Han majority dispatched from the mainland.

Despite these dire statistics for Li, their presence and involvement in tourism have steadily changed the economic landscape on Hainan. Liu and Wall (2005) undertook a survey on the informal sector on Hainan. They found that ethnic tourism can contribute significantly to local economic development because tourists typically purchased locally produced goods and services, and supported small-scale enterprises. They argued that an advantage of ethnic tourism is that it is 'a home-grown, self-reliant initiative to inspire local entrepreneurship' (Liu & Wall, 2005: 706). The establishment of folk villages surrounded by an informal sector reflects a labor intensive form of tourism in which local resources and skills are used to provide services for tourists. Xu (1999) noted that the comparatively low entry level nature of jobs in these activities motivates communities to become involved with tourism whose economic spin-off effects can be enormous. Use of guesthouses, sales of handicrafts and food, and the promotion of ethnic cultures have a direct impact on local economic development.

Private enterprise operations, managed by non-Li people, control the majority of folk villages. While ethnic minorities are seen as a marketable resource, little attention has been paid to cultural preservation. Therefore, a tension between economic development and cultural preservation is evident in the context of Hainan folk villages. Ethnic dance performers are better paid compared to workers involved in more mundane activities. Individual monthly salaries for dancers ranged from 300 yuan (US$36) in Wuzishan Li Village to 1000 yuan (US$120) in Luhuitou theme park. In addition, the villages covered room and board. According to the data collected from the interviews, the average net income of a dance performer was around 5000 yuan (US$602) or 6000 yuan (US$722) annually. Comparatively, the average annual income per capita on Hainan was 7852 yuan (US$946) in 2005 (Statistics Bureau of Hainan Province, 2007). Although the net incomes of dance performers was below that of the provincial average, they were substantially above those common in rural areas after free room and board covered by the folk villages was factored in. The salaries of the managers were significantly higher than those of the performers. Managers of folk villages averaged around 800 to 1000 yuan (US$96 to $120) per month, approximately 50% higher than the dance performers. Nevertheless, managers lived with the dancers under one roof and shared the same food. In most folk villages, the chief director and managers' rooms were adjacent to the employees' dormitories.

Since room and board were covered by the village, dance performers appeared to have more disposable income than many other people. Over 50% of interviewees claimed that they spent their income locally, with little put into saving. Most male dance performers complained of the high cost for desired goods (e.g. buying cigarettes and liquor); about a third (35%) of interviewees stated that they save money for the future; and 15% of them not only save money but also send money home. Those sending money to their families were predominantly married females who did this to support their children's living and education expenses, or to assist their parents. Unmarried female performers also expressed the view that a dance career is short, and, therefore, it is necessary to start saving money and to seek a family with which to settle down.

When asked if tourism development would change Li culture, many Li dancers expressed a positive opinion toward tourism and economic development. One Li dancer in Baoting Areca Manor described the situation as follows:

> This area [Baoting county] is very poor and backward. My family has worked on the farm for generations; however, my parents still barely make ends meet. I am the youngest daughter in the family and have been dancing in this village for a couple of years. Even though my income is not high, I feel this job fits me very well. We present our culture by performing dances. My parents once visited me and felt very happy to see my performance of traditional Li dance.

Tourism generates both direct and indirect employment that can be measured through salaries and their subsequent redistribution. Employee salaries vary directly with the size of the establishment (the larger the establishment, the higher the salary); thus, average salaries vary among geographic areas. Villages close to the cities of Sanya and Haikou offered higher salaries, while the villages in central Hainan offered the lowest. The pattern of higher salaries in urban areas is part of a broader pattern that has resulted in urban growth as ethnic minority people, in general, migrate to take advantage of more favorable employment opportunities.

Folk villages located in the central part of Hainan have experienced a large turnover of dance performers. For example, the Wuzishan Li Village had only three dance performers because many performers had migrated to the main resort areas of Sanya, where dance performances in restaurants and hotels paid much higher salaries. The young dance performers told me that due to their busy work schedule, they were not able to help their parents to farm and had to skip the traditional Li ceremonies and festivals. Given the gradual erosion of tradition in the communities, cultural preservation seemed to have less importance for ethnic dance performers. As stated by one of the dance performers, 'dance reflects our culture and we are also doing so to make a living'. The relationship between economic development and cultural preservation does not seem to conflict. It appears that while traditional dance forms have grown weaker, the broader pattern of Li dance expression is preserved even though it has continually been re-invented in response to tourists' and market demand.

The overwhelming emphasis on economic development has crowded out traditional dance in Li communities. The advent of tourism has had a profound effect on traditional rural economies; however, employment in the folk villages has been one way for young Li to improve their standard of living. Ethnic tourism has enabled dance performers to attempt to bring together traditional cultural values with a need for economic development. Upward social mobility has become increasingly desirable, particularly for those dance performers who look for better opportunities. There is no doubt that ethnic tourism has improved the economic well-being for those involved in it, but it has also transformed the Li communities. Upholding traditions and values in the communities has become a challenge as tourism has become a source of employment for minority people.

Cultural Evolution versus Museumification

The folk village setting is a challenging context in terms of dance performance. On the one hand, the goal of dance presentation is to perform a facet of traditional ethnic culture. On the other hand, the villages provide the impetus for that same dance structure to evolve and change. In Hainan folk villages, performances are shaped to fit the economic interests of entrepreneurs as well as the limited time schedules of tourists. Presentations feature elaborate costumes and designed stage sets that project spectacular visual images. Ethnic dance forms are structurally compressed and improvised sections of accompanying music are shortened or replaced by new compositions. In addition to these performance-related changes, Li culture as a whole is constantly evolving in the face of changes within the environment in which it exists. Phillips and Steiner (1999) suggested that scholars often fail to understand touristic arts performance due to two major factors. First, the underlying assumption is that authentic arts is a functional object for the community and not for market exchange. The dance performance, originally a part of rituals and ceremonies, has transformed into *mise-en-scène*, staged for tourists by tourism businesses and governments. In the context of tourism, cultural evolution is viewed as a distortion of ethnic culture and a development of primitivism. Additionally, traditional arts are often commoditized in response to tourists' preference. Once ethnic arts and crafts are adapted for commercial consumption, they are considered contaminated and inauthentic. The combination of modern and primitive characteristics for the tourist trade has been characterized as an abusive use of ethnic culture, a hijacking of the development of cultural evolution (MacCannell, 1992). By contrast, Maruyama *et al.* (2008) have argued that, given the subjective and dynamic nature of authenticity, the changes or innovations in art forms should be seen as pragmatic ways or creations of new meanings in response to current social realities and demands. In reality, 'living history' is non-existent and museumified primitivism cannot be found.

The attributes of the dance performers themselves are seen as critical indicators of authenticity, and what happens to the performer in the process or as a result of a performance is often deemed to be important in determining the degree of commodification. In fact, both within and outside the tourism setting, the performers' backgrounds and the nature of their involvement are criteria used in the evaluation of authenticity. Daniel (1996) has suggested that there are two important indicators of the authenticity of dance performances: (1) ethnicity of the performers and (2) their dance training. For the first criterion, the majority of dance performers came from local or neighboring communities. Folk villages located on the central route recruited mainly Li people, while villages located on the eastern route generally hired a small proportion of non-Li performers (10–25%). The only exception was the Indonesian Village in which 50% of dance performers were of Chinese-Indonesian origin and the rest were second-generation Indonesian-Chinese who could not speak the Indonesian language. In general, the second generation has little knowledge of Indonesia and can be viewed as local Hainan residents. Unlike the formal sector of the Hainan tourism industry, where ethnic minorities do not constitute a large proportion of employees (Ouyang, 1999), the establishment of tourist villages has not only created substantial employment opportunities for ethnic minorities, especially youth, but has also vigorously promoted such operatives in the informal sector as vendors, drivers and guides. These vendors, the majority of whom are Li, prefer the flexibilities and freedom to the restrictions of the formal sector. The folk villages were generally located in isolation so that the vendors did not need to compete with retail stores. The informal sector provided an excellent opportunity for interacting with tourists who tend to be willing to pay for ethnic goods and souvenirs.

Although proportion of ethnic representation is an important indicator of authenticity, in interviews, the dancers indicated that ethnicity is not the only selection criterion for recruitment. Since a dance troupe operates as a team, likelihood of 'getting along with the team' was the most important selection factor. During recruitment, the village directors paid more attention to dancers' aptitude for learning, their physical appearance and their personality. Some directors even insist that performers from Mainland China work better than Li performers because those from the mainland are 'smarter' than those from the minority. For example, the director of Sanya Li Ethnic Folk Village commented that:

> When we hire the ethnic dance performers, the first thing we consider is the aptitude for learning to dance. In general, the Li have known ethnic dance during childhood, therefore it is much easier for young Li girls to learn these dance programs. However, I have to tell you two things: first, the dance programs we present are not totally ethnic Li dance – they have been modified to fit tourists' tastes and time schedules. Second, some dancers from Mainland China do a better job than ethnic dancers here. They are smarter than the ordinary Li. Thus, ethnicity is an important criterion when choosing the dance performers; however, it is not a must.

The Li dancers generally did not have prior professional training. As indicated above, their educational levels were usually low and they rarely had prior formal training. However, the interviewees indicated that dance training was gained in the following three ways:

(1)   About a quarter (26%) of those interviewed stated that they had received dance training during junior high school. The junior high schools in the Li Autonomous Prefecture generally offer Li dance classes as part of the curriculum. Therefore, some already had training in traditional Li dances when they became dance performers in the folk villages.

(2)   More than half (65%) of those interviewed had learned dance techniques through on-the-job training. For example, a tourist village would hire a choreographer from an ethnic community to train performers in a short period of time. The newly recruited performers experienced what is essentially a 'crash course' requiring intensive exercise in a very short period of time.

(3)   A very small proportion (9%) of the interviewed dance performers had gone through professional training from local ethnic dance schools.

Thus, the majority of dancers received dance training informally. When asked whether such informal training might affect the authentic presentation of dance performances, one ethnic Li dancer in Baoting Areca Manor commented that:

> I think [on-the-job training] is sufficient. The choreographers who the village invited are senior instructors from the central part of Hainan. Although they have never gone through formal education or held

any dancing diploma, they are indeed professional and very patient to teach us. On the contrary, I do not believe in the ethnic dancing schools in Sanya (a coastal resort in the south of Hainan). Many teachers are Han and their understanding of Li dance is different from us.

The comments of the ethnic dance performers reflected a belief that commercialization in dance training is not preferred. Although dance training at an arts school is seen as 'authentic' from a government perspective, it is not widely viewed as 'authentic' by the dance performers. As noted in the comment, many teachers in dancing schools are of Han origin and the dance schools are run by a government that has promoted the institutionalization of Li dancing and singing. In these government-sponsored schools, Li people learn newly developed 'Li' routines that include poetic songs, myths and cultural approaches to life. Thus, such dance training was regarded as encouraging 'manufactured' routines or, at best, a blend of Han and ethnic Li forms.

Most of the interviewed dance performers agreed that what they perform is very different from the present reality of Li villages. A state of museumification was obvious as I experienced in the folk village. One dance performer in Sanya Li Folk Village expressed the following concerns:

When we perform the Li dance, tourists often view us differently. Some tourists from Mainland China used very rude words to describe Li people. They suggested we are ancient, backward and barbarian. In fact, we are exactly the same: we can speak Mandarin, we know the fashion in big cities, and we look like Han.

The dances that ethnic performers present on stage did not represent the authentic evolution of cultural forms. Further, they had limited opportunities to interact with tourists. As a result, they seldom demonstrate that ethnic culture is not static but evolves over time. This situation reflected, in part, the relative lack of control of ethnic communities over tourism development. Perhaps what might be called for is that dance performers move from primarily serving the needs of tourists to adopting a more proactive role in protecting ethnic culture from the effects of tourism.

The relationship between tourism and cultural conservation has both positive and negative aspects. As a tourism site, the folk village is a business enterprise whose 'success' is largely determined by its level of popularity with tourists. Providing tourists with entertainment and a certain degree of excitement is an unavoidable requirement of a tourism attraction. Ethnic dance performances have been widely viewed as a form of entertainment. While many Li have felt that tourism has commodified many aspects of their culture, it has also provided financial resources to assist the preservation of the cultural elements that make Li artifacts and cultural practices attractive to tourists. On the other hand, the Li minority is not well positioned to take advantage of the opportunities presented by ethnic tourism. The development, marketing and delivery of ethnic products are undertaken by private entrepreneurs. The Li minority has played only a minor role in decision making. Li culture presented in the villages has been shaped and modified by touristic influences. In this case, museumification or cultural freezing is not the danger, it is a matter of whether or not change is to be based on the evolution of organic Li life, rather than being based on having elements introduced to dance, art and music that has no real foundation on the actual evolving experience of people. Li control needs to be enhanced so that the Li people will have real power to decide what is appropriate for presentation. But at the village level, this was not the case because non-Li entrepreneurs, for whom economic gain was the top priority, owned the folk village.

Ethnic Autonomy versus State Regulation

The interviews revealed that the major problem for ethnic autonomy is the land ownership, particularly the communities near Sanya, where the resort development peaked in the 2000s. Wang and Wall (2005) documented the forced displacement of the Li to allow development of the golf course in their communities. The local government in league with private business decided to acquire the community green land. A series of problems with the operation have resulted because of the lack of a generalized framework for Li relocation and the inadequate involvement in policy making and relocation affairs of those affected. Monetary compensation was provided for all expropriated land, but the Li lost an important agricultural resource. The displacement programs were involved in settling the Li in nearby areas, moving them far away or relocating them in urban areas dominated by industrial enterprises. The expropriation of the entire area meant that the traditional agricultural resource disappeared. The displacement caused severe socioeconomic, cultural and physical problems for Li communities. Although the monetary compensation from local government provided short-term assistance to the poor communities, from a long-term perspective, the disappearance of agriculture lands forced the Li to look for other income sources to complement the inadequate compensation. The resettlement was complicated by several factors: difficulties in rebuilding traditional agriculture and adapting to a new social setting outside the farmland; and increasing unemployment in urban Hainan. Furthermore, the displacement changed family structure, community structure, neighborhood patterns and a traditional cosmological culture that viewed land as having spiritual significance for the Li. A flow of migrant workers to the major cities resulted. This migration included dance performers who grew up on farms, but ended up working in hotels and entertainment districts. During the interviews, I found that approximately one in three of the dance performers with whom I spoke came from displaced families.

Despite expressing their support for the economic necessity for displacement, the majority of the Li that I interviewed had mixed feelings about their relocation. A major concern for the relocated Li was that they face the risk of impoverishment because of a shortage of financial and economic resources and mismanagement of the operation, including corruption and embezzlement of the compensation funding by local officials. Davies and Wismer (2007) found that on the surface, the Li seem to share the perspectives of government officials that economic development is necessary; however, in private, there is a discrepancy between their public statements and their privately expressed complaints over government controls of land use and restrictions on access to resources. Davies and Wismer concluded that propaganda plays a key role in explaining the contradictions between Li statements and actions. In part, the villagers have had to gloss over the problems they face and are saying what they have been told to say. I encountered a similar pattern in my interviews with dance performers. When the local officials and the site mangers accompanied me for the interview, I always received extremely positive support for economic development, job satisfaction and the ethnic policies toward the Li. However, the answers were totally different when I interviewed dancers alone, particularly when my translator spoke the Li language. Wang and Wall (2007) expressed the view that problems accompanying tourism-induced displacement result from top-down administrative arrangements, which cause deficiencies in the implementation of resettlement and compensation given to those displaced. Local officials generally lacked the awareness, interest or understanding to deal effectively with minority issues. The sense of elitism and discrimination (e.g. Han know far better than Li) was common among the decision makers. Local participation was a foreign concept to officials and the limited formal educational experiences of and legal services available to, resulted in a passive reaction among Li with regard to getting involved in the planning for the displacement.

There are usually two levels of local government on Hainan: (1) the formal – local governance often imposed and supported by the Han majority; and (2) the traditional – community leaders associated with ethnic Li cultures. The latter are characterized by a reliance on the village council of elders in a traditional culture dominated by patriarchy and paternalism. Traditional leaders place a high value on communal and kinship bonds. Decisions are made through consensus building. The Li are much influenced by these traditional community leaders. However, tourism development has gradually changed the structure of Li communities. One dance performer in Wuzishan Li Village explained the situation as follows:

> When I planned to leave the village of Baisha seeking a job, I first had to get my parents' agreement; also, my family was required to obtain agreement from the entire clan in the village. Consensus was not always easy to reach because some village heads were concerned by the changes – they felt I would be in a dangerous position in the outside world. However, last year when I returned to my village, I bought a lot of gifts and brought some money for my family and relatives. They came to realize that it was a wise idea to send me out of the village.

In the Li communities, the immediate effects of economic and technological progress on traditional society are evident. Traditional systems could be maintained in a rural environment where communities were restricted in size and where social units were well integrated and dominated by direct personal relationships. However, in settings characterized by modernization and urbanization, traditional systems have given way to new social and cultural systems. Tourism development in ethnic communities can be seen as imposing a strain on traditional structures as specific cultural traits are eroded and relations between individuals are broadened and become more indirect.

State regulation has encouraged tourism involvement by the Li minority, in particular by young Li, given that the unemployment rate among the Li is exceedingly high. As of my data gathering, ethnic autonomy had not formed a threat to the State. In fact, the government hoped to reduce financial burdens through the development of tourism. Tourism was thus widely viewed as a provider of jobs and as a revenue generator. However, the job prospects for the Li minority seemed to be dim. In general, the Li had little education. Their most common occupations in the hospitality sector were menial, e.g. room cleaners and kitchen helpers. Many young Li people had quit jobs owing to high workloads and discrimination. Work in folk villages was seen as the most satisfactory occupation. One Li dance performer in Baoting Areca Manor described her feelings this way:

> I worked a couple of years in the hotel restaurant as a waitress. It was a restaurant themed Li food and we were supposed to dress in Li costumes. However, I was not happy not only because the workload was very high, but also they [non-Li managers] teased and joked about our presentation. My feeling is much better here [folk village] being a dance performer. Even though the workload is the same or sometimes higher, I feel pleased to showcase our culture and work in the ethnic Li context.

According to Swain (1989), the fundamental challenges to ethnic tourism are: does the ethnic minority group exercise sufficient autonomy; how is their culture marketed; what socio-cultural responses have the ethnic minority group expressed toward tourism; and what are the prospects for future development? The establishment of folk villages has provided a sense (perhaps a false sense given the locus of decision making) of ethnic autonomy for the Li minority. They realize that the Li culture has had a high value when marketed to tourists. Some dance performers voiced the opinion that as long as they stay 'ethnic', they can gain economic improvement and incentives from the local and provincial governments.

Mass Tourism Development versus Sustainable Ethnic Tourism

Community participation and involvement are essential for sustainable tourism development (Tosun, 2000, 2006). The benefits of tourism designed and implemented with the participation of the ethnic communities involved will empower community members, helping them mobilize their own resources, defining their needs and making their own decisions about how to meet those needs (Stone, 1989; Timothy, 1999). However, tensions tend to occur among various stakeholders when ethnic culture is being used as a tool for economic development; the governments may attempt to use tourism to standardize ethnic markers; tourism businesses may seek short-term profits; communities and even tourists may dispute the process of authenticating ethnic cultures. Tosun (2006) proposed a spectrum of the community participation in tourism: spontaneous, induced and coercive community participation. Spontaneous participation tends to be bottom-up, with authentic participation in decision making and self-planning for long-term sustainability. Induced participation is top-down, passive and indirect with only token citizen participation. In other words, the community may participate in implementing and sharing the benefits of tourism, but not in the decision-making process. Coercive participation is manipulated and contrived, representing the lowest level of genuine community participation. The objective is 'not to enable people to participate in the tourism development process, but to enable power holders to educate or cure host communities to turn away potential and actual threats to future of tourism development' (Tosun, 2006: 495).

Mass tourism development is usually viewed as having negative impacts on ethnic communities whether through environmental degradation or negative consequences resulting from direct contacts between tourists and hosts. However, Abercrombie and Longhurst (1998: 40) have suggested 'a limited area of transparency' between tourists and performers through a liminal theatrical space. That space encourages immediate reactions from the audience and permits a level of social interaction that can contribute to an understanding of cross-cultural difference between audience and performers. It can be noted that tourism leads to a loss of ethnic culture through the influence of commodification. At the same time, there is the potential for it to contribute to an increase in knowledge of diverse cultures. However, the majority of interviewed dance performers expressed several concerns regarding the 'limited area of transparency' as it exists between them and tourists before whom they perform. First, they expressed concern about poor tourist behavior resulting from a lack of cultural sensitivity. Dancers said that tourists are often unaware of Li cultural background, norms and folklore. Dance performers are seen as tourist objects, with little respect being given to them during shows. For example, dancers reported the inconsiderate taking of photographs and impolite assertiveness by tourists as they attempted to get the best seats (and best views). Dancers also described how tourists used flashlights to take photographs in the dance hall, while some even jumped on the stage to get a good picture. While dancers found such poor behavior to be disruptive, they were also 'put off' by a more general lack of reverence or interest in cultural meaning and significance behind the performance. Dancers indicated that such limited knowledge and appreciation of the cultural significance of the dances led tourists to make rude comments during performances.

According to the survey, dance performers in general were satisfied with their job because they were respected by other employees in the village. Performers in the Indonesian Village showed the highest level of satisfaction (95%) with their jobs, whereas performers in Wuzishan Li Village showed the least satisfaction (66% felt dissatisfied). Dance performers in villages located on the eastern route generally expressed higher levels of satisfaction than those in villages located along the central route. When asked if they would continue to work in the village, the Tianya Haijiao theme park and Indonesian Village respondents expressed the highest willingness to do so (88 and 95%, respectively). However, only 29% of dance performers in Hainan Village of Chinese nationalities, located on the central route, planned to stay on.

The reasons for such differences can be explained by the business situation on the central and eastern routes. Interviewees in three villages along the central route expressed concerns about the declining volume of tourists (two of the three were actually in the process of closure). For example, villages in Wuzishan, toward the center of the island, were facing a sharp decline in tourists following the opening of the eastern express highway. One female dance performer in Wuzishan Li Village said:

> We used to have 80 employees but now only 25 are left. We used to have 500 or so tourists visit our village per day but now only 20–30 tourists per week. Two years ago, I could earn as much as 800 yuan but now barely make ends meet. Most dance performers had to quit the job or move to [tourist villages in] the east to dance.

By contrast, dance performers in villages located along the eastern route remarked how busy they were during the peak travel season (generally during the lunar Chinese New Year and the winter season in Mainland China). Many complained that they were too busy dancing on the stage to take any breaks. The managers in the Indonesian Village have had to increase the number of dance performances to keep up with the volume of tourist arrivals. Nevertheless, most respondents were pessimistic about opportunities to get more advancement. The only exception was in Luhuitou theme park, where 75% said that there were more training opportunities. Further inquiry revealed that this theme park has an employment offer that if a dance performer keeps working for more than three years, he or she can switch to full-time status with full medical insurance. Most villages provide limited health care for employees; thus, employees are not assured prompt treatment should a medical emergency occur. Dance performers generally lack legal contracts and protection. As a rule, they are required to deposit several hundred yuan by the time they are offered and accept a job and the deposit can only be refunded after working for six months or more. Dancers reported that they were also commonly deprived of public holidays and weekend breaks. The villages, such as the Indonesian Village and Baoting Areca Manor, allow only one two-day break in a month.

Based on the report of dancers in several villages, the above findings reveal that the level of job satisfaction does not relate directly to income; that is, higher income was not associated with higher levels of satisfaction. Rather, the level of job satisfaction was related more to the potential number of tourist arrivals. Because an increasing number of tourist arrivals increases business for the folk village, this, in turn, increases the job security of the dance performers. Thus, from a dance performer's perspective, mass tourism was an important factor affecting job security and advancement.

Summary

Through the narrations of dance performers at various folk villages, this chapter explored the gendered and exoticized character of ethnic dance performance on Hainan. Despite the fact that women tend to be more involved in ethnic tourism than men, they are often depicted as a faceless, voiceless and silent group in scholarly research (Li, 2003). Ethnic tourism is commonly viewed as a process of feminizing Other and selling stereotyped images of cultural exoticism. Hainan is no exception as female dancers are the most identifiable ethnic marker with their roles ranging from performing on the stage to dressing up to greet groups of tourists. They represent what I, in an earlier chapter, called an 'ethnic panopticon', where tourists can gaze and fantasize about the Other in a fixed setting. However, at least one difference exists – here the relationship between Li female dancers and tourists can be described as what Maoz (2005) has called a 'mutual gaze', that is, they are not only viewed, [but] they also closely observe tourists' behavior and act on tourists' expectations. Mutual gazes turned into arts performance become the basis of a lucrative tourism industry, which in turn forms a public culture where ethnic identities are re-enacted, marketed and promoted.

It has been noted that across many settings, there is a tension between commodification (cultural production for cash) and maintenance of traditional ways (uncommoditized cultural production) in ethnic communities. On Hainan, commodification has had positive value to the Li community given that it has been a means of gaining jobs and income in situations where few alternative opportunities exist. The underlying strength of culture can be seen in the contents of the ethnic dance performance provided to tourists, albeit with modifications required by the tourism setting, the limited provision for training and the ethnic origins of the dancers. Clearly, Li dance performance, as an expression of Li culture, has evolved. The original ritual meaning of the bamboo-beating dance has been converted from an outpouring of mourning for the dead to a festival celebration. The selection requirement that bamboo used in the dance have a reddish color has disappeared. As time passes, fewer and fewer Li will remember the original meaning and form of the original dance.

Edensor (1998: 41) posited that ethnic tourist destinations have become 'enclavic and heterogeneous' settings where tourists and the local can co-exist. The gaze is often reciprocal in nature, given that the ethnic minority does not revolt against tourism development nor reject tourists' gaze on them. It became clear to me that maintenance of ethnicity is desired, but it is not the most important issue for village employers. Economic opportunity takes precedence as ethnic communities celebrate and portray themselves through commodification. Furthermore, it was apparent to me that these female dancers are not merely 'passive symbols of beauty or simplicity for tourist consumption' (Li, 2003: 54), rather they can be seen as 'strategic traders' of ethnic culture as they weave tourists' fantasies to promote business. Mass tourism was desired by the dancers because job security and, hence, economic prosperity and job satisfaction are associated with visitor numbers. Thus, the Li minority, as revealed in the views of dancers at folk villages, authenticated selected aspects of its culture through their performances. Commodification of the culture was viewed as a positive element in the pursuit of sustainable development, because it was considered an inseparable part of the desired economic development. To date, however, control of the commodification of culture and many of the associated benefits have not been in the hands of the minority people. Control over cultural resources and access to them by tourists would seem to require a greater delegation of power if ethnic tourism is to avoid turning exotic cultures into commodities and individuals into amusing 'objects' for tourists' consumption (Klieger, 1990). It is possible that celebration of differences, especially if accompanied by sensitive interpretation, may lead to growing pride and reduced poverty for the minority, and enhanced respect from the majority. On the other hand, or even at the same time, novel encounters may gradually become routine for hosts, the Li costume may become a business uniform, as it has already become for the dancers, and cultural presentations may become more and more removed from the reality of everyday life. Of course, numerous forces, in addition to tourism, impinge on culture. What is authentic today may not be authentic tomorrow, as the present becomes the past, and the lifestyles of the Li people themselves change.

Is the Li culture that I saw portrayed in the folk villages of Hainan authentic? This seemingly simple question does not have a tidy answer. In this case, ethnic tourism does not appear to have generated a new or emergent Li culture nor commodified one distinct from an original culture. As Medina (2003) pointed out, 'new channels' are utilized to access traditions that may have persisted across the communities. These new channels encompass 'a limited area of transparency' between dance performers and tourists; or *mise-en-scène* to put dance performance on the stage. The interactions tend to reshape the Li culture, some elements are lost in response to market forces, while others are strengthened through commodification. Ethnic tourism is the driving force for commodification and a powerful force that shapes ethnic identity. On the evidence that has been presented, a strong case can be made that commodification of the ethnic cultures of Hainan have had both positive and negative effects. Authenticity is not a unidimensional concept that lends itself to simple interpretation. Nevertheless, it is possible to explore the issues that underlie authentication, as has been done in this chapter. The task of understanding authenticity is elusive (and often illusive); the investigation of authentication offers a manageable way forward.

Chapter 6
Tourists

Introduction

On 14 November 2008, Inter Press News Agency published a travel report entitled 'Shangri-La under Tourist Siege' by Antoaneta Bezlova. The success of British author James Hilton's book, *Lost Horizon*, has motivated tourists to pursue a mystical utopia, to discover an enclosed paradise of carefree happiness and to flourish free of contamination from the outside world. County Zhongdian in the Province of Yunnan, China, tried to cash in on the area's unique history, culture and nature by renaming itself Shangri-La and asserting that the novel *Lost Horizon* was set there. The neighboring town, Lijiang, has a large concentration of ethnic minority, the Naxi, who make up 70% of the population. Ethnic Naxi have a matrilineal society led by shamans (the Dongbas) who developed their own hieroglyphic writing system that dates back to the 14th century.

In 1997, Lijiang was given UNESCO's World Heritage status, which provided an immediate boost to tourist numbers. From 1997 to 2007, the old town's tourist numbers grew from 1.7 million to 4.6 million. The famous Chinese film director, Yimou Zhang, created a show called 'Impressions Lijiang', presented on a spectacular open-air stage with a cast of 500 amateur performers from 10 ethnic groups. The show tapped into a growing fascination among Han-majority Chinese for the lives and experiences of the country's exotic 'others'. Through ethnic songs and dances, tourists erupted in cheers as they followed gyrating movements and incantations of the Dongbas. At the end of the show, tourists applauded with enthusiasm, 'We like you', 'We will be back!'.

At the end of the program, tourists lined up to receive Dongbas' symbolic blessing. Every spectator scribbled a wish on a piece of paper and dropped it in the Shamans' urn in the hope that their magical spells would make it come true. One couple on honeymoon cheerfully told the reporter that they loved visiting Lijiang because 'people here are so uninhibited and different from our hometown. The natural setting is fantastic. We wanted to have a special place for our honeymoon and we chose Lijiang. It is as close to paradise as one can find in China'.

Finding reality in paradise is often bittersweet. According to Bezlova's article in the Inter Press News Agency, Chinese tourists, mainly the Han majority, are visible on every step of the cobbled streets of this tiny town. They crowd the small artisans' shops, fill the boutiques, spillover into the streets from restaurants and coffee shops and gaze on the exotic cultural presentations. Tourists bring money and jobs to the local economy; meanwhile, old vernacular houses have been razed and replaced by Western-style structures. Newcomers have increasingly displaced the local Naxi minority. Gradually, shops along these quaint streets are run by people from the mainland, not the Naxi people who were forced to leave owing to the high cost of rentals. Commodification of Naxi culture has become so drastic that the UNESCO mission cautioned the Lijiang government in January 2008 that commercial interests have compromised authentic heritage values and there is a possibility of rescinding the status of World Heritage if unbridled development continues.

The report ended with an interview with Aming Duo, one of about 50 remaining Naxi shamans. He sells inscriptions in the Naxi's unique hieroglyphs to tourists at the Dongba palace. 'The problem is that our script was meant to record history and philosophy. Now I'm being asked to write jokes and people's names. It feels like a profanity to my tradition', Aming commented. Despite these changes and criticism, at the end of the interview, Aming confessed to the reporter that he could not survive without the income from this job brings him.

Various studies (Dyer *et al.*, 2003; Reisinger & Turner, 2003; Hinch & Butler, 2007) have pointed to the mutual benefits experienced in cross-cultural, tourist–host encounters. These benefits include the generation of positive attitudes on the part of both tourist and host, increased cultural understanding, reduction of ethnic prejudices and development of pride, appreciation and tolerance. The Lijiang news report evidently illustrated that ethnic tourism provides a joyful and exotic experience for tourists. Additionally, the growing number of domestic tourists in Lijiang indicated their interest in searching for ethnic culture different from their everyday lives.

At a deeper level, tourist arrivals highlight the cultural distance of contemporary China's urban and rural; the modern and traditional, the affluent and poor. The marketing of Shangri-la evokes a romantic, mythical, yet inaccessible image of ethnic people. The honeymooning couple's enthusiastic comments about Lijiang show that paradise, like beauty, lies in the eye of the beholder, having highly subjective determinants. If James Hilton were alive today, perhaps he would be surprised to know that the branding of Shangri-la has become such a powerful, commercial and effective way to attract tourists from every corner of China.

However, intercultural encounters can generate unpleasant conflicts (Robinson & Boniface, 1999). Ryan (2002: 952) pointed out that as ethnic minorities have become both objects of the tourist gaze and commodifiers of tourism product, 'spatial distance' has increased cultural misunderstanding and tensions between tourists and ethnic communities. Tourist arrivals have often had a negative impact on ethnic communities with authentic cultural expression evolving into contrived products for sale. The surge of interest in seeing exotic Others and seeking pleasurable experiences have reshaped the cultural landscape of destination areas. Tourists have economic power vis-à-vis ethnic minorities who live and work in tourism enterprises. The interview with Aming Duo, the shaman of Naxi, pointed out that economic power often overtakes cultural authenticity even when there is an attempt to draw boundaries in host–guest encounters. Aming clearly understood that selling inscriptions with Naxi's unique hieroglyphs to tourists is a 'profanity', to some extent, a prostitution of his culture and heritage; however, Aming admitted that he was also dependent on the income that the practice produced.

For ethnic minorities, commodification is a *fait accompli* where authenticity has already been eroded and corrupted by tourism. Van den Berghe (1994: 17) proposed that ethnic tourism, insofar as it is a quest for the Other, is more or less an example of the 'Heisenberg effect'; that is, the observer affects the observed. Similar to an interview where the interviewees tend to give answers they think the interviewer wants to hear, the quest for authenticity is constantly threatened by the interaction between tourists and those who are the objects of the tourists' interest. He further proposed that tourist–host interactions in the context of ethnic tourism can be summarized as: (a) ephemeral and unlikely to be repeated; encounters are particularly open to deceit, exploitation and mistrust since both tourists and ethnic minorities can easily escape the consequences of hostility and dishonesty; (b) those in which the tourist is relatively ignorant of local cultures and thus often appears incompetent, ridiculous, gullible, exploitable and vulnerable to faulty communication and misunderstandings; and (c) relationships between tourists and tourees that are intrinsically asymmetrical, not only in terms of disparity of wealth (favoring the tourist) and information (favoring the touree), typically casting the tourist into the spectator role and the touree into that of a performer.

The Tourist: A New Theory of the Leisure Class (MacCannell, 1976), though admittedly an older source, presents a fascinating analysis of the tourist in the postmodern era. He used tourism as a point of entry to explore the ethnography of tourist culture and suggested that attractions could be characterized as varying in the degree to which they were staged; that is, the degree to which they replaced the real with 'staged authenticity'. MacCannell viewed tourism as a harmless fetishization of Other, since tourists have sought backstage (i.e. genuine or non-contrived) experiences and demanded authenticity. From a tourist perspective, authenticity is a desired experience, or benefit, associated with visits to tourism sites.

Anticipation of authenticity poses a challenge in ethnic tourism, but its confirmation is widely regarded as the most important criterion for a satisfying tourist experience (Chambers, 1999). For example, Chang's (2006) study of the Rukai aboriginal cultural festival in Taiwan employed cluster analysis to identity three tourist groupings: 'aboriginal cultural learner', 'change routine life travelers' and 'active culture explorers'. She argued that for tourists within the groupings 'aboriginal cultural learners' and 'active culture explorers', promotional efforts should emphasize authenticity and uniqueness of culture, as such groups were likely to be interested in experiencing backstage aboriginal customs. The study demonstrated that authenticity remains a motivating factor, though it possesses an elusive nature. King (2009: 49) further suggested that instead of jettisoning the concept of authenticity, there is a need to 'personalize it, address its socially constructed nature, and recognize that tourists can perceive authenticity to their satisfaction even when it is staged'.

Postmodernist tourism scholars (Stebbins, 1996; Moscardo & Pearce, 1999; Cohen, 2004) have suggested that genuineness or authenticity of a tourist setting is not a tangible asset but, instead, is a judgment or value placed on the setting by the tourists. An authentic experience may be achieved despite compromise of cultural values or modifications to cultural products and activities presented to tourists (McIntosh & Prentice, 1999). Tourists' perception of authenticity is highly subjective but can be segmented, analyzed and induced (Xie, 2004). Not all tourists seek authenticity, many recognize the inauthenticity of the experience, but still enjoy it (Cohen, 1988; Moscardo & Pearce, 1986). Tourists' 'fun gaze' (Ooi, 2002: 87) accepts kitsch, commercialism and cultural inauthenticity. Attractions centered on the 'fun gaze' are understood as constructed spectacles, in which tourists are in a playful search for enjoyment. In this approach, the main concern is the illusion of authenticity rather than a definitive reality (Yang & Wall, 2009).

Despite a heated debate on tourists' perception of authenticity, there is a dearth of research on domestic tourists who are the main component of the ethnic tourism market in many developing countries (Li, 2004). Such central questions as 'what kind of perceived authenticity is most important for tourists' and 'what is the true meaning of authenticity' remain neglected issues. Previous research on ethnic tourists has usually relied on individual case studies, with the result that insights have been less cumulative than they might otherwise have been. In other words, few comparative studies facilitate understanding of cultural tourists in different locations. Second, the majority of research has assumed that tourists visiting culture-oriented destinations can be considered 'cultural tourists'. In fact, many tourists participate in package tours that include a series of recreational activities, such as sightseeing, shopping and observing cultural performances. Such tourists usually lack the time and depth of experience to understand the more complex and intricate aspects of ethnic culture.

This chapter identifies a range of critical issues for tourists visiting folk villages on Hainan. By using quantitative surveys in three selected villages (Baoting Areca Manor, Sanya Li Folk Village and the Indonesian Village), tourists' perception of authenticity, their assessments of the villages and products, and levels of satisfaction with their experiences were compared. The primary purpose of this comparative study is to delineate the profiles of domestic tourists on Hainan and their views of authenticity of ethnic cultural presentations. Important issues related to economic impacts, service quality and enhancement of cultural integrity have been raised in prior investigation of tourists' experience. Feedback from tourists can be used to identity issues in ethnic tourism and can suggest directions for tourism-related planning. The chapter first introduces domestic tourists on Hainan, including a background of three folk villages in which the survey was undertaken. It then reports the results of a sample survey of 586 visitors to the three folk villages. Tourists' opinions are summarized and their perceptions of authenticity are compared and evaluated by statistical analysis.

Domestic Tourists on Hainan

Hainan Island is reputed to be the 'Chinese Hawaii' and is attracting hordes of Chinese seeking sun and fun. Mass tourism is the most popular form of tourism on Hainan. An overwhelming majority (96%) of tourists comes from Mainland China (Hainan Tourism Administration, 2006) on package tours, the easiest and cheapest way to travel to and within Hainan. Travel agencies generally get a series of special deals when organizing tours. Frequent, frenzied price cutting by the tour operators on the mainland has created a perception that Hainan is a cheap and affordable destination. Price wars during the slow season in summer are particularly intense. Hostilities in the fierce package holiday price wars produce no winners. For example, a six-day package from Shanghai to Hainan, including round trip airfare, accommodation and food, costs as low as ¥1500 (US$214), while a one-way airfare from Shanghai to Hainan costs around ¥1200 (US$171). Independent travel to Hainan often results in a higher cost in both airfare and accommodation.

A large proportion of tourists are attracted by the exotic tropical climate on Hainan. The island has projected its image as a romantic, Wild West frontier with a sun-sea-sand-sex indulgence by tourism bureaus. The sheer numbers of Chinese tourists mean that once-unspoiled, inaccessible locations, like Tianya Haijiao, Wuzhishan and Wuzhizhou (a tiny, exclusive, white-sand island just offshore northeast of Yalong Bay), have been developed with Disney-like fervor to entertain throngs of tourists dressed in loud Hawaiian shirts. With the upgrade of the central and eastern highways, tourists can be spotted on almost every moving bus. Massive tourism development in the 2000s witnessed a significant increase in the number of hotels and man-made attractions. Tsui (2009) sarcastically commented that Hainan is quickly evolving from the 'Chinese Hawaii' to more closely resembling a 'Chinese Miami'; that is, a place full of shiny resorts and artificial attractions.

The typical package tour encompasses a series of such recreational activities as traveling to two main hubs, the cities of Haikou and Sanya, shopping at local jewelry stores, dining on seafood near Sanya Bay, etc. Visits to folk villages are part of the tours arranged by travel agencies, but are regarded as a fringe activity not receiving much attention. This lack of importance is especially obvious when tourists have limited contact with local people. They are very much separated from the cultural spheres in which ethnic minorities live.

Since travel routes are designed by statutory agencies and tour operators, the provision of kickbacks has become the most important factor in choosing the village to be visited. In addition, the number of tourists visiting a folk village is controlled by the ease of access to the site and the effectiveness of its promotion. The longer the village has been in existence, the more likely it is to receive large tourist numbers, with less successful ones having closed. Some villages have been developed along the eastern highway to provide such convenience. The displays in most villages tend to be identical so that it is unlikely that tourists will want to visit two or three villages on one trip.

As tour operators have not viewed village tours as an important program, the vast majority of tourists from Mainland China are not prepared for a visit to a folk village. Tourists appear to have little information on ethnicity and the experience they have in the village is totally arranged by the tour operators. Tourists from Mainland China typically seem to be interested in local ethnic traditions as a form of entertainment, but expect to remain inside an environmental bubble, stay in modern accommodations, speak their native language with a tour guide and be transported by an air-conditioned bus (Nyaupane *et al.*, 2006). Interactions between tourists and ethnic minorities are brief and take place in controlled settings. In general, their stay at the folk village lasts around 40–60 minutes. Activities include attending a dance performance, walking around the village to shop and having a snack of ethnic food. Some tourists pay extra money to participate in ethnic ceremonies, such as a mock wedding. The relationship between tourists and ethnic people is thus highly transitory. To make matters worse, tour guides do not play a significant role in explaining and interpreting the ethnic culture of the village, but normally entertain tourists with fictional anecdotes, freely admitting that they know the stories are based on imagination rather than an informed knowledge of ethnic culture. Some tour guides simply stand at the exit and wait for their clients to return, resulting in the tourists having a superficial experience of the folk village.

For most tourists from Mainland China, mention of the ethnic Li evokes images of a convivial bamboo-beating dance, colorful costume and promiscuous sexual relationships. Ethnic Li are viewed as 'unspoiled natives' representing exotic imaginations of the past. These images are largely derived from the mass media, which influences their expectations. From the perspective of what Baudelaire (1970) has termed *flâneur*, Chinese tourists have embarked on brief and aimless trips to Hainan, wanting to experience ethnic presentations only in passing. *Flâneur* is a set of mutual gazes between tourists and tourees with differing expectations. Striking a somewhat self-congratulatory stance, tourists view themselves as cosmopolitan and modern as opposed to the backward and primitive minority. On their part, Li people view tourists as rich people who have both higher social and economic status. The stereotypes of domestic tourists, in turn, have shaped the ethnic Li's own view of themselves. They find a social exchange that 'asks' them to fit a caricature of themselves on stage: one that requires them to be backward in order to preserve their 'authentic' culture. Stereotypes, both positive and negative, are reinforced by tourist-oriented performances, working against the present-day ethnic minority's struggle for social, economic and political autonomy. Despite the fact that the ethnic Li have been assimilated by the Han majority for decades, tourists come, expecting that 'pure' ethnic and traditional customs will be readily available in the folk villages. Locked into an unequal power relationship, the ethnic minority is pushed to fulfill tourist fantasies. The appeal of cultural otherness to tourists is an impetus to the development of creative ways of packaging and manipulating cultural stereotypes and identities.

There are three prominent villages on Hainan that attract a disproportionate number of tourists: (a) Baoting Areca Manor, (b) Sanya Li folk village and (c) the Indonesian Village. The three are highly representative of ethnic cultures on Hainan. Baoting Areca Manor is located in Baoting Li and Miao Autonomous Prefecture. The county has been one of the poorest regions and the manor was the main tourist attraction. It is surrounded by tall areca forests, where the Li have lived for centuries. The manor was a joint venture between the private sector and local government. It claimed to be the largest folk village on Hainan in terms of size and employees. The manor not only served as a model culture with which tourists could instantly identify, but it also functioned as an ethnic interpretive center to showcase the culture to tourists in a manner that the Li preferred. For example, in the early 2000s, the village had a small craft gallery for exhibiting Li artifacts. Although the display was rudimentary, it strove to reflect the authentic rural life of the Li. The manor also provided a set of elaborate 30–40 minute performances, such as the bamboo-beating dance, harvest celebration ceremony and Li wedding ceremony for tourists. However, the manor was highly commercialized with hundreds of vendors selling a range of goods from ethnic souvenirs, crafts, silver ornaments, and teas to local herbal preparations. Owing to the road conditions of the central highway, tourists generally visited the manor by tour buses. The number of tourist arrivals averaged around 500 per day. They typically spent an hour or so touring the village, watching dance performances and shopping.

By contrast, Sanya Li Folk Village was located on a southern exit of the eastern highway. In a convenient location for tourist arrivals, the village was built in 1996 after the completion of the eastern highway; however, it was not in the Li Autonomous Region. The village was owned by a private entrepreneur. Its theme was very close to that of the Baoting Areca Manor, but it paid more attention to the 'work, life, love and festivals' of the Li. The village offered a variety of dance programs such as the Lunar Third of March ceremony (a sort of love parade of the Li), depicting the vanishing customs of the Li. Tourists could participate in a mock Li wedding or rent Li clothing inside the village. The number of tourist arrival averaged 600 per day and the majority visited the village for 40 minutes and then moved on to the city of Sanya, the famous seaside resort in the south of the island.

The Indonesian Village was unique since it portrayed the Chinese-Indonesian diaspora who settled on Hainan after anti-communist riots in Indonesia. The diasporic communities worked primarily on tropical agricultural farms, including rubber and coffee plantations. The village was located in the County of Xinglong, a well-known spa destination on Hainan. Xinglong Overseas Chinese Farm leased the land to the village, which, in return, hired Chinese-Indonesians to perform and manage the village. The original idea was to showcase images of Indonesia in the hope of instantly becoming 'the most successful folk village on Hainan' (Hainan Tourism Administration, 1999). It was estimated that 60% of tour buses visited the village and that an average of 2200 tourists a day arrived in early 2000 (Xie & Wall, 2008). The main attractions of the village were Indonesian folk dances and songs. The village was closed in 2006. The reasons for the closure will be detailed in Chapter 7.

Tourist Surveys

Folk villages on Hainan are purpose-built tourist attractions, in which the theme is essentially ethnicity, e.g. Li or Chinese-Indonesian. The establishments accentuate selected ethnic elements for display and provide a context for ethnic minorities to interact with outsiders. Since these villages cater to tourists' needs and wants, they are seen as important stakeholders in authenticating ethnic cultural resources. Photography during the tour is the leading authenticating action of tourists (Finley, 2004). Individuals, armed with cameras, engage in intense and constant photographic activity that documents ethnic points of interest, members of the group or details of the villages. It is anticipated that tourists will search for cultural differences and will interpret ethnic presentations in their own ways. The result is that they can misinterpret, overlook or even be unaware of many cultural aspects of the settings they visit. On the other hand, the myriad of tourist interpretations of a single cultural product reflects the reality that ethnic culture is not symbolically closed, but is open for tourist's consumption in various ways (Ooi, 2002).

In 2000, a tourist survey was conducted in Baoting Areca Manor, Sanya Li Folk Village and the Indonesian Village. The research was followed by short-term visits and informal observations in 2008 and 2009. The reasons for choosing these three villages, besides their popularity with tourists, were: (a) both Baoting Areca Manor and Sanya Li Folk Village were similar in scale and theme, showcased the Li culture and were among the largest folk villages on Hainan. Both villages provided convenient transport access and attracted a substantial number of tourists. (b) The Indonesian Village differed significantly in the culture displayed: it showcased the Chinese-Indonesian diaspora who escaped from Indonesia during the anti-communist riots in the 1960s. The inclusion of the Indonesian Village permitted a comparison of visitors' responses to different cultures: Li and Indonesian.

The tourist survey for the three selected villages had three sets of questions. The first set of questions collected information about the respondents' visit to the village (e.g. type of transport, sources of ethnic cultural information and reasons for their visit) and their socio-demographic characteristics. It also asked about their previous knowledge of Li or Indonesian-Chinese peoples. The second set of questions focused on respondents' perceptions of authenticity, their expenditures, and measures of the importance they gave to different aspects of ethnic experience. The final set of questions measured overall satisfaction with the village experience.

The survey took place on weekends and public holidays to ensure the availability of large numbers of tourists. Data were gleaned in the morning and afternoon to cover both peak and off-peak periods (morning and late afternoon). A research assistant from the University of Hainan and I were stationed at the exit and parking areas of the village. We approached tour guides and drivers because the majority of visitors were in package tours and it was deemed appropriate to get permission from the tour guides prior to undertaking the survey. Tourists were then approached and asked to participate in the survey. Pencils and questionnaires were ready to be passed out if they agreed.

A total of 586 responses were obtained: 226 in Baoting Areca Manor, 134 in Sanya Li Folk Village and 226 in the Indonesian Village. The response rate varied between each village. The Indonesian village recorded the highest response rate with 90% of tourist participation, compared with 75% in Baoting and 55% in Sanya. The low response rate in Sanya Village was due to the limited time available for tourists to fill out the questionnaires. Most tourists were only given 40 minutes in Sanya Village and tour guides were anxious to take tourists to the city of

Sanya for sightseeing and shopping. Thus, a significant portion of the questionnaires gathered at Sanya turned out to be incomplete and could not be treated as providing valid data. Statistical analyses, using the Chi-square procedure, were carried out to test for significant differences in the responses among the three villages. Specific comparisons of the three villages were completed with all alpha levels set at $P < 0.05$.

Socio-demographic Characteristics of Tourists

Chi-square analyses indicated that the tourists' profiles from the three villages were very similar. The overall sample had more males than females (i.e. the Indonesian Village had 63% male respondents, Baoting 60% and Sanya 59%). Such gender imbalance can be explained by the fact that Hainan tourism has long been male oriented. Images of sun-sea-sand-sex and beautiful minority women, which dominate the packaging of the island, attract more male tourists than females. Although the majority of tourists' ages ranged from 20 to 40, a slight difference existed among the three villages regarding the percentage within that age range: Baoting had the largest number in the 20–30 age group (46%) and the smallest number in the 41–50 age group (15%). It is not known why this difference in age composition between sites was found. Chi-square analysis indicated that no significant difference in tourists' incomes existed among the three villages ($\chi^2 = 14.6$, df $= 10$, $P < 0.20$). The average income of surveyed tourists was around ¥400–800 (US$58–117) per month.

In terms of education, respondents in all three villages reported a high education level (58% of respondents in the Indonesian Village, 56% in Baoting and 54% in Sanya claimed undergraduate degrees). Administrative and government staff were major occupation groups: 55% of respondents in Baoting, 58% in Sanya and 64% in the Indonesian Village. Persons working in the civil services generally have high educations and participate in package tours organized by the government as an employment perk and a means of promoting group solidarity.

In terms of ethnicity, the overwhelming number of tourists reported that they were Han (over 98% of respondents). This is not surprising given that most tourists came from Mainland China and the number of international tourists continues to be small. Ethnic tourism attracts predominantly Han people wishing to see exotic minority peoples. One can conclude that, with the possible exception of age, tourists to the three sites had similar characteristics. In summary, the majority of respondents were highly educated people between 20 and 40 years old, with relatively high incomes, coming from the economically developed areas of China. Given this homogeneity, should differences in the responses to other questions be found among the three villages, those differences were unlikely to be explained by the personal characteristics of the tourists.

Perception of Authenticity

The perception of authenticity is closely related to tourists' preconceived images (Waller & Lea, 1999). Schouten (2006) indicated that authentic experience often does not represent a good tourist experience, with more authentic experiences associated with a higher level of complaints from tourists. Wynn (2007: 15) observed that both tourists and tourees are locked in a dialectic, where 'authenticity is lost and sought, authenticity voyeuristically consumed and thereby eroded'. Using an analogy of wine oxidation, I suggest that just as air contact causes loss of aroma and formation of an unpleasant odor, the encounter of tourists and ethnic minority in a contrived setting tends to instantly contaminate cultural authenticity and lower its value. From this perspective, tourism can, literally and figuratively, be described as a 'devourer' of culture that is destroying the very thing it has sought to preserve.

Most tourists to Hainan participate in package tours and pay most expenses prior to the trip. Touring a folk village has been a part of recreation programs designed by tour operators on Hainan, and tourists are not required to pay directly for watching such cultural displays as dance performances. Thus, it is difficult to judge the issue of commodification solely from the visible financial exchange. Table 6.1 provides the reasons for tourists visiting the villages. It is evident that 'on tour' was the major reason for their visiting the folk village. Over 70% of respondents in both Baoting and Sanya villages indicated that a village tour was a part of the tour program arranged by travel agencies. Almost

Table 6.1 Tourists' reasons for visitation

Reason	*Baoting (%)*	*Sanya (%)*	*Indonesian (%)*
Tour program	70	75	58
Personal desire	20	17	31
Others	10	8	11

$\chi^2 = 13.6$, df = 4, $P < 0.05$.

one third of respondents in the Indonesian Village reported the trip as 'personal desire'; however, most participated in the package tour for its convenience. The Indonesian Village was closer to and more accessible from the main city, Sanya, and this may have slightly increased the proportion of independent travelers, i.e. tourists not coming as part of a pre-paid tour. Therefore, we can see that variations existed among these villages with reference to the motivations tourists indicated for their visits.

Tourists in the three villages exhibited similar views on the issue of authenticity ($\chi^2 = 8.2$, df = 4, $P < 0.10$), with no significant variation among the villages vis-à-vis tourists' perceptions of authenticity. Table 6.2 compares the tourists' perceptions of authenticity in the three villages: 40% of respondents perceived Baoting as an authentic presentation of ethnic culture, 38% in Sanya and 37% in the Indonesian Village. However, a substantial proportion of respondents did not view the folk villages as authentic (24% in Baoting, 15% in Sanya and 16% in the Indonesian Village). At the same time, a large proportion of respondents claimed 'don't know', with 37% of respondents in Baoting, 47% in Sanya and 47% in the Indonesian Village expressing this view.

The findings suggested that a majority of tourists did not know ethnic culture well and that their perceptions of what was presented were blurred and uncertain. A large proportion of tourists had little knowledge of ethnic culture and they judged authenticity against stereotyped images. One view of the results was that tourists were using stereotypes as the basis for their judgments of authenticity. Furthermore, only a fraction of tourists in all three villages was familiar with ethnic cultures prior to their arrival on Hainan or the folk village (Table 6.3). A great majority judged their knowledge of ethnic cultures as 'superficial' (64% in Baoting, 58% in Sanya and 59% in the Indonesian Village). At the same time, nearly 25% of respondents in each village chose 'don't know' when describing their knowledge of ethnic cultures. Chi-square analysis also

Table 6.2 Perception of authenticity

	Baoting (%)	*Sanya (%)*	*Indonesian (%)*
Authentic	40	38	37
Inauthentic	24	15	16
Don't know	37	47	47

$\chi^2 = 8.2$, df = 4, $P < 0.10$.

Table 6.3 Knowledge of ethnic cultures before arrival

Knowledge	Baoting (%)	Sanya (%)	Indonesian (%)
Very familiar	3	2	2
Familiar	12	12	15
Superficial	64	58	59
Don't know	21	28	24

$\chi^2 = 5.0$, df = 6, $P < 1$.

indicated no significant difference in the level of knowledge at the three villages ($\chi^2 = 5.0$, df = 6, $P < 1$). Tourists to Li and Chinese-Indonesian cultures were equally unfamiliar with the culture of the villages they visited.

Of those who indicated that they were familiar with ethnicity, the sample in each of the three villages showed a similar pattern: a relatively high knowledge of ethnic dance/song, with 40% in Baoting, 41% in Sanya and 46% in the Indonesian Village, respectively. Such a high degree of knowledge of dance/song can be understood as the results of images of dancers and singers who had been widely portrayed in the mass media and tourism advertising. In general, tourists may be aware of spectacular presentations, such as the bamboo-beating dance, but not of other aspects of history or culture.

Tourists on Hainan were ill-prepared for a tour of a folk village because their reported appreciation and comprehension of ethnic cultures was low. In fact, they generally were more concerned with their enjoyment of the performance or that of the overall trip, rather than the authenticity of what they were viewing. While ethnic music, Li costume or Indonesian folk songs might have raised the interest of tourists, the majority still reported that they knew little of ethnic cultures after their village experience. Of those who expressed familiarity with ethnicity, the majority indicated that they relied on spectacular images from the media to evaluate authenticity. These images centered on dance and song performance or folklore widely shown in the mass media. Instead of encouraging cross-cultural communication, the village tour implicitly reinforced stereotypical images of ethnic Li. Those stereotypes persisted because tourists and hosts were unable to acquire much information about the other culture in a short period of time (Cohen, 1993). Stereotypes produced not only physical distance but also attitudinal separation, as both tourists and hosts have different ways of judging each other based on their own experience and values. Most of the time, tourists' judgments were shaped by how the village or the show was presented. Since they were not aware of other aspects of ethnic history or folklore, tourists were more likely to impose their own cultures on others or to use unfamiliar categories improperly. As suggested by Hall (2007), a growing preponderance of the 'fake' or 'inauthentic' is not necessarily objectionable to tourists. Fakery is essentially an attempt to replicate meanings of objects. The results were false understanding because of unrealized expectations, as a large number of tourists expressed 'don't know' and 'no opinions' toward ethnicity. Inauthenticity can be seen as an attempt to fill a vacuum in tourists understanding with an exotic, enticing experience. Given the reality that most of these tourists came to the villages with little or no knowledge of the cultures of the minorities, it seems reasonable that they would place the importance of entertainment over that of expanding their cultural knowledge. These tourists could not be viewed as true 'cultural tourists'; rather, they were incidental tourists to an ethnic tourism attraction.

Perception of Interesting Sites

Tourism businesses cater to tourists' tastes so it should come as no surprise that folk villages provide selected cultural expressions to meet tourists' expectation. Figure 6.1 shows sites of interest to tourists. Respondents were given a list of possible attractions in the village and were asked to check as many as appropriate to their interests.

A chi-square test was calculated and significant differences were not found among the villages ($\chi^2 = 49$, df $= 10$, $P < 0.05$). Both architecture

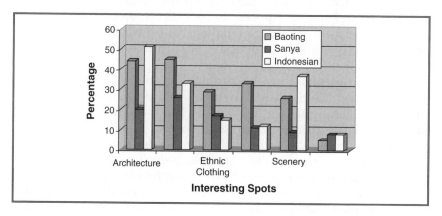

Figure 6.1 Interesting sites in folk villages

and dance performance were ranked most highly in the three villages. The dance performances in both Baoting and Sanya were ranked the highest among interesting features by 45 and 26% of respondents, respectively. Li dance performance is famous in China, particularly the bamboo-beating dance. Tourists were fond of the colorful ethnic costumes and the sheer joy of the dance movements. Both villages had orchestrated excellent dance programs performed at a high level of excellence. The architecture in the Indonesian Village was ranked as the highest attraction there and over 50% of the respondents thought the buildings were 'very exotic'. Many tourists commented that touring the village provided an excellent opportunity for learning about Indonesian culture and folklore without going abroad. Comparatively, the percentages of expressed interest from respondents in Sanya Village were lower than in the other two villages. Perhaps this was because tourists spent less time touring the village as travel agents were anxious to move them on to the city of Sanya for shopping and dining.

Tourists expressed a high degree of interest in ethnic customs and folklore. However, some felt frustrated that they were unable to find any help in deepening their understanding. For example, tourists indicated that they would have liked to learn about ethnic architecture, but nobody explained it to them. Tour guides and village operators did not sufficiently explain ethnic culture during the tours. Even the village employees did not know how to clearly explain the significance of the Li 'boat-shaped house'. At the same time, many tourists found 'exoticness' to be a good indicator with which to evaluate the quality of the tour. Remarks such as 'we like to see different clothing' and 'we want to know why they are wearing short skirts,' reflect the curiosity of tourists and their interest in ethnicity. Apparently, tourists had an unclear picture of Li culture, and many concluded after touring the village that this ethnic minority was economically and socially backward because they were not 'modern' at all.

These misconceptions can be attributed to tourism middlemen (i.e. tour guides and travel agencies) who did not play a sufficient role in interpreting ethnic cultures for tourists. There are two kinds of tour guides on Hainan: a *quanpei* (comprehensive tour guide) and a *dipei* (local tour guide). The typical *quanpei* is a Han person contracted by travel agencies and accompanies the tour from beginning to end. A *dipei* is typically a local minority person hired by the tourist site, who does not control the travel itinerary. Ethnic Han guides normally have a higher educational level than the minorities; however, they often have limited knowledge of ethnic culture. Tourist site managements tend to avoid hiring a local minority person in order to save costs. My investigation suggests that this preference for the *quanpei* is based on tourists' ethnocentrism; that is, the belief in the superiority of the Han culture as compared to that of the Li. What tourists found in the folk village were museumified elements of ethnic cultures. Their visits tended to reinforce previously held stereotypes, based on images derived from the media. As suggested by Suvantola (2002), tourist discourse and its tendency to portray Other as exotic relics to gaze at, are, in fact, the main reason that meaningful intercultural contact does not occur. Village businesses routinely cater to tourists' interest in the exotic in order to produce a 'hyper-reality' that heightens contrasts between tourist and host cultures. Eventually, these cultural differences turn into unfounded negative perceptions of the minority group by some tourists. Gessner and Schade (1990: 258) characterized these misunderstandings as 'an already complex situation is exacerbated by ambiguities, lack of awareness and/or the misunderstanding of cultural behavior standards, of language or of relational dimensions such as confidentiality or status'.

Economic Impacts

Tourists have significant economic impacts on the folk villages. Village businesses rely heavily on the number of tourist visits. The average on-site expenditure per surveyed respondent was ¥143 (US$17) in Baoting, ¥65 (US$7.8) in Sanya and ¥108 (US$13) at the Indonesian Village. The average expenditure of each respondent may include outlays for more than one person. Conservatively, it is assumed that each surveyed respondent represented three visitors who spent money in the village. Thus, one can extrapolate the economic impact on the villages by multiplying the average tourist expenditure by the number of tourist arrivals and dividing by three. It is roughly estimated that gross tourist' expenditure is around ¥8 million (US$0.9 million) per year in Baoting, ¥4 million (US$0.47 million) per year in Sanya and ¥28 million (US$3.33 million) per year in the Indonesian Village. Although such rough estimates do not represent a comprehensive and accurate picture of the economic impact, they indicate that the economic impact on the folk villages is very significant.

Table 6.4 lists some of the most popular souvenirs purchased during visits to the three villages. A large proportion of souvenir purchases can be categorized as local specialties, such as tropical fruit (e.g. mango, areca, lychee), herbal tea or Chinese medicine. Many tourists were interested in authentic handicrafts and trinkets made by ethnic

Table 6.4 Souvenir rolls of film purchased in folk villages

Items	Baoting (%)	Sanya (%)	Indonesian (%)
Local specialties	35	34	35
Ethnic trinket	13	15	0
Ethnic clothing	4	4	5
Silver/jewellery	8	4	1
Photo-taking	2	1	2

$\chi^2 = 27.3$, df = 8, $P < 0.05$.

minorities; however, they expressed difficulty in finding high quality and representative ethnic souvenirs inside the villages. Furthermore, no tourists purchased 'ethnic trinkets' in the Indonesian Village, accounting for the significant statistical difference in souvenir purchases among the three study sites. This may be explained by a challenge of cultural expression of the Chinese-Indonesian diaspora – there was no representative souvenir product in the village.

Although tourists spent substantial amounts of money in the villages, purchasing of craft souvenirs was reported at a relatively low level. Instead, tourists spent more money on agricultural products, such as fruit, teas and herbals. One of critical issues in cultural preservation is tourists' propensity, or lack thereof, to appreciate ethnic products and purchase souvenirs (Asplet & Cooper, 2000). These results suggest that the ethnic souvenir market on Hainan was still in its infancy but had much potential. Although tourists expressed a desire to seek craft souvenirs representing the village, availability of culture-related merchandise appeared to be limited in the three villages. In particular, the Indonesian Village had not developed a single souvenir to meet tourists' interests. It is essential for these villages to develop high-quality souvenirs that faithfully represent local minority cultures. There is an important niche market to be developed in the production of ethnic souvenirs.

It is evident that tourists inject a substantial amount of money into the folk villages through purchasing souvenirs and participating in ceremonies. They have important and significant economic impacts on the island. Local tourism income is directly related to the number of tourist visits. However, the growth of tourism has had a negative effect on the preservation of traditional culture in the villages. Commercialization of ethnic cultures was highly visible in the villages where, in effect, traditional forms were for sale. Tourists in the villages were actually consuming traditional cultural expression.

Service Quality

The most common form of tourism on Hainan is mass tourism. Most tourists are not interested in becoming more informed about the cultures they view, and have little knowledge of sustainable ethnic tourism. The visitation of folk villages was organized by tour agencies and tourists had little time to appreciate ethnic cultures. The number of repeat tourists was virtually non-existent. Thus, tourists had limited expectations for the folk village experience and had limited insightful suggestions for future development. However, tourists expressed their opinions toward service quality during the survey. Thus, it is reasonable to suggest that service quality is seen as an important aspect of sustainable ethnic tourism development.

The perception of service quality by tourists is particularly important for the evaluation of the host institutions (Walle, 1998). Cultural differences influence service providers and tourist interaction. Differing tourists and hosts perceptions of service provision may have important implications in the assessment of service quality. Qualities such as being friendly, prompt and helpful may have different meanings in different cultures, resulting in differences in perceptions of what quality is in cross-cultural situations. Therefore, it is important to recognize and respond to varying expectations when seeking to further the goal of sustainable development. Since tourists' expectations are shaped by their culture, their culture is the basis for expected service standards. While it can be argued that tourists' expectations are also shaped by such other factors as media, the influence of culture on individuals is arguably the most important.

Table 6.5 presents mean ratings of satisfaction (ranging from 1 = very unsatisfactory to 5 = very satisfactory) in the three village sites. Overall, the ratings in the three villages were very similar ($\chi^2 = 0.09$, df = 16, $P < 1$): an above average rating of overall quality of 3.1 in Baoting, 3.2 in Sanya and 3.5 in the Indonesian Village. Among all the aspects of their visit, the respondents gave highest marks for the quality of the tour guide, with 3.8 in Baoting, 3.7 in Sanya and 4.2 in the Indonesian Village. This was perhaps surprising given the lack of interpretation provided by tour guides at the folk villages, but probably reflects the fact that they interact with tourists across the entire tour that may last several days.

Table 6.5 Mean ratings of satisfaction in folk villages

Attribute	Baoting	Sanya	Indonesian
Village location	3.6	3.5	3.8
Architectural design	3.2	3.2	3.5
Dance performance	3.4	3.3	3.6
Ethnic clothing	3.5	3.5	3.6
Souvenir quality	2.7	3.0	3.2
Staff quality	3.1	3.3	3.9
Tour guide quality	3.8	3.7	4.2
Ticket pricing	2.6	2.8	3.3
Overall impression	3.1	3.2	3.5

Note: Rating scale ranged from 1: very unsatisfactory to 5: very satisfactory.
$\chi^2 = 0.09$, df $= 16$, $P < 1$.

Tourists expressed least satisfaction with ticket pricing (2.6 in Baoting and 2.8 in Sanya). Many tourists in Baoting also felt dissatisfied with the quality of souvenirs with a mean rating of 2.7.

When asked about the future prospects for folk villages, the majority of tourists replied, 'keep it original' or 'improve service quality'. Tourists who enjoyed performances and village tours were more likely to perceive high service quality than others who did not have positive experiences. They believed the current form of mass tourism on Hainan would continue in the near future. Distinctions between mass tourism and sustainable tourism were not important from tourists' perspectives. Tourists visited the village as a part of the tourism programs and had few ideas for the most desirable direction for village development in the long run.

Future Development

Ethnic autonomy from a tourist perspective can be examined along the dimensions of power, control, information and knowledge. An ethnic community that might otherwise appear to be weak, nevertheless possesses the strengths inherent in being on its home territory and knowing about its resources and potential. My observations in the villages showed that domestic tourists on Hainan regard ethnic autonomy and

Table 6.6 Suggestions for future development

Suggestions	Baoting (%)	Sanya (%)	Indonesian (%)
Village expansion	30	35	46
Detailed introduction to ethnic culture	23	20	19
Strengthen authenticity	7	11	12
Improve sanitation	13	7	3
Lessen vendor annoyance	13	9	3
Fair ticket pricing	7	11	8
Lessen commoditization	3	2	3

$\chi^2 = 13.7$, df = 12, $P < 1$.

state regulation as a pair of dichotomies. On the one hand, state policies may change the authenticity of ethnic cultures; on the other hand, many tourists believe that the prosperity of folk villages could not be sustained without the support of governments.

Table 6.6 presents tourists' views of the appropriateness for a variety of possibilities for future development in folk villages. Questions presented to the respondents were open-ended and responses were grouped into categories during the analysis. A chi-square test indicated that no significant differences existed among the three villages concerning the tourists' preferences. The option of 'village expansion' was ranked highest by the tourists. In particular, 46% of respondents in the Indonesian Village thought village expansion would be the best option for future development. Many suggested the possibility of including other ethnic themes such as Thai or Philippine cultures in the village. Tourists indicated that expansion should not only enhance the existing facilities, but also improve service and accessibility. The majority of tourists expressed high interests in these folk villages, particularly compared to other folk villages they had visited, such as the theme parks in Shenzhen, a city next to Hong Kong. Interest in village expansion can also be seen as reflected in the idea that tourists would like to see high ethnic autonomy in the village so that the community would control the presentation of Li culture.

Furthermore, respondents expressed an interest in having the interpretation of ethnic culture strengthened in the villages, with 7% in

Baoting, 11% in Sanya and 12% in the Indonesian Village seeing this as a desirable direction for future development. Some tourists wrote that they felt lost in the village because they were surrounded by countless vendors. Others wanted to learn more of the ethnic cultures through signage, video introduction and detailed interpretation. For example, tourists indicated that a Li interpreter is needed to explain the background of the folklore and customs prior to attending the dance performance. Respondents in both the Sanya and Indonesian villages expressed concerns regarding authenticity (11 and 12%, respectively). Some tourists even declared that 'if Li people ran this village, it may be more authentic' than, as they were told by tour guides, being a joint venture with the government.

Issues related to sanitation improvement and vendor annoyance were each raised by 13% of respondents in Baoting village. Many tourists complained about the poor toilet facilities and indicated that they were pestered by numerous vendors in the village. An average of 9% of respondents in the three villages remarked on the high price of admission. Most tourists were not required to purchase tickets since the tour was arranged by tour operators. However, when they saw the ticket price on the entrance bulletin board, a number of tourists expressed the opinion that it was overpriced. As has been described previously, it was common practice to give tour guides kickbacks in order to get them to bring tourists to the villages. In point of fact, admission prices had been raised to offset the cost of these incentives to tour guides, even though the giving and receiving of kickbacks is illegal. When asked whether government involvement in the folk villages would be beneficial, a great majority of tourists stated 'don't know' (60%). A quarter of respondents said 'Yes', adding that government involvement can help regulate the tourism market, in particular, the activities of the informal sector in the village. Some tourists complained that no warranty of products existed to fall back on if village souvenirs proved not satisfactory. A typical statement reflecting this concern is, 'What if I bought fake jade or rotten fruits in the village?' Many tourists wanted the local government to regulate the vendors in order to protect the consumer. Apparently, tourists had no idea that the villages were entrepreneurial operations. In fact, folk villages on Hainan present a more complex picture: villages were not operated by the ethnic minorities and state regulation of the folk villages was weak.

Summary

One of the primary goals of ethnic tourism is to help tourists experience the everyday life of ethnic communities. The experience of intercultural dialogues and exchanges is particularly important for tourists whose experiences can be restricted by contrived, fixed attractions, such as folk villages. Ironically, these villages could serve as 'meeting places' where tourists might learn to appreciate ethnic cultures; or could serve as a conduit in helping them overcome biases and building positive views of the Other. The development of tourism might also be conceptualized as encouraging debate about the characteristics of ethnic culture and how it might accurately be presented to tourists (Kolas, 2008). In reality, presentation of the everyday culture of ethnic peoples has never been accomplished by ethnic tourism: ethnic performances mimic authentic culture and cater to tourists' preference for viewing a contrived collage of ethnic images. Tourists' visits are so bounded and spatiotemporally fixed that the pursuit of authentic culture is replaced by illusion.

This chapter has provided an analysis of tourist surveys in three selected villages, and offered some insights into the interests and experiences of tourists at these ethnic tourism attractions. It is normal for tourists of another culture to be both fascinated and apprehensive about the different cultural and social structures of ethnic communities featured in tourist attractions. The findings showed that there was a significant correlation between tourists' perceptions of the authenticity of the presentations, and their level of satisfaction with those presentations. However, the surveys raised an interesting question: how can tourists know and understand ethnic cultures (in this case the Li and diasporic cultures) when their visits are controlled by tour operators who do not have significant knowledge about the places they visit? Perhaps the answer lies in the reality that the development and structure of ethnic tourism on Hainan is unique. Tourists to the island have distinctive characteristics in authenticating cultural resources as identified in the following points.

Firstly, visits to folk villages on Hainan were organized by tour operators as a part of recreational sightseeing. Tourists came from Mainland China with the preconception that Hainan is an island resort. They were not prepared for ethnic tourism, and their knowledge of ethnic cultures was limited and superficial. Commodification of ethnicity was acceptable for tourists, in fact, many of them enjoyed the setting despite its overt commercialization. Tourists expressed an interest in authenticity, but their knowledge of what that interest implied was limited. A large proportion of tourists were primarily interested in relaxation and fantasy rides. Encounters between tourists and hosts were brief as person-to-person exchange was minimal. The illusion of authenticity was largely derived from blurred and fluid images presented in the mass media. I have argued that tourists on Hainan should not be viewed as ethnic or cultural tourists, rather they are recreational tourists who happen to have an incidental experience in an ethnic tourism attraction.

The surveys suggested that cultural experience was virtually the same in the three villages, regardless of the culture of the village (Li or Chinese-Indonesian) and their locations (the central route or the eastern route). Statistical analyses indicated that the socio-demographic characteristics of tourists visiting the three villages were similar. The length of time spent touring the villages was the same across the three sites, and tourists similarly gained only superficial impressions of the ethnic cultures presented. Some minor differences were found among the three villages. For example, in the Indonesian Village, owing to its high publicity and exoticness, the architecture received wide recognition and the overall service quality was ranked higher than at the other two villages.

Although tourists had a significant economic impact through their purchase of souvenirs and tropical fruit, they did not view themselves as directly involved in the process of cultural preservation. These findings are consistent with those of recent studies (McIntosh & Johnson, 2005; Yang & Wall, 2009) indicating that tourists' responses to authenticity in folk villages focus on local settings (situational authenticity) and to tourists' fulfilling personal needs (behavioral authenticity). Most importantly, tourists expect to see quaintly 'museumified' aspects of ethnic cultures and do not generally realize that ethnic culture evolves with time. Quality of service is an important issue for the development of mass tourism. The concept of sustainable development was still foreign for tourists and few insightful suggestions relating to the authenticity and preservation of ethnic culture were found during the surveys.

What can be learned from this research on Hainan's folk villages? Few tensions between hosts and guests appeared to exist at the time these data were gathered. Not all tourists to ethnic attractions ranked experiencing a different ethnic culture as a high priority, because the decision to visit might not have been their own. Grazian (2003) has noted that different types of tourists measure authenticity according to somewhat divergent sets of criteria, and that the search for authenticity is hardly ever a quest for some actual material thing, but rather for what tourists in a particular social milieu imagine the symbols of authenticity to be.

My data indicate that having an authentic experience was low on the list of preferences, though tourists were interested in and prepared to learn about minority cultures. They seemed to enjoy the spectacle, and the selected presentation of cultural attributes reinforced a stereotypical view of ethnic groups. Perhaps this failure to move their interest in learning about minority cultures beyond a shallow reinforcement of stereotypes could be addressed by the provision of a more sophisticated interpretation. Many tourists would be more receptive to this. Having minority persons serve as tour guides would not only result in a more rounded and balanced portrayal and appreciation of minority culture, it would also enhance the quality of tourist experiences. At the same time, such involvement could create additional employment opportunities for minority people.

Chapter 7

Tourism Businesses

Structure of Tourism Businesses

On 2 March 2009, *China Daily* published an update of tourism on Hainan. The city, Sanya, located in the southern tip of the island, was described as experiencing massive resort development: multinational hotel chains, such as Ritz-Carlton, Banyan Tree, Le Méridien and Mandarin Oriental had all opened resorts there. The global economic downturn did not seem to have slowed the development of Sanya's high-end travel market. Boqing Li, deputy mayor of Sanya, proudly told the reporter that 'we will re-identify the city's travel market and make a change in the city's tourism industry development pattern from the low-end toward the upper-end'. Sanya, according to the local government, is being positioned to become a luxury travel destination of international appeal to rival Bali and Phuket. It is striving to move its travel market upscale to attract more 'elite overseas holidaymakers'. Rather than being identified as the 'Chinese Hawaii', Boqing Li described Hainan as aspiring to become an 'Asian Miami', a hub of international cruise lines, and 'a paradise for the rich', featuring a luxury marina with 72 berths. The Chinese real estate company, Antaeus Group, was reported to have already invested 2 billion yuan (approximately US$292 million) to build a seven-star hotel, a 200 m skyscraper, located on Phoenix Port Island in Sanya. The impetus for this prospect was derived from Burj Al Arab hotel in Dubai, which attracts worldwide attention. 'If Dubai can build it, we (Chinese business) can do that too' the group manager was quoted as saying.

Despite the extravagant hotel and resort development, the report ends with the subtitle 'cultural tourism'. Minsheng Liao, director-general of Sanya Culture Bureau, commented that 'tourists can not only enjoy sandy beaches and bright sunshine, but also explore diverse local cultures'. The scope of cultural tourism, according to the Sanya Culture Bureau, ranges from the Crown of Beauty Center, Sanya's indoor theater, which was home to the Miss World Contest, to the Nanshan Buddhist Temple with its giant Kwan-Yin statue in the sea. Surprisingly, ethnic minorities were not discussed in the report for cultural tourism development, even though ethnicity has become a popular and marketable resource incorporated into the travel itineraries of many agencies. From a business perspective, it is unlikely that ethnic tourism would attract such investment as that provided by the Antaeus Group, which is building a seven-star hotel to compete with Burj Al Arab in Dubai. Additionally, ethnic tourism is also unable to produce a generic identifiable product, such as the Kwan-Yin statue in the Buddhist temple. The goals of being an 'Asian Miami' or 'a paradise for the rich' have clearly avoided the involvement of the ethnic minorities, who comprise almost 10% of the island's population. The absence of ethnic minority involvement in tourism planning also reflects a misconception on the part of both governments and businesses that the demand for ethnic tourism is rather low. Ethnic tourism is widely viewed as 'small potatoes' as compared with sightseeing and other forms of tourism.

Shaw and Williams (1994) pointed out that the tourism industry tends to be dominated by a few large businesses operating alongside a large number of small and independent ones. The majority of tourism businesses are seen as small and medium enterprises (SME), which serve as intermediaries to help tourists interact directly with local people at ethnic attractions. From a structuralist perspective, the interface between the tourism business and the host community is a rather obvious source of potential conflict. Tourism businesses have profoundly influenced ethnic identity by creating a dynamic tension between exogenous forces and local traditions. Such businesses are a growth engine for economic development in which the ideas of destination are commoditized through marketing and promotion; they are also the cultural brokers who (re)construct ethnic performance for tourists. Meanwhile, tourism development has caused physical incursion into ethnic communities. Also, the direct consequences of commercialization and modernity have had a marked impact on ethnic cultures. Tourism enterprises, such as tourist folk villages, not only hire a significant number of local ethnic employees to serve tourists, but also authenticate ethnic cultures to suit tourist needs and wants; that is, they determine what, how and when aspects of ethnic culture are portrayed and performed. Conflicts occur when 'cultural carrying capacity' reaches the tipping-point of the acceptability of tourism in physical, perceptual, economic or social terms (Parris, 1996; Robinson & Boniface, 1999). Tourist attractions, souvenirs and other tourists' paraphernalia promote conflicts over spatial representation (Edensor, 1998). Therefore, Page *et al.* (1999: 454) suggested that where the tourism industry is dominated by small businesses, it is necessary to understand 'how they develop, function, conduct business and interact with tourists and non-tourists'.

In general, tourism scholars have classified businesses into two broad categories: formal and informal sectors. The differing character of the development of the formal and informal sectors has implications for the participation of ethnic minorities in tourism. Ethnic minorities can find employment opportunities in the formal sector such as hotels and state-run organizations, but the vast majority of opportunities are situated in the informal sector, ranging from street hawkers to managers of the folk villages. Given the wider spectrum of employment in tourism, the classification of formal and informal sectors appears to be an over-simplification. For example, Cukier's (2002) fieldwork in Bali, Indonesia, found that most ethnic minorities working in the informal sector were not marginalized economically; rather, their incomes were often higher than in the formal sector, such as front desk employees. By contrast, informal sector workers tended to be entrepreneurial, mobile, independent and not controlled by the formal sector. The established assumption that the informal sector would eventually disappear as tourism develops was not supported, apparently, because as ethnic minorities move up to other occupations within the formal sector, the employment opportunities remain strong in the informal sector with new migrants moving in to fill those slots. Because of the limitations of the formal/informal framework, this chapter changed to focus on the ownership of the businesses using three categories: (a) state-owned business, (b) joint state-owned/private ventures and (c) privately owned business. The following elaborates these three categories in the context of Hainan Island.

The majority of the tourism industry on Hainan is made up of state-owned business, such as accommodation, transport, attractions and support services, whose workers include tour operators, travel agents, hotel developers and government promoters and regulators. Given the political structure in China, state-owned business generally enjoys numerous privileges. For example, state travel agents on Hainan have special arrangements with the airline companies that provide below-market airfares for package tours. State-owned business can also influence the prices of hotels, transportation and park entrance fees. The involvement of ethnic minorities in state-owned business is limited. Since state enterprises are tightly controlled by the Han majority on Hainan, ethnic minorities have often been discriminated against and viewed as 'outsiders' by the businesses.

Joint venture business on Hainan is mainly found in the hospitality industry. The majority of starred hotels on Hainan are joint ventures between the government and external sources of investment. Under the government's support for tourism development, the inflow of external investment in the mid 2000s enhanced the variety and quality of the hotel business as evidenced by the recent hotel boom in Sanya. The main sources of foreign investment came from neighboring affluent locations, such as Hong Kong, Taiwan and elsewhere in Southeast Asia.

Liang *et al.* (2003) undertook an investigation of ethnic Li living in Shuiman, a village near Wuzhishan located in central Hainan, a joint venture between a tourism company and the village. The development of Shuiman was supposed to be built on mutual aid and cooperation. The tourism company agreed to employ many villagers in a variety of roles, while the villagers' collective control of their lands was transferred to the company in return for compensatory payments for resources such as crops and trees grown on them. However, as is often the case with joint ventures between ethnic minorities and tourism enterprises, problems arose. There was an aura of forcible eviction involved in the demolition of ethnic communities and compensation for displacement was not fully implemented (Wang & Wall, 2007). Ethnic communities located near the joint venture hotel were hired to work only in menial jobs. While many of the Li were engaged in performing dances and folk songs in the hotels and the tourist attractions, such work was contractual and the performers did not have the same benefits as full-time employees.

Privately owned business predominates in small tourist attractions, such as the tourist folk villages. Ethnic tourism on Hainan is a typical combination of entrepreneurship and small businesses, which receive little support from the local government. These enterprises are part of the informal sector. They are typically fragmented and parochial, yet they play a critical role in the survival of ethnic tourism. The number of employees in these folk villages tends to be small, ranging from 50 to 200. Although several folk villages have claimed that they are a joint venture between the private sector and government, the proportion of government investment is negligible. The purpose of asking government to be a partner is to ensure authoritative support in the village's operation. The main purpose of a joint venture is to enjoy a series of preferential policies from the local government, such as tax exemptions and land leases.

During the early phases of tourism development on Hainan, folk villages were located primarily along the central route where the majority of the ethnic Li reside. The location of many of these villages was remote and difficult to access. Since the establishment of the eastern highway in 1994, folk villages have gradually moved to locations along the highway in order to offer convenient access to tourist buses from two main nodes, Haikou and Sanya. Thus, transport routes played a major part in determining the development and popularity of many folk villages. However, several folk villages located on the central route lasted only a few months and then disappeared. One of the villages I visited had only 4–10 tourists per week and was practically defunct. The shifting locations of folk villages have made researching their role in ethnic tourism problematic.

In recent years, ethnic folk villages were built as part of recreational complexes, such as Sanya Nanshan Buddhism cultural tourism zone. However, a closer look at these villages revealed that dance performers wearing Li clothing were not of Li origin, that the 'traditional' dances have become 'manufactured' routines and that ethnic clothing was, in essence, a business uniform. I characterized these newly built villages as 'artificial' since their original buildings had been transplanted and the ethnic culture and heritage presented was actually a fabricated prototype.

This chapter strives to understand authentication from a business perspective, as observed in two selected folk villages on Hainan. The first village is Areca Manor located in Baoting (central Hainan), which represents the ethnic Li culture. The other is the Indonesian Village located in Xinglong (eastern Hainan), where the largest Chinese-Indonesian diaspora is found. Although the Indonesian Village was closed in 2006, it was one of the best villages on Hainan and lessons can be learned for its closure. Background material for these two villages was introduced in Chapter 6. Both were chosen for a variety of reasons: stability of operations; similarity in size and operation; locations on an original ethnic site and presence of ties to a local ethnic community; and similarity in their developmental patterns.

Stability of operation

Areca Manor is located in Gansheling of Baoting Li and Miao Autonomous Region, about 28 km from Sanya and is close enough to be visited on a day excursion. The Indonesian Village was strategically located near the eastern highway, between Haikou and Sanya. It was an ideal location for tour buses to stop for an overnight stay.

Location on an original ethnic site and close ties to an ethnic community

Areca Manor was set up in a forest where ethnic Li communities have lived for hundreds of years, while the Indonesian Village was built on the original Overseas Farm where Chinese-Indonesians have settled since the 1960s. Moreover, both villages have had close relationships with the local communities. Areca Manor received food and electricity supply from the neighboring Li communities. It has become the largest employer in the region, while the Indonesia Village received similar support from the Overseas Farm in Xinglong.

Similarity in size and operation

Both are similar in terms of number of employees and the physical size of the villages. Areca Manor has about 100 employees while the Indonesian Village has about 107. Areca Manor attracted about 3,500 tourists per week while the Indonesia Village attracted 15,000 per week. The difference in the tourist arrivals of the two villages is largely due to transportation. Even though the central route was upgraded in 2005, the central region is still widely viewed as difficult to access.

Similarity in the process of enterprise development

Areca Manor was developed as a joint venture with the local government, showcasing ethnic Li cultures. When it was developed, the Indonesian Village was claimed to be a totally foreign-backed investment because the owner of the village holds a Hong Kong Special Administrative Region passport through marriage. Areca Manor has evolved from an authentic portrayal of Li culture to a large theme park specializing in the Chiyou tribe, an imagined tribe that has never been found on Hainan; the Indonesian Village, on the other hand, changed from performing Chinese-Indonesian diasporic culture to a potpourri of Southeast Asian exotic shows.

This research was conducted through personal interviews with the owners, site managers, employees and community members of the two villages. The interviews in Areca Manor focused on five continua that have previously been presented, e.g. authenticity versus commodification; cultural evolution versus museumification; economic development versus cultural preservation; ethnic autonomy versus state regulation; and mass tourism development versus sustainable ethnic tourism. During the interviews in the Indonesian Village, I focused on the issues of positioning ethnic identity, the ownership of cultural property, the degree of cultural commodification for touristic purposes and the perceptions of authenticity from village business and ethnic communities. These issues are closely tied to the five continua and have been raised by Robinson and Boniface (1999) as major challenges when ethnicity has been used as a marketable resource. They also contribute to an understanding of the complexity of authenticating ethnic tourism from a business perspective.

Baoting Areca Manor

Authenticity versus commodification

The manor was established in October 1995, when tourism was just starting on the island. The site was located in the lush green forest of the central route (see Plate 7.1). Historically, most Li communities have been located in this region. My initial request for an interview with the owner of the village was turned down for various reasons, e.g. the owner had gone to the Burma and China border to look for a new theme park, he was out of town or he was busy, to mention just a few of the excuses offered. I was finally given a chance to talk to him and the interview turned out to be surprisingly good and informative. I was even granted permission to conduct a tourist survey, in and outside the village with the assistance of site managers.

The owner, Tianfu Chen, is not an ethnic Li, but rather a Han from Mainland China. He called himself the 'head' of the manor. He and his business partners raised the funding and started the folk village business in the early 1990s. Inspired by the theme park boom in Mainland China, Chen decided to use the ethnic Li and Miao as foci for tourist folk villages. The initial attempt to develop a village was near Wuzhishan where the

Plate 7.1 The gate of Baoting Areca Manor

largest ethnic Li population in the central route is concentrated. According to Tianfu, the opening of the folk village received a cold reception from both tourists and the local government. The inaccessibility of the village to tourist buses forced the business to close within three months. During the closure of the village, he and his partners had a major division of opinion regarding the future of the development. One of his partners, Yiming Li, believed the future of the folk village should focus on ethnic groups other than the Li and Miao. She eventually left for Xinglong to run the Indonesian Village. Her departure was contentious, centered on differing financial perspectives. Each blamed the other for the problems that developed during the early stage of the village's development.

In the early 2000s, the objective of the manor was to 'faithfully portray the life, customs, and conditions of the Li minority'. The 'inhabitants' in the folk villages were all of Li ethnicity. They demonstrated such traditional skills as the manufacture of embroidery, the singing of traditional Li songs in their own languages, playing a range of traditional musical instruments, folk dancing and the presentation of Li folklore. The village benefited from its geographic proximity to the Li communities that supplied both labor and services. The concept of the manor was, by and large, a living community designed to help tourists understand the everyday life of the Li. It also had a small and primitive showroom to introduce Li culture and history in the area. The façade of the manor was designed based on traditional Li boat-shape housing. Mr Chen told me that although the manor was never a top tourist attraction on the central route, it nonetheless attracted a significant number of tourists who were truly interested in experiencing Li culture. The manor expanded faster than almost any other village over the past decade. To Mr Chen, the location of the manor was proof that his village was authentically representative of Li culture.

In 2005, Areca Manor decided to change its business model from portraying a purely ethnic Li and Miao culture to one that would present a combined focus on wilderness and ethnicity. Part of the reason for these changes was the result of the wide support of the local government, which wanted to develop 'ecotourism' and 'wilderness' given that the area while scenic, was less developed than Sanya. The shift of the ethnic theme, according to Mr Chen, was a 'mind change' and a 'new emphasis' in tourism investment. Previous Li ethnicity had been presented authentically, but the shift in direction for the manor was intended to create a new tourism product in order to attract more tourists as they were on the way to Sanya.

A new ethnic tribe, called the 'Chiyou tribe', was deliberately created. This artificial tribe was supposed to have come from Northern China. Similar to the Kombai tribe in Papua New Guinea, the Chiyou were described as primitive tree people of the Stone Age. Tools were made from stone, men and women dressed in grass skirts and hunted wild animals. In a typical event offered to tourists, soon after the tour group arrived, a 'Chiyou' dressed troupe, acting in a stereotyped 'tree dweller' fashion, came out of the jungle. Then they used spears to kill a pig that had been tied up at the performance hall. Thus, the manor evolved from being a living museum focused on the Li people, to a theme park centered on the life of a cultural group found only in Chinese folklore. The central purpose of the manor became the offering of spectacular and attractive entertainment. A poster at the manor's entrance offered the following description of the park:

> This is a Forest Kingdom where Chiyou tribe lives. These people are primitive and still live in Stone Age. They live in trees and wear deep blue clothing to cover most of their bodies. You can learn bow-drill fire-making with Chiyou individuals, and you can experience how they eat raw and bloody meat. Don't forget they are the lost people and you shouldn't miss this opportunity to visit them.

I questioned this change of the thematic focus during my second visit to the manor in 2006. To me, it seems strange to move from an authentic portrayal of Li culture to presenting something totally fictional. I shared my concerns with Mr Chen and the site managers during the tour. One of the managers pointed out that using Li as a tourism product has increasingly become a passé and anachronistic remnant of pre-modern authenticity. Tourists, I was told, are looking for something new and stimulating. The manor faces fierce competition from numerous theme parks recently built in the Sanya area. Most of those parks have a section devoted to such ethnic Li performances as the bamboo-beating dance; therefore, it has become extremely difficult to attract tourists who have already watched the performance in Sanya. Mr Chen indicated that there was a strong need to find an interesting product to draw tourists for day excursions. The combination of a wilderness setting and a performance by a caveman-like tribe became an instant hit for tourists who wanted to escape beach life in Sanya.

The change of the manor's theme has also altered the remaining programs performed by the Li. In order to create space for the Chiyou tribe show, the Li dance hall and the showroom were moved to the edge of the manor. The size of the dance hall was greatly reduced and the performance was shortened from 30 to 10 minutes. The Li performances have been gradually marginalized. In 2008, the manor decided to lay off all full-time Li performers, and hire part-time performers from neighboring areas. These part timers are paid per show and do not have any fringe benefits provided by the manor. As suggested by the managers, the layoff decision reinforced the declining tourist interests in Li performances. On the other hand, the decreased focus on Li culture confirms that the new tourist attraction, the Chiyou tribe show, is working extremely well.

In my view, the manor has become a world of 'kitsch'. I observed two separate shows in the dance hall. The first performance, supposedly centered on Li culture, was entitled 'the matchmaker'. A female emcee introduced twin girls dressed in beautiful Li costume. She told the audience that these twin Li girls had just reached puberty and they were eager to find 'prince charming' and to have romantic trysts with the audience. The audience roared and several male tourists stood up and made catcalls to the twin girls. Two tourists were finally chosen, one was old, the other was young, and they both started to learn how to hold the girls' hands like a 'lover' in a traditional Li way. Some off-color jokes were cracked by the master of ceremony and I saw that the twin girls' obviously blushed. However, enthusiasm in the dance hall was palpable, as the show continued to demonstrate how Li women 'empower' a man in the bedroom.

Another presentation was of a supposed fire ritual of the Chiyou tribe. The actors dressed and behaved like New Zealand Maori fire poi, spinning and dancing with fire. At the end of the performance, one of the actors was invited to put out the fire with his bare feet. The audience cheered as the fire became only smoke and ashes, but nobody knew if the bare feet of the actor were unharmed or actually burned.

During the interview, Mr Chen constantly reminded me that tourists on Hainan do not actually want the truth but want to be entertained. Though performances have become a matter of story-telling, Mr Chen asked why should the manor spoil this enjoyment for them? Flying in the face of Mr Chen's comment is the unavoidable realization that the difference between authenticity and commodification means little in the running of the village. The issue of authenticity is inextricably linked to market demand for performances presented as 'authentic'. From this perspective, the dividing line between authenticity and commodification becomes blurred, and thus an authentic village like Areca Manor can be commoditized to the point where the balance between historical and socio-cultural veracity has been lost.

This matter of balancing authenticity and commodification raises broad issues that extend into difficult questions of cultural integration, best practice and political control. The village enterprises have provided an entirely new context for the expression of Li culture and identity, even though these expressions were rather limited. Areca Manor previously marketed its tourism product as 'authentic Li', but has now shifted to be a presentation of the 'authentic Chiyou tribe'. Common to both of these iterations was that the manor has presented the exotic and primitive to tourists who generally have no idea of ethnic culture. Given that, the discourse of authenticity can be seen as more or less an academic vocabulary, rather than a concept that is actually based in reality.

Cultural evolution versus museumification

From a business perspective, tourism functions neither as a destroyer nor as a preserver of ethnic culture. Rather, as Oakes (1998) has noted, tourism is part of the contradictory process of cultural change associated with modernity. Cultural evolution is an ongoing process influenced by modernity, commodification and identity. As summarized by Wood (1993: 58), ethnic culture is 'the specification of links between an invented present and an imagined past' and is 'constantly being symbolically recreated and contested'. The meaning of cultural evolution, according to Wood, is not a unitary thing whose process can be specifically identified, rather, cultural evolution is characterized by constant reformulation.

One of the perspectives from which to observe cultural evolution is through the lens of a 'brochure image' (Gotham, 2007). The 'brochure image' is an important advertising media and one of the most researched aspects of tourism marketing (Pritchard & Morgan, 2001). Brochure images are a form of 'text', combining narratives, concepts and ideologies of a business (Jenkins, 2003). Advertising effectiveness is the outcome of tourism businesses that portray the authenticity of ethnic culture (Taylor, 2001). Most tourists have little knowledge of ethnic culture and brochures serve as a first impression of the village. The brochure image is also widely used to attract tourists by mass media and such tourism middlemen as tour operators and guides. The design and endorsement of brochures reflect how the tourism business market and promote ethnic culture as they present the culture to the public (Chang *et al.*, 2005). In particular, the use of gender images in tourism brochures has been widely discussed as an approach to understanding the marketing and promotion of cultural tourism (Sirakaya & Sonmez, 1999). In essence, a brochure can be seen as an organization's business card and the content of brochures using folk villages illuminates business attitude toward cultural evolution and socio-economic change.

Although virtually all travel agencies on Hainan include a folk village as an attraction in their brochures, only about 10% of the brochures I collected provided some information on the ethnic minorities featured in the villages. As of my observations in the Fall of 2009, two types of brochures are available on Hainan – small village brochures printed to give to tourists during their visits and tour itineraries designed by each village for tour guides and bus drivers. The latter includes instructions for the village tour and suggests appropriate tips for tour guides. Some itineraries append coupons for free food and cigarettes in order to attract tour guides and drivers.

The brochures of most villages that focus on the Li culture highlighted the recreational aspects of Li culture. The ethnic Li have been specifically marketed to Mainland Chinese tourists as overly primitive and tantalizing to voyeuristic interests. For example, tourists' attention is drawn away from the cultural impacts of modernization on the villages and their natural environment. Nearly all village brochures assert authenticity by claiming that 'typical' ethnic performances are offered for tourists to observe and record on their travel tour. The brochure of Areca Manor before 2005 explicitly stated that 'Li women will dress up in full ceremonial costumes for tourists to take photos'. Most village tour itineraries clearly indicate that tourists will see traditional Li culture, including colorful ceremonial costumes, dance performances, Li wedding ceremonies and cockfighting demonstrations. However, no brochure noted that fees would be charged for taking photos of Li woman or attending enactments of Li wedding ceremonies.

There is a clear contrast between Li culture performed for tourists as passive observers and opportunities for tourists to actively experience or the less common presentation in which tourists participate in the Li lifestyle. A few brochures referred to social interaction with the Li, mainly by drinking rice wine or by joining in dances. For example, the brochure of Sanya Li Folk Village invited tourists to join in everyday indigenous activities: 'Feel free to join the Li minority in their daily chores like weaving clothes, feeding their livestock, washing their clothes and swimming in the river'. In fact, such tempting descriptions rarely turn into reality.

All the brochures mention dance as a key tourist attraction, e.g. the bamboo-beating dance or, in the case of the Indonesian Village, an Indonesian folk dance. However, none of the village brochures depicted tourists dancing or interacting with their Li hosts. The Li people are presented as objects for tourists to view. Tour itineraries largely describe Li dance as a tourist spectacle, *'mudu chuantong Li wudao he yingyue'* ('Witness the Li dance with traditional music'), although a few invite tourist participation, e.g. *'jingqing chanjia tamen de dachaiwu'* ('do not hesitate to join them in doing the bamboo-beating dance'). It was also indicated that convivial tourists might also 'join the tribal revelry in the dance hall' and 'imbibe the locally brewed rice wine *"Shanlan Jiu"'*.

The word authentic was not widely used in the travel brochures. Instead, the word 'traditional' was often used to describe Li housing, the welcome ceremony, Li dance and rice wine. However, most tour itineraries referred to Li customs, such as the welcome ceremony, or the appearance of Li housing as 'primitive'. On the other hand, authenticity is widely ascribed to tourist meals available in the village, apparently relating to where and how the food is eaten rather than the culinary content. Brochures stated that tourists will experience *'Lizhu shenyan – chaoxishang jiuchan'* ('a Li feast – a natural-style dinner on the mat-covered floor'), or tourists will simply 'dine Li style'. Other brochures used the more fanciful term 'jungle feast' to describe snacks 'served in native style at the riverbank' with food cooked in bamboo. This was the only reference to Li culinary traditions.

Some folk villages further linked authenticity with the type of travel and the distance traveled. Areca Manor was described as a 'real adventure' where tourists can experience the 'natural lifestyle' and search for authentic Li customs. The search for authenticity relative to the distance traveled serves as a marketing device to sell the village tour. The brochures described the villages located on the central route as 'more primitive' since they are 'located deep in the *Wuzhi Shan* (Five Finger Mountain)'.

The paradox between cultural evolution and museumification was evident on Hainan. The ethnic Li, designated as one of 55 ethnicities by the government, has mostly assimilated as a part of pan-Han culture, and most of their distinctive ethnic symbols have disappeared. Many earn their living catering to the tourist industry in tourist villages and hotels. Cultural evolution poses a serious problem for the tourism business, as explained by Mr Chen:

> The Li culture has changed. If we showcase the modern lifestyle of the ethnic Li minority, tourists would be disappointed. In fact, there is little difference between Li people and Han people nowadays. Our problem is the presentation of the folk village – does it truly reflect

the modern lifestyle or ancient lifestyle? The final choice was a mixed bag of both modern and past.

Folk village businesses on Hainan have realized that the influence of cultural evolution, particularly, acculturation, makes it difficult to maintain the theme of the folk village. Li traditions have indeed changed and thus are in need of updating for public display. This inevitably raises questions about the veracity of presentations identified as authentic. Examples can be seen in some villages near Sanya where traditional ethnic clothing has, in effect, become a business uniform identifiable as Li. In some folk villages located in Sanya, almost 70% of the dancers wearing ethnic Li dress were not Li. The actual Li dancers commented that the ethnic dress is only for performance, not for daily life. One of the site mangers in the Areca Manor explained the situation to me in the following way:

> The reason they wear ethnic dress is to make sure they are different from ordinary tourists. To some extent, the performance has to be ancient, distant, and fossil. However, sometimes tourists developed a distorted image that the ethnic Li minority was totally pre-modern and backward. They felt it was exotic to watch the ethnic dance performance, yet expressed little appreciation. They bought many ethnic souvenirs, yet knew little of the value of those souvenirs.

Tourists often expected that the Li in the villages would be quaintly traditional and in a state of 'museumification', that is, viewed through the lens of 'ethnic panopticon'. The folk villages on Hainan provided an interesting picture: those wearing traditional Li dress might not be Li, while those wearing Han dress might not be Han. The presentations of the folk villages were in a high state of 'museumification', portraying traditional aspects of Li cultures, which are assumed to be ancient, exotic and fossilized. The villages were like theme parks where 'front stage' and 'back stage' are totally separated. The tourism business paid more attention to meeting the expectation of tourists, and presented selected aspects of Li culture in an entertaining way. What was left for tourists was an incomplete and superficial image of Li culture.

Economic development versus cultural preservation

Tourism is a process of economic development and integration in which the idea of place is commodified through the marketing of standardized images and cultural markers. Tourism also injects a whole new set of possibilities that may be appropriated by local communities as they reconstruct a sense of place. Folk villages on Hainan have occupied an ambiguous space between the broad contending forces of cultural preservation and commercial tourism development. The provincial government has established a framework that encourages both market-oriented economic development and the preservation of symbols of cultural diversity. Because the idea of ethnic authenticity based on cultural distance from the Han has been sanctioned and institutionalized by the tourism industry, a contradiction has surfaced between commercialism and the preservation of ethnic authenticity. Managers of folk villages were not aware of the possibility of an avoidable contradiction between cultural preservation and economic development. Village entrepreneurs have attempted to promote the development interests by catering to tourists' perceptions of authenticity, and in the process have ignored the reality that the cultures they present have continued to change and evolve.

Tourism businesses can play a key role in balancing economic development and cultural preservation. My observation is that village revenues are not generated primarily from admission tickets, but from the sales of tropical fruits, ethnic souvenirs and Chinese herbals by vendors inside the villages. In general, tour guides have received a large proportion of admission revenue as a kickback for bringing tourists to the village. For example, in Baoting Areca Manor, the entrance fee was ¥80 (about US$12), and the majority of tourists came from package tours. Tour guides and drivers would receive about ¥70 (about US$10), a kickback for taking the tourists to the manor. The system of *huikou* (kickback, commission) has been extremely popular among tour guides and drivers. The fact is that tour guides with most travel agencies were unpaid or meagerly paid. Receiving entrance fees' commissions and kickbacks through tourists' expenditure has not only been tolerated by travel agencies, but has also been a means for the guides to survive financially.

The *huikou* scheme has had major impacts on both tourism businesses and tourists. The folk villages' success has largely been determined by the number of tourists received. Travel agencies and tour guides tightly controlled the flow of the tourists and selected the folk village they wanted to promote. Owing to the scattered distribution of folk villages along the central and eastern highways, competition to attract tourists was fierce. To some extent, a reliable flow of tourists can determine village survival. For most folk villages, accepting the *huikou* scheme has not been a choice, but a must. Behind every prosperous village lies the story about how much *huikou* is embedded in business practice. Some folk villages even agreed with tour guides and drivers that, regardless of the number of tourists, as long as they bring in tourists to the village, they can get a certain amount of payment. Tourists' purchasing has been a big business for both folk village and tour guides, since both can figure the approximate revenue generated by buying souvenirs and ethnic silver ornaments. To compete for the business of travel agencies and tour guides, virtually every village needed to return a certain percentage of the revenues to the guides. This led them to shorten the cultural presentations to ensure that tourists would have sufficient time to shop. The tour guides waited at the exit of the village and by the time the bus started to drive to the next attraction, they had received an envelope filled with cash reflecting the sales and the number of tourists. The managers of the Areca Manor complained that some tour buses would threaten sites to pay higher *huikou*. The folk villages needed to negotiate the amount of kickbacks on a regular basis with tour guides as tourism fluctuated over time.

Li (2004) argued that commission-oriented behaviors and operations in Chinese ethnic tourist attractions have led to a diminishing consideration of tourists' interests and to a deterioration of ethnic tourism product quality. Without mutually acceptable commissions, travel agencies or tour guides are able to alter their itineraries, bypass the folk villages and, ultimately, threaten the survival of the village business. The *huikou* practice has hindered tourists wanting to experience authentic folk villages, since the villages visited are determined by the tour guides who get the most commissions. Owing to lack of transportation options, tourists have to rely on travel agencies to arrange their visit to folk villages. Instead of choosing the most representative and authentic folk village, tour guides have been more interested in profit sharing with the village business. Thus, tourists have been seriously shortchanged by the *huikou* scheme that plagues Hainan. Profit squeezing has inevitably forced the villages to expand space for vendors, and to shrink the areas allotted to ethnic performance in order to maximize revenues.

In Baoting Areca Manor, the ratio between the size of the performance site (i.e. dance hall, wedding hall, ethnic pavilions) and the area allocated to vendor stands was roughly 3:7, which indicated that commercialization in villages has been given high priority. The vendor stalls within the village, selling an array of goods, e.g. fruits, ethnic ornaments, herbals, jades and ethnic prints and crafts, have become the mainstream of tourists' experience in the village. Most of these vendors were Li people from neighboring communities. Their businesses hinged on the volume of tourist arrivals since the vendors were charged fees to set up their stands in the village. One of the vendors in Areca Manor pointed out to me that:

> The [Baoting] village charges ¥300 to ¥400 per stand per month and the rest is mine. The business thus depends on the number of tourists. Years ago, tourists bought a lot of mango and papaya, also a lot of expensive pearl jewelry. Now the competition has become very high, and the business has become difficult, especially because many tourists have complained that the pearl jewelry is fake and over-priced. [Tourists] have become smarter and smarter. They bargain the price fiercely and buy little. However, as long as tourists come, I don't worry about the business too much.

The folk villages have thus become a combination of ethnic presentations and sale outlets with the major revenue coming from the vendor stalls. In addition, the entrepreneurial mindset had filtered down to little Li girls and boys, whose parents were the dance performers in the village. I tried to take a photograph of one cute girl, who was about 8 years old, dressed in Li costume. Though I was a distance from her, she noticed me immediately. Instead of refusing permission to photograph her, she smiled, greeted me in Mandarin, and struck several Li dance poses (probably mimicking her mother) to invite me to take more photographs. I took about five in total and was ready to thank her for her hospitality. Before I could leave, she suddenly grabbed my hand saying 'you owe me 5 yuan, sir, each photo of me costs 1 yuan!' (see Plate 7.2).

Tourists have complained that Areca Manor has become a big 'flea market' instead of an ethnic theme park. Economic development appears to have been the top priority, while cultural preservation was treated as a form of tokenism. For example, when asked whether the village management had taken cultural preservation into account, one of the site managers in Areca Manor offered the following perspective:

> I am not sure what kind of cultural preservation you refer to. This is a tourist-oriented village and our business relies on the incoming tourists. My understanding of cultural preservation is to showcase the Li ethnic cultures by dance programs, songs, and costumes. Apart from these, I am afraid we don't have much influence on cultural preservation. Cultural preservation should be taken care of by the government.

Cultural preservation seems to be an irrelevancy in the village context. In fact, cultural resources were exploited for commercial purposes and

Plate 7.2 Smiling girl in folk village

preservation could actually hinder ongoing economic development. Furthermore, tourism businesses on Hainan have put a positive spin on the commodification of culture. Cultural preservation was often referred to as focused on the 'quaint' customs of the Li people and other 'exotic' ethnic groups. By establishing tourist folk villages, the businesses believed that they provide entertainment opportunities for tourists as well as highlighting key distinctions between Li culture and the tourists' cultures. In the economic realm, the businesses believed they created ethnic employment and income for the ethnic groups.

Although the rich culture and natural resources of Hainan provide the context and environment for tourism, further refinement of the tourism enterprise, in my view, is necessary to strike a more favorable balance between the exchange of cultural experience for a financial return, and the creation of a situation in which the villages can promote cultural preservation through the careful management of their cultural resources.

Ethnic autonomy versus state regulation

State regulation on Hainan is moderate at best. The establishment of a Special Economic Zone provided a relaxed environment for tourism business. The goal of state deregulation was to minimize government intervention in the economy with few state-operated enterprises. The development of folk villages has been viewed as a 'grass-roots' phenomenon and has received little attention from the government. The interviews I conducted with officials from the Hainan Tourism Bureau suggested that little information on folk villages can be obtained from the provincial level of government, e.g. none of the officials with whom I spoke knew the exact number of folk villages on Hainan. The reasons for this information gap can be summarized as follows.

(1)   The operation of folk villages was a relatively insignificant aspect of provincial tourism planning. In general, these folk villages were run by private businesses and required little investment from the province. The location of many of these villages was remote, and difficult to access before the establishment of the eastern freeway. The majority of villages were located in the mountainous central region where the journey from Haikou to the center took at least five hours.

(2)   The tourism image of Hainan was primarily based on sun, sea, sand and sex. The development of ethnic tourism was still novel and had been seen as an 'add-on' program. Therefore, the state held a *laissez faire* attitude toward folk villages. In fact, the provincial government made little effort to support folk villages. The Li and their culture had long been marginalized economically and politically. The government had yet to fully realize the importance and potential of ethnic cultural resources, especially for the international market.

(3)   Policies for the development of folk villages came directly from the local government of the area in which the village was located. There was little influence from central government or provincial regulations. Business relationships between the local government and folk villages have been seen as the most critical issue. The owners of folk villages also participated in administrative positions in the local government in order to have some influence in local politics. They participated in the local economic development meetings and provided financial support for certain projects. Some villages even invited local officials to join the business in order to ensure local administrative support for their business operation.

Healthy relationships between the local government and the villages often furthered the interest of the owners. Local officials could alleviate tax burdens for the villages and provide a series of preferential programs to support the business. Mr. Chen offered the following rationale for designating Areca Manor as a joint venture with the local government:

Tourism business in Hainan is seasonal: it rises to a peak from October to the Chinese New Year (generally occurring in February). However, summer is a slow season. The [local] government here tends to help out our business. For example, it provides a tax break in summer to alleviate our financial burden. Also, the government gives us some preferential policies when our business is going to expand. Generally, the land use fee would be much lower if we expand the physical size of the village locally. Nothing works out without governmental support.

Tourism businesses did not view ethnic autonomy as a threat: on the contrary, ethnicity was viewed as a marketable tourism resource. For example, the village businesses located in the Li Autonomous Regions boasted of their 'authenticity' and 'quaintness'. The managers of Areca Manor proclaimed that it was the only authentic folk village, not those in Sanya or Haikou, since there was too much commercialization at those sites. When authenticating the ethnic resource for tourism purposes, the village applied a clear-cut criterion to make sure that the Li minority people are different from the Han majority people. Instead of showcasing the integration of the Li minority into the one happy Chinese cultural family and stressing the unity of the Chinese peoples, folk villages on Hainan highlighted the uniqueness of the Li culture and customs through entertainment. Li culture has been forged and its lost tradition has been reinvented with a new look by the village businesses. Although state regulation serves to strengthen cultural integration and economic development, village businesses on Hainan were very interested in authenticating ethnic resources for the touristic gaze.

Mass tourism development versus sustainable ethnic tourism

Sustainable development is meant to meet the needs of the present without compromising the well-being of future generations. It is relevant for tourism mainly for two reasons (Gunn, 1994): first, the basic premise of sustainable development is that it is possible to foster growth while also requiring that the growth be positive, providing net social and economic benefits. Second, sustainability requires that development is rooted in a stable and continuing resource base. Sustainability is characterized by the protection and survival of (a) the business enterprise, (b) the minority culture, (c) the natural environment, (d) small communities and their local decision-making powers and (e) mass tourism relates positively to all the factors identified above. Thus, sustainability is based on the balance between stability and change. Ideally, a tourism enterprise, such as an ethnic tourism site, should provide tourists with a rich, accurate and entertaining understanding of cultural resources (Gunn, 1994). The key to success vis-à-vis sustainability is that the facility within the ethnic community should evoke a fascinating and memorable tourist experience, while avoiding degradation of the cultural resources of the 'real' community. It is at the site itself that the specific issue of balancing resource protection with development changes from policy to action, particularly with regard to such issues as location, theme and carrying capacity. Tourism unavoidably involves socio-economic development. It is consumptive like other industries, and the level of consumption is determined by the model used in pursuing the development of tourism. At certain levels of consumption and with careful planning, tourism may be able to operate in a sustainable fashion.

Mass tourism is dominant on Hainan as 96% of tourist arrivals come from Mainland China. Tourism revenue primarily comes from domestic as opposed to international tourists. As already noted, Hainan has been associated with enjoying sea-sand-sun-sex experiences. The island is not seen primarily as an ethnic tourism destination. Although a folk village tour has become an integral part of most tour programs, the full cultural potential of the folk village has yet to be realized by tourism agencies. Since the main revenue of folk villages is generated from tourist expenditures inside the village, the number of tourists has become the most important issue. I have seen that the villages used a variety of incentives to attract potential tourists, particularly through incentives offered to tour guides and bus drivers (e.g. kickbacks, commissions, free meals, etc.). The resulting reality is that visiting folk villages has not been controlled by the tourists, but by such culture brokers as tour guides, travel agencies and tour bus drivers.

The meaning of sustainability seemed to be unclear to most village managers. They believed it was a buzz word, lacking substance. In particular, sustainability was regarded as a lofty goal set by the provincial government, not by the folk village. As one of the site managers stated:

> I think it is a complex issue when you put your finger on sustainability. Our village is a privately-owned business influenced heavily by the policies of local government and the number of tourist arrivals. Without strong local support and tourist flow, it seems unlikely that a sustainable folk village could be established.

It appears that sustainable ethnic tourism development has not received attention from tourism businesses due to uncertainty regarding local policies and sufficient tourist arrivals. Although ethnic culture's important role was recognized by both tourism business and local government, cultural resources have been seen as a way of generating profit for both the entrepreneurs and the local government. This emphasis on profitability, as previously noted, resulted in fierce competition among some villages near the city of Sanya. Some of the villages changed their attitude toward ethnic cultural preservation, instead, moving toward the exploitation of ethnicity for economic purposes. Perhaps because of the short period of time in which ethnic tourism has operated on Hainan, sustainable ethnic tourism development has yet to be established.

Indonesian Village

The Indonesian Village was founded in 1996 in Xinglong as a joint venture between the local government and Hong Kong, the latter being the primary investor. The land was leased from the Overseas Chinese farm and the diasporic community provided labor and infrastructure support. In return, the Indonesian Village would give high priority to the community's employment. The establishment of the village received tax relief from the local government as a way to support agricultural industry and to economically revitalize the Chinese-Indonesian communities. The establishment of the village, which was born of a desire to portray Indonesian culture, received a warm reception by the diasporic community in 1996 (see Plate 7.3).

The community generally supported it and was optimistic that tourism growth would yield benefits for individuals. The desire to experience Indonesian culture was palpable among tourists, but they wanted to see as many programs as they could in a short span of time. Xinglong is strategically located half way between Haikou and Sanya along the eastern highway; therefore, it has become a necessary stop for tour buses. Tourists were excited by the opportunity presented by the village, but not many were aware of the history of the diasporic community. The tour guides in common parlance refer to the village as *Huaqiao Cun* (the Overseas Village), a refuge for overseas Chinese exiled from Indonesia. The reasons behind the exiles and the history of the diaspora had never been adequately explained. The resettlement of Chinese-Indonesians in Xinglong was presented as a 'job opportunity' to work in the rubber plantations, apparently suited to the refugees since

Plate 7.3 Gate of the Indonesian Village

rubber is a tropical product commonly grown in Southeast Asia. The diasporic community was referred to *'yinni huaqiao'* (Indonesian overseas Chinese) in order to distinguish other *'huaqiao'* who have long been cited as successful examples of transnational entrepreneurs and wealthy investors in Mainland China. Nonini (1997) suggested that diasporic refugees from Indonesia and Malaysia have been largely neglected in Mainland China due to their perceived 'non-elite' and 'unsuccessful' status. The description of 'having no position' both in the prior host land and the homeland has impacted the general judgment of the diasporas' identity.

Ethnic identity

The Indonesian Village was widely regarded as a tourist destination with the goal of 'experiencing Indonesia without traveling to Indonesia'. It offered a variety of recreational programs for tourists. The aesthetic and folk aspects of Chinese-Indonesian traditions were highlighted and brought to the fore as representative of authentic Indonesian culture. The village provides an opportunity to revive the memorable rituals and dances that Chinese-Indonesians grew up with, but their performance in the village was largely perceived as 'entertainment' rather than 'authentic culture' by tourists. The most famous dance performance was that given by first generation Chinese-Indonesians, generally older adults. The stage became the focus of the tour since other attractions were commercial activities surrounded by numerous vendors selling such products as tropical fruits and Chinese herbal medicines. Desmond (1999) has pointed out that the public display of ethnic individuals, e.g. how they look, what they do, where they do it, who watches and under what conditions, is profoundly important in structuring identity categories of race, gender and cultural affiliation. These displays on stage, as an integral part of the arts performance, create a lucrative tourism enterprise where ethnic identity is sold and enacted. The shows in the village were in three parts that lasted for 30–40 minutes. These were: (a) Indonesian dance, (b) Indonesian folk songs and (c) a tourist participation program. The Indonesian dance was comprised of the umbrella dance (*tari payung*) and the candle dance (*tari lilin*) from West Sumatra. The umbrella dance was the most striking cultural offerings of the village since the performance was lavishly decorated and the story of protecting a lover was easy to understand. The candle dance showed women dancers balancing flickering candles on saucer plates in their hands to the rhythm of the music. It symbolizes that both a bride and a groom can achieve their aspirations in married life together. Both dances were popular among the village residents as the majority of Chinese-Indonesians in Xinglong came from Java and Sumatra. Later, Balinese dance was added, performed by second generation Chinese-Indonesian because their youth and agility allowed them to perform the choreography. Tourists were encouraged to participate in the dance performance in the final part of the show and the interaction between tourists and the dancers often went well. The dance performances played a significant role in diasporic identity by showcasing culture and heritage and for the wider tourists who tended to know little about the diasporic community. One of the dancers commented to me that traditional dance and the musical instruments played on stage brought back memories of his youth and the music helped him recall the 'good old days' before the exodus from Indonesia.

However, tension arose when a growing number of tourists and guides expressed a strong interest in Balinese dance performance, particularly the revised version of *Legong*-style dance. The colorful costumes and exotic movements of the dance were particularly attractive to tourists. The village managers were asked to spend more time on the Balinese dance by shortening the umbrella and candle dances generally performed by first generation villagers. Simultaneously, some of the Indonesian chants and rhythms were combined with Chinese love songs and music to cater to tourists who did not understand the original lyrics. Thus, a changed form of cultural expression emerged in the village. Balinese dance performed solely by second generation, mainly young females, came to dominate the dance performance. The underlying assumption was that, since tourists stay only a short time, the performance needed to be changed somewhat so that they could have more time to shop in the village. Furthermore, Balinese dance was enthusiastically received by most tourists, and was widely viewed as a popular, identifiable and 'authentic' Indonesian dance. These changes created a heated debate between the dancers and the village managers. Concerns were expressed that the majority of the Chinese-Indonesians in Xinglong were not from Bali. Moreover, villagers pointed out that dance performance had become a potpourri with the various dances neither Indonesian nor Chinese. The first generation dancers questioned whether 'the emerging authenticity' helped tourists to understand the 'real' diasporic identity better. As one senior dance performer told me:

> The manager required us to perform Balinese dance, but it is so foreign to me since I have lived in Xinglong for many years. The Balinese dance should be performed by young girls but I am too old to do so. I dislike acting as a Balinese and it does not make sense to me... I came from Padang (West Sumatra) originally.

My interviews revealed a generational gap between the first generation of diasporic Chinese-Indonesian and the second generation who was born and raised in Xinglong. The second generation was young, around 25–35 years old and could not speak Indonesian. According to the local government, the second generation was not even qualified to be called 'huaqiao' (overseas Chinese), but was identified as typical Hainanese. The attitudes of the second generation were totally different given that their main interests centered on work and career. This second generation tended to dislike agriculture employment, but enjoyed working in the village. The village offered an intensive course to teach basic Indonesian to the second generation. The main purpose of the language lessons was to allow the younger generation greet and speak some basic Indonesian words, so that tourists would believe that the village was authentic. Most importantly, the second generation participated in Balinese-style dance performance. When asked about how her generation differed from the first generation, one female dancer answered as follows:

> It was an ordeal for my parents to resettle on Hainan Island and I have no idea what happened in Indonesia. When I grew up as a little girl, people call me *"xiao huaqiao"* (little overseas Chinese) and I thought it was funny. I really don't care about my parents' identity – I am a Hainanese and this is my home. If I am asked to perform and I can get money, I can do it without a problem.

Her comment reflected the complexity of tourism-identity in this diasporic community; that is, cultural identity differed between the generations. While the first generation raised objections to the content of the dance program, the second generation viewed the performance as a commercial practice that allowed them to make a living. In a similar vein, McIntosh *et al.*'s (2002) study of Maori folk villages of New Zealand illustrated that even with good intentions to be representative and authentic, there is a predisposition to create a so-called attraction-based identity, which eventually slips into a commercialized version of a cultural display. The cultural performances in the Indonesian village were commonly commodified for tourism purposes. The diasporic identity has increasingly become a challenge to interpret and showcase for the second generation.

Perception of authenticity

An understanding of the community's perceptions of authenticity is crucial to tourism planning and development (Wall, 1996). This is particularly important for ethnic tourism because it focuses on the cultural elements of tradition and customs. In the case of the Indonesian Village, the management of ethnic tourism was seen as a major problem because Chinese-Indonesians were not included as real partners in running the village. Private enterprise and non-diasporic individuals controlled the village. Ms Yiming Li, the owner of the village was originally from Mainland China, but has Hong Kong residency. Therefore, investment in the village was approved as a joint venture and was supported by the local government as a way to revitalize the economy. In the early 2000s, when the number of tourist arrivals surged, the Indonesian Village on Hainan achieved its peak. It became routine for tour buses along the eastern highway to Sanya to include a short stop in the village to watch 'exotic' Indonesian performances and to purchase 'authentic' crafts and souvenirs. The number of dance performances increased to 15 to 20 times per day in order to serve the influx of tourists. Catering to tourists with entertainment and a certain degree of excitement was an essential element of the village's success as a tourist attraction.

With the popularity of the village, the owner and managers believed the expansion was necessary to attract more tourists and to increase business. In addition to presenting *en masse* Chinese-Indonesian culture in Xinglong, the village management decided to change its name to '*Dongnanya fengqin cun*' (Southeast Asian Scenic Village) in 1999. According to the owner, the change reflected the trend of ethnic tourism on Hainan. She asserted that a growing number of tourists wanted to experience a diversity of cultures and that the Indonesian Village would be vulnerable if it offered a single tourism product. The diasporic Indonesians were seen as a marketable resource, yet management's perception was that enthusiasm from tourists would diminish gradually; therefore, there was a need to add new tourist products.

After the name change, the size of the village was greatly expanded and exhibitions about Thailand, Malaysia and Vietnam were added. Since Xinglong does not have any of these ethnic groups, the settings were largely built on imagination and imitation. In particular, the managers of the village traveled to Thailand and brought back some ideas for redesigning the village. One of the bizarre additions was 'ladyboy dance' featuring costumed, transgendered performers dancing on the stage. Although the ladyboy dance has little relation to Thai culture, it was widely viewed as 'exotic' and 'stimulating' by Mainland Chinese tourists who had virtually no contact with transsexuality.

The name and performance changes impacted the perception of authenticity within the diasporic community. The initial enthusiasm with which the village was greeted, waned because the identity of the community was abruptly transformed. Although Indonesian dance was still an integral part of the programs, its diluted content turned the village into what some might see as a lowbrow theme park. Villagers' irritation escalated when the community refused to renew the land lease, asserting that the village did not represent their culture anymore. The community petitioned the local government to take action on the land dispute with the village because it was built on a former plantation site. One of the Chinese-Indonesians told me in private that the programs in the village have steadily become '*pian ren de*' (cheating, inauthentic) and the displays a 'circus'. As more tourists appeared to be interested in the 'exotic' ladyboy dances as a form of cultural entertainment, the Indonesian dance and songs, performed by the first and second generations, were sidelined. The village as a vehicle for presenting

Chinese-Indonesian culture disappeared. This resulted in artificiality and conflicting perceptions of what constitutes the 'authentic' Chinese-Indonesian culture. The community decided to reject the presentations when the practice of ethnic tourism bore little relation to authenticity.

Conflicts between village and community

The success of the Indonesian Village changed business in Xinglong. The region was extremely poor and received little economic benefit from tourism on Hainan since tourists passed through and had nothing to do with the town. Besides selling fruits, crafts and spa services in hotels, tourist-related activities were virtually non-existent and the infrastructure was too backward to attract any investment. Although the commodification of Chinese-Indonesian culture was initially viewed by the community as a positive process, the control of development and many of the associated aspects have not been in the hands of its village members. The cultural resources of the diasporic community have been seen as a way of profit making and the interests of the community did not seem to be respected. There has been a constant concern about contamination of culture by outsiders who do not share the values nor appreciate the community. Antagonism surfaced in the community because the Indonesian Village did not represent the culture of the Chinese-Indonesians; rather, it became a theme park where diasporic was presented along with other cultural elements that have no relationship to it.

Community involvement in ethnic tourism can be examined using two perspectives: the decision-making process and tourism benefits-sharing (Timothy, 1999). It is believed that active community involvement in tourism development will contribute to more sustainable tourism. However, many community members complained of having little decision-making power in the village. Most tourists came in package tours controlled by the travel agencies and almost all of them came from Mainland China (Xie & Wall, 2008). The diasporic community had limited opportunity to interact with tourists and the village became only a window of opportunity to start a tourism business, rather than a vehicle for broader economic development. The owner of the village did not seem willing to communicate with the community and lacked the knowledge of how to present Chinese-Indonesian culture. Although the village was linked to the wider economy and changes that occurred were not solely due to tourism, the Chinese-Indonesian community became increasingly frustrated by the village and the local government because they had little input on how their own culture was being advertised and promoted to tourists. Using Tosun's (2006) spectrum of community participation in tourism, 'coercive community participation' would be the most appropriate way to describe the character in this particular community: its culture was manipulated and distorted by the management of the village. Additionally, the local government made little effort to preserve the culture, involving the community members as passive recipients of exogenous influence.

The diasporic community felt strongly that they had helped establish the village yet they did not receive a fair share of the economic benefit. It became a central attraction in Xinglong, but their input was ignored by the village's management and the local government. At the beginning of 2000, with fewer Chinese-Indonesians employed in the village and the name changed to cater to tourists, the community believed that their support for the village had been betrayed. That tour buses chose to stop only in the village caused a major concern that other business not associated with the village might not be able to survive.

Tensions between the community and the village ran so high that a revenue-sharing plan was proposed as a necessary step to salvage the deterioration in managing community relations. However, the proposal received a cold reception from the village with the managers arguing that the business had appropriately been transformed into a diversity of Southeast Asian themes. While acknowledging the diasporic community's help to set up development of the tourism undertaking, I was told by one of the managers in the village who is in charge of staffing:

> The location of the Village was originally an overseas Chinese farm. Without our investment, it would still be farm land. The success of the Village certainly attracted a lot of attention from the neighboring communities and all wanted a piece of shared profit. However, we spent "blood and sweat" (*xuehan*) in the Village and don't owe them anything. Our business will be fine without them

Negotiations between the community and the village broke down. Village management accused the diaspora of greed, and laziness as the main reason for their economic backwardness. It also expressed discontent that local government purposefully sided with the community in seeking revenue sharing. Ms Li, the owner of the Indonesian Village, attributed the problems to the lack of support by local government for suppressing unhealthy competition and to its whimsical policies:

> The local government supported the development of Indonesian villages in 1995 and provided a package of preferential policies.

However, since our business is doing exceedingly well, some officials want to change the existing policies and try to tax this and that. Terrible things happened when the local government decided to build another Indonesian village in the downtown of Xinglong in order to get a portion of the profits. Can you imagine of having two exactly similar theme villages in such a small township? I think these officials were influenced by the Overseas Farm and have caused a difficult time for our future business.

However, without the support of the diaspora community and local government, village management faced a shortage of electricity and water. The initial agreement that the community would share the same electricity grid was suspended. The village replaced electricity power generators to continue its business. While community involvement in tourism would seem to suggest that local people have a degree of control over resource and benefit sharing, in the case of the Indonesian Village, it was seen that the benefits had not been dispersed across the community. The deteriorating partnership with the private enterprise contributed to the growth of tensions that eventually impacted tourism businesses. It eventually forced the village to close in 2003. The Indonesia Village briefly reopened in 2006, only to close again.

Reflections on the Indonesian Village's history

Saïd (2003: 18) once called identity as 'a generalized condition of homelessness', a term that implies identity has increasingly become mobile, hybrid and deterritorialized. The diasporic identity is more malleable than others since it oscillates between homeland and host land. In modern society, the integrity of identity can also be affected by tourism encroachment and tourists' demands. Ethnic tourism promotes the distinctiveness of diasporic identity, while at the same time, generating a tremendous amount of tension among communities, tourism businesses, governments and tourists.

Ghai (2000: 12) used the word 'asymmetry' to describe power inequity when different stakeholders exert influence on ethnic attractions. For example, in the case of the Indonesian Village, the local government played an encouraging role in the development of the diasporic community, but its support lay in the hope of receiving financial benefits from tourists. Authenticity was not a high priority among many tourists who visited the village, though many were interested in and prepared to learn about diasporic culture and dance performance. Paradoxically, their interests often led to changes in the original performances to create a spectacular *mise-en-scène*. The Chinese-Indonesians were represented as a discrete entity with distinctive folk customs related to costume, dance, music, culinary practices and religious belief. Exotic images were flamboyantly proliferated along the eastern highway that the village represented authentic Chinese-Indonesian culture as reflected in its dance and singing. The majority of Chinese-Indonesians had little experience with Balinese style of dances, but was asked to re-enact such dances so that tourists would enjoy the 'real' Indonesian culture. A new form of dance was produced, mixing elements from Balinese, Sumatra and Javanese dance. Dance elements were taken out of one context and placed in another (Clifford, 1988). Although this conceptualization of authenticity raises questions about identity and ownership, it also transforms cultures into 'alienable objects, where a potential exchange-value of a performance assumes priority over any use-value of a performance' (Clifford, 1988: 4).

Village businesses were supposed to play a key role in balancing economic development and cultural preservation, but in reality, economic development was the top priority and the diasporic resources were exploited for commercial purposes. While the community strived to utilize cultural presentations to preserve its identity and authenticity, the commercial interests of the village's management inevitably reshaped the cultural landscape. Furthermore, the differences between first and second generation village residents demonstrate that diasporic identity is fluid and continues to evolve. The older generation took the cultural displays and the contents of the performance seriously while the younger generation enjoyed the entertainment aspects of the village as performance was largely designed for commercial purposes.

The mismanagement of the Indonesian Village can be attributed to management's narrow focus on profit taking and its disregard of the importance of community involvement. The original intention of the village was to promote the Chinese-Indonesian culture, however, it gradually morphed into a theme park where the value of diasporic culture was deemed less important. The name change to Southeast Asia Scenic Village revealed an obvious attempt to attract more tourists; however, once again the change lacked consultation with the diasporic community and its place attachment to Xinglong. From the perspective of the community, the village was viewed as a special location where interaction with tourists could take place with results broader than the sole issue of economic gain. The marginalization of the diasporic culture by the village managers thus caused tension and detrimental effects in the long run. The dispute over land and profit sharing were the consequences of the changing perceptions of the community and its attitude toward ethnic tourism development.

The development and demise of the Indonesian Village has implications for ethnic tourism development. As suggested by Ying and Zhou (2007), the ideal 'community involvement' approach for tourism development does not seem to work in China; rather, it has been characterized by a quandary centered on 'controlling' or 'being controlled' for the ethnic communities. The powerlessness of Chinese-Indonesians on Hainan Island aggravated the delicate relationship among village business, local government and tourists. Perhaps the lesson of the Indonesian Village is that an ethnic attraction will not be successful unless it understands the complex interplay of identity, authenticity, commodification and sustainability. In particular, the efficacy of community involvement should be regarded as a central issue in ethnic tourism. The true ownership and power relations of the ethnic attraction remain a challenge for future development.

Summary

Collins-Kreiner and Olsen (2004) suggested that existing research tends to overlook the extent to which tourism businesses operate and transform authenticity, experiences and spirituality into commodities for sale. This chapter fills the gap by examining two folk villages' business operation vis-à-vis authenticating ethnic cultures and identities (one for ethnic Li, another for Chinese-Indonesian). We have seen that there were similarities and differences between the two villages in their attempts to employ ethnicity as a marketable resource. At the time of writing this chapter, Areca Manor is still in operation while the Indonesian Village has been closed due to the land dispute with the diasporic community. When the tourism industry took off on the island, the owners of the two villages worked closely together to develop ethnic folk villages. However, they departed because they held different business orientations: Mr Tianfu Chen was initially committed to maintain a focus on Li culture as a foundation of the village, while Ms Yiming Li saw the village as a point of departure that shifted away from a narrow, authentic portrayal of Li culture. Unlike the newer folk villages located where ethnic peoples are largely absent, both villages were established where ethnic communities reside. They were the pioneer villages to draw the attention of tourists and to serve as a model for ethnic tourism development on Hainan. Both played a prominent role in presenting ethnic images and cultural exoticism to the public. Areca Manor and the Indonesian Village were also credited with providing an important source of employment for local ethnic people. Most importantly, longitudinal study of both villages provided a record of how tourism businesses operated and evolved that could be examined.

Areca Manor has shifted from an authentic Li village to an entertainment center. In a similar vein, the Indonesian Village has changed the portrayal of the original Chinese-Indonesians to a potpourri of Southeast Asian 'kitsch'. The commodification of ethnic resources swiftly got out of hand and the villages became overdeveloped, marginalizing ethnic communities and residents. Both have changed the names and themes of the villages as tourism triggered a surge in tourist arrivals. Clark (2009) pointed out that perhaps naming and renaming of indigenous tourism sites is an important first step in place marking, and that such changes play a vital role in the development of tourist attractions. However, if the naming of sites creates misunderstanding and conjures expectations that are not met, then it can become a management problem that adversely affects the images of the attractions. Frenzied competition created a new set of identities to draw in tourist money. The name change for the Indonesian Village aggravated tensions associated with the diasporic identity and community involvement. It also diluted the uniqueness of the village as the only village built on original diasporic farmland. Although the name change from Areca Manor to 'Chiyou tribe' reflected a marketing strategy to cater to tourists, it nonetheless sharply downgraded its authentic image as the representative of Li culture.

Tourism businesses walk a fine line, balancing cultural preservation and economic development; however, in the case of the two ethnic villages examined, the latter appeared to be most important while cultural preservation was largely neglected. The management of the folk villages insisted on 'livening things up' so that the tourists would not get bored. The villages failed to see the significance of the profound, long-standing cultural differences that exist in ethnic cultures. Instead, the folk villages became a combination of ethnic presentations and sale outlets for the numerous vendor stands. Ethnic presentation is in a state of 'museumification', portraying traditional aspects of ethnic culture as ancient, exotic and fossilized. Tourism businesses pay more attention to meeting the expectations of tourists and to presenting selected aspects of ethnic culture in an entertaining way. Also, the effect of state regulation on village business was minimal. The operation of folk villages has been viewed as a grassroots phenomenon and ethnic autonomy was not viewed as a threat. Authenticity appeared to be a flexible notion to the managers of the folk villages. The manipulation of ethnic dance programs and other ethnic cultural events to serve economic interests resulted in the loss of authenticity and educational value: spectacle and entertainment seem to have been valued more highly in both villages. Since the businesses depended on the number of tourist arrivals, mass tourism was used to exploit ethnicity for economic gain of the enterprises. Sustainable cultural tourism was not widely appreciated nor even addressed.

At a deep level, both villages experienced identity problems. The authentic tourist attraction built on fixed ethnic identity was never fulfilled. Ethnic Li has been assimilated by the majority Han to the extent that its distinctive identity is on the verge of disappearance. Portraying the Li as an arrested and museumified identity has misrepresented the reality of Li life. Chinese-Indonesians, on the other hand, have been caught in what Ibrahim (2008: 235) called 'spectre of "and"'; that is, being overseas Chinese on Hainan while possessing a body that is read in the dominant social imaginary as a diasporic Indonesian. Since the marketing of ethnic tourism dislikes uncertainty and hybridity, this in-betweenness became hurdles to be removed by the village management. The differing perception of authenticity between first and second generation Chinese-Indonesians illuminated the problems of keeping the original diasporic identity and maintaining the uniqueness of culture and heritage.

Chapter 8
Equilibrium

Introduction

Kolas' (2008) book entitled *Tourism and Tibetan Culture in Transition: A Place called Shangrila*, explored the intricate relationship between tourism, culture and ethnic identity in Shangrila, a Tibetan region in Southwest China. She conducted an investigation of an ethnic tourism program called 'Visit to a Tibetan family'. Tourists who wanted to taste Tibetan food, see traditional costumes and experience folk music, initiated the program. The tourism service department controlled by the Han responded by introducing a combination of sightseeing and family visits. Tourists not only have first-hand knowledge of Tibetan life and culture, but also have a chance to observe a Tibetan family's everyday life. The home setting was cozy and friendly. The tour guide first introduced traditional aspects of Tibetan customs to tourists. The *po cha* (Tibetan butter tea), barley wine and roasted mutton were served to show family hospitality. Finally, folk songs and dances were performed in an impromptu way that tourists could participate in. It provided an excellent opportunity for tourists to take a rare glimpse of 'back stage', 'authentic' Tibetan family life.

Despite the popularity of the program, a Tibetan tour guide told Kolas in private that it has nothing to do with 'real' family life. These houses were carefully selected by tourism agencies and tour operators under the strict control of the government. What the tourists see is not authentic, but fabricated specifically for what tourists expect to see. Later, Kolas questioned her Tibetan friend whether the dance performances at the 'Tibetan family house' were similar to those that local people would dance at bonfire parties or at home. The reply was a definite no. However, Kolas argued that dances performed by her friend's sister and other villagers during the festival were similarly 'inauthentic'. To this, her Tibetan friend explained: 'that's no problem, since the festival was not for tourists, it was for ourselves'.

Kolas' case study revealed an enduring problem of understanding the concept of authenticity, that is, what is authentic, and for whom is it authentic? An ethnic minority is a subaltern social group, a term used by

Bhabha (2004) to emphasize the importance of social power relations. 'Subaltern' connotes an oppressed minority group, and represents a direct challenge to the hegemonic power of the majority group. Tourism is an enterprise of major economic and social significance that is controlled by the majority group. The interpretation of the ethnic authenticity presented is often imposed by the majority; therefore, ethnicity becomes malleable and subjective, making ethnic identities and cultures more than elusive. The psychological pressure to modernize (Norberg-Hodge, 1991) and the promise of economic gain (McLaren, 2003) by the majority group have led to a series of social changes in ethnic communities. Authenticity is part of these changes and is determined by the dominant force in power relations. Such 'authenticity' represents a mode of survival that an ethnic minority learns to adapt to in response to pressures from the majority group. In other words, the establishment of authenticity runs on a one-way street from the majority to the minority with no way to turn around.

As described in Kolas' Tibetan case study, cultural presentation becomes tantamount to ethnic identity even though it has been reconstructed as a marketable commodity for tourists. The 'Visit to a Tibetan family' program was controlled by the government and standardized by tourism businesses. To some extent, ethnic identity has been commoditized as a bait to lure tourists' dollars. McLaren (2003: 47) asserted that 'the commoditization of culture for the sake of earning tourist dollars is bad enough: it is reprehensible when it does so at the expense of an [ethnic] people's misery?' This suggests that tourism should be viewed as a threat to ethnic cultures and identities, and the development of 'authentic ethnic tourism' is an oxymoron. However, the borderline encounters between tourists and ethnic minorities are not the sole factor contributing to the manipulation of cultural authenticity. Additionally, a variety of internal and exogenous forces are also at play. A binary of 'good versus bad' criticism of tourism tends to overlook the multifaceted, often contradictory, nature of tourism activities. Authenticity falls in the interstices of society that origin can never be found.

In his observation of the evolution of New Orleans' traditional Mardi Gras, Gotham (2007: 205) commented that instead of viewing tourism as a threat to authenticity, it would be helpful to take a more complex and nuanced understanding of the various stakeholders' relationship to tourism. He suggested that instead of regarding authenticity as immutable and primordial, it might be useful to examine the process of authentication 'focusing on how and under what conditions people make claims for authenticity and the interests that such claims serve'. He further suggested that the concept of authenticity has always been fluid and hybrid, and that it is constantly being shaped by various stakeholders. Each stakeholder group struggles to establish its legitimacy as a cultural authority; thus, all authenticities are potential victims of these creative changes and struggles. Kolas (2008: 29), in her book on tourism in Tibet, echoed Gotham's arguments that ethnic tourism is an 'evolving project' fuelled by tourist demands, state policies and the various agendas of tourism businesses and visited peoples. It is a forum in which ethnic identity and authenticity are negotiated. The different stakeholders have their own preconceptions about the 'ethnic minorities' in question, the 'essence' of their cultures, and the needs and wants of tourists. Ethnic identity and authenticity are the central characters, the protagonists on the stage which each of the stakeholders seek to define.

Both Gotham and Kolas' arguments reinforce the central argument of this book that has viewed ethnic tourism on Hainan through the lens of four identified stakeholders – governments, ethnic communities, tourists and tourism businesses. This exploration has demonstrated that authentication provides a useful approach to understanding the complicated interplay of interests and influence that have shaped ethnic tourism on Hainan. In contrast to the subjectivities and peculiarities inherent in identifying what is 'authentic', focusing on the process used to define 'authentic' (that is, authentication) appears to be a pragmatic approach to identifying the value-laden role each stakeholder plays in determining what ends up being presented as 'authentic' ethnic culture to tourists.

I have suggested that the distinction between authenticity and authentication can be viewed through two separate prisms. First, authenticity can be viewed as having many different meanings depending on the contexts. Using Bhabha's (2004) concept of 'subaltern', we would note that authenticity is often defined in a fabricated and unequal host–guest situation. In such contexts, it is hard to pin down, objectively and precisely, what is authentic because the concept is constantly shifting and being transformed. The difficulty with understanding authenticity, according to Yang and Wall (2009: 251), flows from the reality that it embodies 'more than a simple idea underlying the originality of objects, but involves various perspectives, value statements, judgments, stereotypes, and spatial and socio-political influences'.

In tourism literature, authenticity is not a fixed entity, but a flexible notion to be continuously negotiated and molded into *ad hoc* resources, or assets to be spent in order to achieve economic priorities. It needs to be defined not only in terms of the provenance of material and non-material aspects of a culture, but also by subjective criteria as applied by various stakeholders. Furthermore, authenticity is constructed, experienced and managed by a variety of 'cultural mediators' (Ooi, 2002). In other words, it is a state of being that can only be judged by stakeholders involved in the process.

By contrast, authentication is a traceable and measurable concept. It can be characterized as a way of 'cultural translation' (Bhabha, 2004), a product of interplay between, for example, minority and majority cultures; tourees and tourists; local and national political authority. Thus, authentication is an interactive process, characterized by multiple discourses. Bhabha (2004: 210) described the process of cultural translation as:

> a way of imitating, but in a mischievous, displacing sense – intimating an original in such a way that the priority of the original is not reinforced but by the very fact that it can be simulated, copied, transferred, transformed, made into a simulacrum and so on: the "original" is never finished or complete in itself. The "originary" is always open to translation so that it can never be said to have a totalized prior moment of being or meaning – an essence.

A second perspective for understanding the authenticity/authentication issue is that authentication serves as a process of translating 'originary' for tourist consumption. It is a process not solely exercised by majority groups, but participated in by a wide array of players. It closely resembles the game of 'rumor', where a communication line of several people is formed who verbally pass a sentence from one person to the next, each whispering into the other's ear. After having been communicated, heard and re-communicated many times, the original sentence is often dramatically changed, both in terms of its form and content. The result of authentication can never bring back the 'originary', but it does convey a message through different people, albeit the point of departure and last iteration will never be the same.

Most importantly, authentication serves as a process of 'multi-layered Othering' (Li, 2003). Tourism creates a system of ethnic relations that involves different cultures, class backgrounds and interests. For example, governments set up policies to guide tourism development, ethnic communities are the attraction being gazed on by tourists, tourists are attracted by the Otherness of the natives and the pursuit of authenticity, and tourism businesses endeavor to benefit economically from the host–guest interaction. Van de Berghe (1994: 122–123) argued that the complex system of interactions among all these groups can be seen as a special form of ethnic relations, since these interactions clearly take place across ethnic lines. He called the system 'super-ethny' as each group is processing its own agenda. Authentication should be viewed as a palimpsest, an indigenous process, an overlay of power struggles and conflicts among various stakeholders. It involves a dialectical relationship between socio-economic, political and cultural forces. Li (2003: 57) suggested that the process of Othering always 'reflects and involves an issue of self-defining and positioning when confronting the packaged stereotypes of [ethnic] cultures, tourist consumption, and the implied unbalanced power relationship'. Ultimately, the purpose of authentication involves creating an equilibrium within which each stakeholder can find an appropriate position to gaze on, and be gazed at, by the Other.

This book has proposed five continua: authenticity versus commodification; cultural evolution versus museumification; economic development versus cultural preservation; ethnic autonomy versus state regulation; and mass tourism versus sustainable tourism. Four stakeholders – governments, ethnic communities, tourists and tourism businesses – are identified and juxtaposed on each of the five continua. Also, the five continua serve as yardsticks to assess the degree of authentication exercised by each of the four stakeholders. Chapters 4–7 have detailed the views of stakeholders on each continuum. By borrowing Giddens' (1984) 'structuration theory', Barth's (1969) 'boundary maintenance' and Wallace's (1956) 'mazeway resynthesis', I have argued that authentication is a dynamic and interactive process in which a balance of forces defines a state of equilibrium. The objective of this chapter is to summarize and compare the positions of stakeholders on each of the five continua in the context of Hainan. It illustrates a conceptual scheme for the analysis of authentication in terms of ethnic tourism development.

A State of Equilibrium

Ethnic minorities in China comprise 123 million people and almost 10% of its population. They straddle China's borders and live in peripheral areas. For centuries, ethnic Li have been found in the central part of Hainan, the location of large, productive agricultural areas. The establishment of autonomous regions on Hainan was intended to preserve the culture and heritage of the minority, and to allow them to enjoy a certain level of land rights. When Hainan became a province of China in 1988, traditional agriculture on the island was gradually replaced by tourism. A hotel boom uprooted hundreds, if not thousands, of Li families from their original areas of residence. The displacement was sanctioned and encouraged by governments at various levels. A range of social and cultural changes was brought about by tourism development in the 2000s. For example, the folk villages built along the highways were not controlled by the Li, but by Han entrepreneurs. Also, while tourists have generated considerable economic benefits for the communities, the preferences of entrepreneurs have skewed the form and content of ethnic offerings (e.g. dance, music, artifacts) toward an emphasis on material reflecting the history of the groups. Economic development as an external force has changed the original social system, pushing ethnic minorities out of the equilibrium. Some important rituals and customs have been adapted for tourists in ways that have significantly changed their original meaning and form. Ethnic Li were turned into caricatures and eventually had to fight stereotypes. The Li have been caught on the horns of a dilemma; that is, while tourism represents a way of improving their economic status, the Li have to give up many central features of their traditional culture to meet the preferences of tourists.

Although ethnic tourism does not mirror the operation of all socio-cultural changes, it can be viewed as representing a microcosm of the positives and negatives in modern life. The interests of socio-cultural change and traditional culture are not necessarily antithetical. For example, change may bring positive consequences that counteract the negative aspects of traditional culture, though of course the reverse may be true as well. While ethnic tourism brought modernity and financial improvement for the Li, it also brought diluted identity and the danger of losing cultural meaning and coherence. An important variable with regard to establishing a beneficial balance between economic benefit and maintenance of cultural integrity appears to be the degree to which the ethnic group actually benefits economically from the development of ethnic tourism. Wu (2000) commented that in the development of ethnic tourism, positive effects for the ethnic group center primarily on economic issues, while negative effects relate more to the cultural aspects of community. A central reality of ethnic tourism is that these two consequences of ethnic tourism (that is economic benefit and loss of traditional culture) unavoidably interact: ethnic tourism relies heavily on the 'Otherness' of traditional culture, while it is also characterized by pressure to adapt that very traditional culture to meet the expectations and preferences of tourists. Thus, ethnic tourism is a two-edged sword for traditional peoples – it represents a way toward economic progress and security, while at the same time, representing a threat to the group's cultural legacy.

Ethnic tourism implicitly attempts to maintain an equilibrium among the needs of stakeholders. On Hainan, the process of authentication has yielded both positive and negative consequences for each stakeholder. Various levels of government hoped to nurture 'commercial consciousness' for ethnic communities so that they might be financially independent. Additionally, an increase of income in ethnic communities was intended to foster a sense of identity and autonomy. Tourism businesses established the folk villages to promote ethnic culture, but gravitated toward touristic presentations that mixed traditional and contrived elements. Commonly, ethnic communities strive to improve their standard of living through tourism, but almost all the costs are born by the communities while the benefits mainly leak out to the outsiders. As Wood (1997) has observed, there are multiple stakeholders mediating the relationships between tourism and ethnic communities. Such relationships are complicated, but each party strives to gain an advantageous position. Wallace (1956), in his 'mazeway resynthesis', suggested cultural distortion can convert into cultural revitalization, as each stakeholder moves toward a new stable equilibrium. Wallace indicated that this movement toward a balanced, self-regulating system does not happen overnight, but is reached through a process of *longue durée*.

I have suggested that the five continua proposed in this book can be viewed as overlapping and interacting, as shown in Figure 8.1. The dot in the middle of Figure 8.1 represents a position that is neutral vis-à-vis each of the five continua. This placement represents a situation in which a stakeholder is located in a middle position on each of the five continua. Any particular position should not be regarded as necessarily superior or

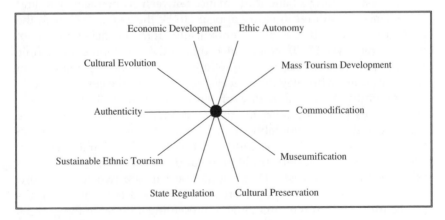

Figure 8.1 State of equilibrium

inferior to any other. Rather, any position will reflect the goals and objectives of those being evaluated and, thus, is likely to vary between stakeholders. In fact, these continua are used as yardsticks to describe the positioning of each stakeholder. My research in folk villages found that during the authentication process, governments, ethnic communities (dancers), tourists and tourism developers occupied different positions with regard to each of the five continua. For example, the national government placed more emphasis on state regulation to curb ethnic autonomy, while tourism developers were more interested in economic development than cultural preservation. Tourists had no opinions about the ethnic presentation, so their experiences in the folk villages tended to be superficial. Dance performers placed emphasis on better pay; however, cultural preservation does not seem to be an important issue to them. Thus, the four stakeholders exhibited four distinctive patterns with regard to the process of authenticating ethnic culture. The fact is that these patterns are fluid, and subject to change, in itself, an indication of the vibrancy of the authentication process.

A comparison of the interests of the stakeholders in Hainan tourism is presented in Figures 8.2–8.5. My research used both quantitative and qualitative methods: results of tourist surveys in Chapter 6 were reported using numbers, percentages and statistical tests, while views of ethnic communities and tourism business developers and managers were gleaned using qualitative methodology, reported in a descriptive manner (e.g. quotations from interviews with dancers and village managers). These figures do not portray quantitative measures but are the results of

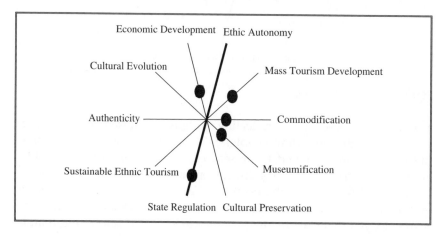

Figure 8.2 Governments' perspectives

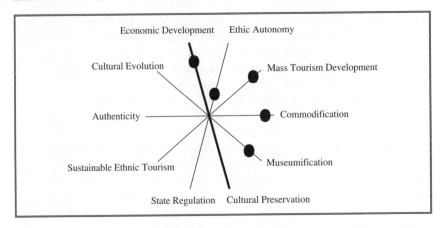

Figure 8.3 Tourism businesses' perspectives

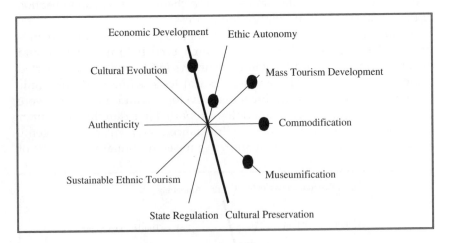

Figure 8.4 Tourists' perspective

a qualitative assessment reflecting judgments based on the data presented in the preceding chapters. At the risk of oversimplification, these figures are designed to present the position of each stakeholder group with respect to various dimensions of the authentication process.

In each of the figures, the position of a specific stakeholder group is indicated on each continuum by a small dark circle. Of course, it must be acknowledged that stakeholder groups are not homogenous and that, in reality, there may be considerable variation in these locations for any

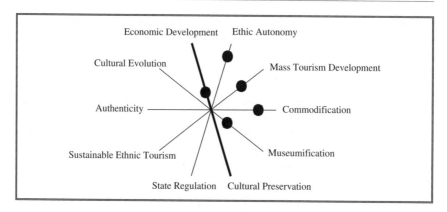

Figure 8.5 Ethnic community's perspective

segment of a stakeholder group. The emphasis here is that what is being presented is the *relative* position of each group on each continuum, rather than the precise location of its position. Because not all continua are of equal importance to all stakeholders, the dimension of greatest importance to each group is given greatest prominence in their figures by a bold line. The following sections will summarize the findings in the preceding chapters and illustrate the interests of each identified stakeholder group vis-à-vis the authentication process.

Governments

Hainan is an island located in the South China Sea. Historically, it was hardly on the radar of the central government. Local officials were dispatched from Mainland China to govern the *man-yi* (Chinese word for barbarian ethnic minorities). The relationship between local and central governments was never close. Perhaps owing to its peripheral location as well as the ignorance of the central government, ethnic culture had been maintained exceedingly well until the advent of tourism on the island in the late 1980s. The establishment of Hainan as a province has added a new layer of administration: the provincial government. The globalization of island tourism has increased the visibility of Hainan and it has become a popular tourist destination compared favorably to Hawaii, Miami or the Canary Islands. Tourism has precipitated cultural changes in ethnic communities as a result of an influx of tourists. Ethnic culture has evolved to an ethnicity-for-tourists with commercialized folk villages mushrooming along the highways in central and eastern parts of Hainan.

The extent of the various governments' roles in tourism varies. Overall, Hainan has enjoyed a flexible political environment and tourism has long been viewed as an important strategy for economic development. Ethnic tourism has been regarded as an integral part of travel itineraries featuring sightseeing and beach fun. Also, the island has been a testing ground as governments look for alternative economic and stimulus plans. Governments, as the largest of the four identified stakeholders, have been responsible for constructing and regulating ethnicity by providing official ethnic designations, and allocating resources in response to political considerations.

In this book, governments have been separated into three levels: national, provincial and local. National (central) government supports economic development and encourages ethnic minorities to improve their economic status by marketing their cultures. Tourism is used as a force for legitimizing and authenticating ethnic culture. Ethnicity of minority groups can be refashioned in response to tourists' expectations and preferences. Hollinshead (1999b: 267) called this kind of modification 'the legerdemain of tourism', through which material symbolism has been constantly interpreted in various time periods. Ethnic attractions in the era of commercialized tourism are often used by governments to further their agendas. For example, the building of theme parks served the purpose of portraying the unity of ethnicities under the leadership of the Communist Party; and folk villages were endorsed by high-ranking officials as a means of authenticating its concerns for preserving cultural heritage. Xiao (2006) discussed China's tourism development and policy through a discourse analysis of the public statements of the former paramount leader, Deng Xiaoping. Xiao's analysis revealed that the Chinese leader's comments had an immediate stimulus effect on tourism, with the result that governments at various levels started to promote his ideas and strategies. Tourism was seen as an industry that required effective policy and planning in its administration. The process of sanctioning the importance of tourism as a vehicle for preserving ethnic cultures reflects the power of a top-down administrative structure to shape public policy and action. The impact of such a strategy often results in the commodification, Disneyization and rationalization of those very ethnic cultures (Gotham, 2007).

National policies have encouraged minorities to become more 'developed' and 'modernized'. The direction of such evolution can be seen as a process of 'Hanification', in which an ethnic minority is subsumed into the Han majority. National government places great emphasis on job creation, with ethnic tourism viewed as one of the best ways to minimize the high unemployment rate. Economic development has been given prominence while cultural preservation has not received much attention from the national government. Also, the meaning of sustainability for minority groups appears to have been very different from what is conceptualized in developed countries where social-cultural and environmental issues have been given greater priority. Sustainable tourism development has been a kind of 'window dressing' used by the central government to present itself as supportive of the interests of minority cultural groups.

The national government has paid increasing attention to controlling the manner in which ethnic autonomy is defined. The concept of 'national stability' as the foundation of ethnic policies has, in fact, created 'internal colonization' in which ethnic minorities are viewed as inseparable members of the Chinese family whose head is the Han. The anti-Chinese violence in Tibet and Xinjiang (Uighur) in 2008 and 2009 has underlined the significance of state regulation vis-à-vis ethnic minorities. Often, the national government's accelerated attempts to forcibly alter ethnic identities have fueled growing resentment among minority peoples. Ethnic autonomy has increasingly become synonymous with advocating 'separatism'. The national government's fear of instability is palpably reflected in the reality where travel and tourism have been constantly regulated to discourage authentic contacts with ethnic minorities. Ethnic tourism is held up as an indication of the openness of the Communist government, and as an indication of its leniency toward minorities (Xiao, 2006). However, it is important to note that ethnic tourism is under the tight control of the national government in order to ensure its positive image to both domestic and international tourists.

Hainan did not become a province until 1988 when the national government made it a Special Economic Zone. Not surprisingly, the new provincial government focused on economic development. It was especially ill-equipped to understand ethnic minorities on Hainan because many provincial officials simply did not accept or even grasp the idea of 'ethnic autonomy'. Tourism has been identified as having great potential for the island's economic development given that it is the largest island in China with an abundance of natural and cultural resources. It has become Hainan's dominant economic sector, replacing traditional farming and agriculture. Its tropical location is a major advantage for mass tourism development, particularly with regard to attracting mainland tourists with packaged tours. Economic development surged in recent years, spurred by a combination of massive subsidies, external investment and rapid urbanization. Hainan has been transformed from a pristine island into an entertainment destination. Interviews with provincial officials indicated a strong desire to become a destination specifically targeted to rich people and international tourists. Sustainable tourism, as part of the eco-province plan, has not been effectively implemented. The reasons for this lack of success can be attributed to the fact that the Li minority did not have a part in shaping the rising tide of economic development. Their umbrage over job discrimination and loss of community lands for resorts and hotels grew. These dissatisfaction was combined mismanagement of social welfare and misguided environmental policies. Ethnic tensions have often been caused by the minority communities' lack of power in the decision making that has shaped economic development. As sensitivity toward cultural identity has been ignored by the provincial government, the ethnic Li have become more vocal in expressing their dissatisfaction and in emphasizing their distinctiveness.

The primary criterion used in identifying cultural authenticity from a local government's perspective lies in the consideration of a group's current location compared to the traditional site of the ethnic community. Commodification and museumification are encouraged by the local government if the site is right; that is if the site is located away from the group's traditional home territory. Given that the folk villages built along the highways were not located on sites traditionally occupied by ethnic minorities, development of them as ethnic tourist attractions was not limited by concerns for preserving ethnic authenticity. Tourism has been viewed by local government as an opportunity for constructing ethnic displays that are attractive to tourists. This approach to ethnic tourism development has led to conflicts between the Han and Li.

Although in some parts of Hainan, tourism is still being expanded, the local government has tended to ignore the recognition that its impact on ethnic communities has serious consequences with regard to their cultures. Focus has been on the belief that rapid development of tourism holds out the prospect of substantial benefits to Li communities. It is also anticipated that ethnic tourism can support a growing number of minority people who could sell a range of products from ethnic souvenirs to local fruits. Local government has welcomed the transition from agriculture to tourism as a means of stimulating the local economy. While the local government has clearly been aware of the possibility of erosion of ethnic identities through tourism and tourist interaction, it has played a passive role in the challenge of finding a balance between power, policy and place.

Because it is extremely difficult to identify the various governments' perspectives on a single diagram, each of the three levels, i.e. national, provincial and local, is presented separately. However, given the general variation among the three government levels vis-à-vis ethnic tourism, there are two similarities. First, economic development has been widely regarded as an effective way to improve the standard of living in ethnic communities. I have repeatedly read such statements issued by the national government as, 'before the foundation of Modern China (pre-1949), the productivity of ethnic minority as low as that of a patrilineal/matrilineal clanship, today their backward condition has been improved'. As I noted in Chapter 3, the pursuit of modernity and the elimination of backwardness have become such a priority of Chinese governments that the risk of losing culture has been given less importance. Acceptable cultural evolution is viewed as minorities becoming more 'Han', thus becoming a part of the Republic family. Sometimes fossilized ethnic images and presentations are useful in making the distinction between 'Self' and 'Other'. Therefore, in some respects, governments are inclined to maintain class and racial distinction as a profitable tool for tourism.

Second, the priority that state policy sets on economic development is the root cause for commodification and museumification of ethnic cultures. According to Gotham (2002: 1737–1739), the rise of the tourism industry has been dominated by the primacy given to 'consumption' over 'production'. Framed as style, taste, travel and 'destination', the tourist experience is one in which image, advertising and consumerism take primacy over production per se. Governments at various levels play critical roles in commodifying ethnicity and turning it into tourism-as-spectacle, assuming that such presentations will bring in revenue and employment most effectively. In addition, the eclipse of exchange value by sign value has impacted on the tourism industry. Governments, as the largest stakeholder, package local traditions, ethnic culture and heritage to such an extent that people lose the ability to distinguish between the 'authentic' and 'illusion'. The core of ethnicity embodies a complex of symbols and meaning, a code of transmitted social values. Ethnic identity becomes greatly malleable when economic goals are prioritized above a concern for maintaining the integrity of that identity. In fact, in China, governments have realized the connections between tourism's cultural manifestations and their impact on ethnic communities, and have used ethnic tourism as a strategy to attract more investment and as propaganda to, domestically and internationally, polish its images.

Based on the above findings, in Figure 8.2, I have drawn a heavy line on the continuum of state regulation and ethnic autonomy to emphasize its significance to governments in China. I have placed small dark circles near the center but toward the economic development, mass tourism development, commodification and museumification end of the continuum. However, I locate the dark circle closer to state regulation to reflect the preference of the governments. These positions represent the governments' perspectives when authenticating ethnic tourism: they focus on state regulation, support economic development and mass tourism, and consent to the degrees of commodification and museumification of ethnic cultures. I would note that this figure does not represent only one level of government, but all three levels of governments.

Tourism Businesses

The term 'tourism businesses' in my examination of Hainan refers to small enterprises that built and managed the folk villages on the island. I have described business practice in two folk villages: Baoting Areca Manor and the Indonesian Village. Village businesses on Hainan are largely privately owned with little assistance from the government in their development. They are, essentially, located in the informal sector, which plays an intermediary role of helping tourists interact with the minority in a village setting. They are the 'ethnicity-commodifying enterprise of enchantment', which promotes, evokes, stimulates and shapes the salience of ethnic boundaries (Rodriguez, 2003: 192). MacCannell (1992: 176) suggested that ethnic tourism as a part of modern mass tourism tends to involve two seemingly contradictory scenes: 'the international homogenization of the culture of the tourists' versus 'the artificial preservation of local ethnic groups and attractions'. Folk villages are purposely decorated to present an air of authenticity, 'a reification of the simple social virtues', and 'the ideal of "village life" into something to see'. MacCannell observed that while the village is not damaged, its original function is transformed and is no longer based on ethnic relations, rather it becomes an element in the recreational experiences of tourists coming from the outside. He called these kinds of folk villages, 'pseudo-communities for touristic attention'.

Touristic folk villages were located on Hainan along the central and eastern highways. The relocation of folk villages to sites near the highways indicates that the primary consideration was maximizing the profitability of the tourist attractions. The rise and fall of the first village, Fan Mao, demonstrates the common cycle through which authenticity moves toward commodification on the island. The original way that the Li culture was presented was swiftly replaced by shoddy imitation and distorted authenticity. Instead of tourists having to go out of their way to visit, the village sites were moved to be more easily accessed by tourists; thus, the demand side trumps the supply side interests. Newer folk villages were located where the Li did not traditionally live, rather than in places where they were a majority. By borrowing Boniface and Fowler's (1993: 121) 'the moving object story' and Urry's (2006: ix) the metaphor of the sandcastle, I suggest that constructing authenticity is a mode of resistance against the mobility of the folk villages that sought tourists along the highways. These villages were not just 'pseudo-communities' but 'touristic communities' (Grünewald, 2006) representing an ethnic theme park and a Disneyization of ethnicity. As Root (1996: 82) observed, tourism businesses not only attempt to 'promote an unlikely equivalence between the past and the present but also engineer particular kinds of folkloric experiences as a way of drawing tourist dollars'. Folk villages on Hainan exemplify the complexities of using tourism as a means of economic development.

I have presented five continua describing ethnic identity, perception of authenticity and conflicts at Areca Manor located in a Li residential area. Also, I have similarly described the communities at the Indonesian Village, a tourism site established on an agricultural area occupied by people of Chinese-Indonesian diasporas. The owners of the two tourist sites had known and worked together during the early years of the theme park boom. Both villages have gone through a checkered history of development. Economic success and mass tourism development had been prioritized and commercialization was common in every corner of the villages. The impact of state regulation has been moderate. To some extent, both villages earned the support of the provincial and local governments through joint venture programs. Ethnic presentation has been viewed as a useful marketing strategy to attract tourists.

In the 1990s, Areca Manor was regarded as the best village to showcase Li culture and rituals. In addition to authentic Li dance and folk performance, the village set aside a small showroom to portray Li life and customs of the region. However, in the mid 2000s, the manor decided to create a set of presentations to attract adventure- and thrill-seeking tourists. Li culture was marginalized and the number of dancers was reduced with many dancers relocated to other villages. Commodification of the Li culture was rampant inside the village with hundreds of vendors selling a wide range of products to tourists. Kickbacks and commissions to tour drivers and guides were widespread in the Areca

Manor since it relied heavily on tourist volume to generate incomes. Although the village business initially played a key role in balancing cultural preservation and economic development, the latter appears to have become most important, and cultural preservation a form of tokenism.

The Indonesian Village, on the other hand, evolved to become a potpourri of Southeast Asian kitsch by diluting its unique diasporic identity. The village added the presentation of Thai cultural elements, and invited ladyboys to perform on the stage. The purpose of the change was to produce a new product in order to draw more tourists. However, the change fuelled dissatisfaction in the diasporic community, which wanted the village to truly represent its history and culture. The community also disliked the idea that it was excluded from participating in the management of the village. This marginalization of the diasporic culture by the village managers caused strains and detrimental effects. A particular source of tensions between the village entrepreneurs and the communities was a perceived disproportionate share of village income claimed by management. A final aspect of the tension between the diasporic community and village management was disagreement over land use. The escalating dispute eventually caused the closure of the village in 2006.

The changes that took place in the development of both villages reflect a fundamental problem of the involvement of Li and Chinese-Indonesian peoples in tourism practice. In recent decades, government policies have exerted significant pressure on the ethnic Li. These pressures have tended to move the Li and other ethnic minorities toward assimilation with the Han majority, thereby weakening their identity. Many of the authentic elements of Li cultures, such as tattoos and wedding practices, are either in danger of becoming lost, or have been irreversibly lost. The Chinese-Indonesian community faced a particular challenge in that they were regarded as Hainanese rather than Indonesian. This was particularly true with reference to the second generation of the community. Tourists will be disappointed to find that much of the ethnic distinctiveness is gone, which is bad news for the tourism business. In return, the perceptual shifts prompted village business to modify its product to meet tourist expectations. Instead of presenting the authentic sides of Li and Chinese-Indonesian from the 'back stage' life of the communities, the tourism business chose to create experiences for tourists that were more fantasy than fact vis-à-vis the culture of the ethnic groups – a path to nowhere. From the perspective of tourism businesses, authentication is a process of deterritorialization (removed from its territory). The original content of ethnic identities is decoded and recoded into a new entity. Tourism businesses then sell the reconstituted, commodified form of the cultures. The themes of the village are determined by outsiders with values and agendas that tend to differ from those of the ethnic communities. Commodification of ethnic cultures ultimately degrades or destroys them.

Therefore, I have taken a strong position regarding the issue of economic development versus cultural preservation, as seen in the context of tourism businesses on Hainan. This is reflected in Figure 8.3, where I have placed the dark circles toward the economic development end of the spectrum. My observation of these villages over the past 10 years illustrates the significant influence of economic considerations on business decision making. Forster (1964: 217–227) argued that tourism businesses have created a 'phony folk' with a 'phony folk culture'. Forster has asserted that the paradoxes often observed in ethnic tourism are due to the 'commercialization of courtesies', whereby a 'moral nexus' (social interaction) becomes converted into a 'cash nexus' (commodification). As sign value has replaced exchange value in postmodern society, Forster bemoaned the tendency for the tourism industry to turn common social interactions into commodities to be bought and sold, threatening to destroy cultural authenticity. The folk villages on Hainan illustrate what Forster predicted, namely, that commodification, mass tourism, museumification and the manipulation of ethnic presentations are the consequences of a 'cash nexus'.

Tourists

Martin Heidegger's (2008) seminal work, *Sein und Zeit* (Being and Time), compared the conditions of 'home' and 'homelessness'. Heidegger stated that 'non-authentic' being is a falsely reassuring sense of living 'in one's own home', while true 'authentic' being is totally estranged from 'average everydayness'. To apply Heidegger's theory to the experience of tourists, authenticity can only be found outside one's usual environment. Ethnic tourism represents typical 'authentic' being since it presupposes an 'uncontaminated' environment where tourists and tourees can meet for a given period of time. The villages visited are set apart from modernity. Tourists on Hainan are unaware of ethnic culture, as visiting a folk village is a fringe activity. In reality, ethnic presentations are artificially recreated exoticism and the recapturing of cultural purity is a rarity.

To make matters worse, tourists may well become their own victims in their quest for the authentic because they authenticate what they expect to see or experience. Tourists tend to believe what they encounter is 'inauthentic' or 'spurious', whenever the experience diverges from their ideals. Typically, tourists' search for ethnic authenticity is guided by stereotypical fantasies involving cultural differences. Often, tourists are influenced by mass media that authenticity is an *a priori* knowledge. Surveys in three selected Hainan folk villages indicated that tourists should not, in fact, be considered 'cultural tourists'. That is, they came to the villages mainly as a secondary activity to other attractions on Hainan, such as visiting Sanya beaches and Haikou resorts, rather than being specially interested in exploring ethnic cultures. The majority (96%) of tourists came from Mainland China on package tours, which are the easiest way to travel to and within Hainan. Although the tourists showed interest in ethnic cultures, they had little knowledge of ethnicity, at best, having only blurred images taken from the mass media. They usually lacked the time and the depth of experience to understand the more complex and intricate aspects of ethnic culture. The pursuit of contact with ethnic authenticity was important for only a few, and generally of little consequence to these casual tourists. It would be more appropriate to call them 'coincidental cultural tourists' whose knowledge of ethnicity was superficial and who were not well prepared for a tour of a village.

Figure 8.4 presents the tourist's perspective with regard to the continua. Their view of the folk villages tended to be open-ended. They displayed a distinct pattern with regard to the continua, indicating that while they looked for a non-contrived ethnic presentation in the villages, they had no definite opinions about the ethnic presentations other than expecting to see presentations that could be described as centered on fossilized aspects of the culture. While they expressed an interest in viewing an 'authentic' ethnic-controlled village, their experience was significantly shaped by the decisions of tour guides. They also hoped that the government would regulate the village businesses, especially that of the informal sector, regarding the chaos and price gouging. Such conflicting interests suggested that tourists had little understanding of the nature of ethnic tourism and were heavily influenced by the accessibility of the site and the way the village had been promoted. In general, their opinions with regard to the five continua appear to be neutral (or unknown). Tourists contributed a significant portion of the economic income of the folk villages through their purchase of souvenirs and tropical goods; however, they did not view themselves as directly involved in the process of cultural preservation. Most importantly, tourists expected to see quaintly traditional aspects of ethnic cultures, but did not realize that the ethnic culture they encountered were representations that had been shaped and modified in response to economic considerations. What they saw was actually a 'museumified' presentation of ethnic culture.

The heavy line drawn in Figure 8.4 represents the continuum of cultural evolution versus museumification. I have placed the dark circles in the center, suggesting that the majority of tourists were unprepared to appreciate ethnic cultures. Their contradictory responses reflected a lack of interpretation from tour guides and villages. Dance performances, folk songs and mock weddings are markers of ethnic identity that tourists can easily identify. An ethnic costume could be rented in the village for a fee that allowed virtually every tourist to become 'Li' or 'Indonesian' for a short period of time. They experienced the wide range of vendors and sellers in the village as an annoyance, pushing them to demand a more non-commercial environment. Tourists were not against commodification, but did not want to experience unbridled overdevelopment. Also, tourists can be viewed as passive observers because opportunities for them to actively experience or participate in the ethnic culture seldom occurred. While they valued authenticity, they judged the authenticity of their experience in the villages on the basis of limited and/or inaccurate information. Consequently, villages endeavored to meet the touristic gaze and expectations by turning ethnicity into 'hyper-reality' (Eco, 1986). In the Hainan context, once again we can see the reality that touristic authentication involves a struggle between front stage and back stage, resulting in self-denial of Other's progression.

Ethnic Communities

This book focused the research on ethnic communities to a specific group – ethnic dance performers in the folk villages. Dance performances are spectacles and the dancers constitute a young and beautiful subset of Li people, immediately indicating the obvious fact that such entertainment cannot truly portray the broad intricacies of a complex culture. In part because of this, Li dancers are appropriate individuals to consult concerning the authenticity of ethnic tourism as they share aspects of their culture with tourists by interacting with tourists. The dancers are, I believe, positioned on the interface between tourism and culture on an ongoing basis, and are familiar with the compromises and trade-offs required to provide an attractive tourism product.

The island of Hainan has been characterized by extremely uneven patterns of development. While cities like Sanya and Haikou have experienced massive urbanization, the regions where the majority of ethnic Li reside remain poor. Ethnic tourism has improved the standard of living in the communities, but has also contributed to a situation of imbalanced wealth distribution. For ethnic Li, as for all people, finding a job and making a living are essential. Thus, economic development seemed to be the most important consideration for dance performers. Many dancers were attracted by the better pay offered in tourism, compared with such traditional alternatives as farming. Employee salaries were found to vary directly with the size of the village. Additionally, salaries varied widely across different geographic locations. Such imbalances have resulted in migration to urban areas by many Li seeking to take advantage of the employment opportunities found there. Folk villages located in the central part of Hainan have experienced a large turnover of dance performers. Cultural preservation does not seem to be an important issue for ethnic dance performers. In fact, ethnicity was not deemed an important factor in their choice of becoming dancers, instead such employment was viewed as a good way to make money.

Li dance programs have gone through a series of evolutions in order to respond to tourists' schedules and tastes. The most well-known program, the bamboo-beating dance, has evolved from a ritual performed at funeral ceremonies to a popular show for celebration. Formal aspects of the dance have been modified, e.g. the original importance of using only red bamboo has been lost. Also, in the process, the content of the dance has been transformed and reconfigured. Finally, government policy vis-à-vis ethnic minorities has resulted in 'invented traditions' being incorporated into dance and other aspects of traditional Li culture. Because of such decontextualization of the bamboo-beating dance, it was rendered inauthentic. However, my research showed that the dance was so popular that it has become the linchpin of Li culture and identity with tourists. It is held in such high esteem that it is a 'must see' for any tourist interested in Li culture.

For dance performers, many other evolving aspects of their culture are not presented on the stage. Ethnic arts performance has increasingly become *mise-en-scène*, style over substance. Certain aspects of Li culture are typically viewed in isolation and outside an appropriate context. Dance performers find that the portrayal of their culture is limited and the aspects that are presented are manipulated to be attractive to tourists. Further, many dance performers have limited opportunity to interact with tourists or to demonstrate that Li culture is not static but evolves over time. The result of this is that dance performances are widely viewed by dancers as a form of entertainment and museumification, designed to cater to tourists rather than having any real cultural significance.

As noted, dance performers in the villages have been mostly young attractive females whose performance emphasizes the romantic and exotic aspects of the Li lifestyle. Using females in the village is viewed as enhancing the authenticity of the presentation, adding to its pre-modern appearance and increasing its appeal to tourists. However, these performers are not representative of the Li community as a whole. They are paid relatively well, but the reality is that they will have employment only as long as tourists visit the village. Thus, their performances have been highly commercialized and turned into a commodity included in the price of a tour package. Therefore, commodification and the profitability of the village as an enterprise pursuit of economy have assumed major importance for dance performers. While the establishment of folk villages provided a sense of ethnic autonomy for the Li, the reality is that control of the villages as a vehicle for cultural expression and preservation resides elsewhere. Communities realized that Li cultures have been marketed to affluent tourist markets beyond Hainan. Dance performers believed that as long as they 'stay ethnic', they could continue to benefit from economic improvement and incentives from the government. Mass tourism was seen as a welcome strategy since the business prospect for dance performers hinges on the number of tourist arrivals.

In describing the position of the Li dancers with regard to the five continua, I have decided to emphasize the continuum of economic development versus cultural preservation in Figure 8.5. This ethnic group placed great stress on enhancement of economic opportunities to the extent that they were prepared to compromise cultural authenticity for the benefits of economic development. That perspective is indicated by the heavy line connecting economic development and cultural preservation. I have moved the dark circles toward ethnic autonomy, mass tourism development, commodification and museumification. From the ethnic minority perspective, the desire to re-establish the 'authentic' has been paralleled by a willingness to adapt to commodification and the museumification conceptualization of authenticity.

Summary

Meethan (2001: 92) once attributed cross-cultural conflicts to modern capitalist society that causes alienation and a consequent loss of authentic social relations and traditional material culture. This alienation, in turn, produces an urge to find the 'Holy Grail of authentic otherness'. In other words, a conflict is created when the mainstream of society constructs 'traditional' cultural identities, which are imposed on the Other. Ethnicity is typically found as a cardinal source of social conflict (Graham *et al.*, 2000). The process of authentication of ethnic cultures by various stakeholders serves this need of the tourism system. Conflicts results because each of the various stakeholders seek to establish equilibrium of the system. Furthermore, stakeholders try to find a balance between inspired fantasy and the faulty 'authentic' experience. Examination of the manner in which authentication often proceeds highlights the conflict associated with power imbalance and divergence of interests/values.

The diagrams describing the process of authentication are meant to provide a broad perspective for understanding the stakeholders' roles in ethnic tourism. As I mentioned in Chapter 1, ethnic tourism can be conceptualized as an 'ethnic panopticon' set in a changing social and economic milieu. Each stakeholder has an opportunity to gaze and be gazed by others and strives to find an optimal viewpoint, which I called 'positioning'. Juxtaposing the five continua, the preferences and attitudes of the four stakeholder groups showed clear difference of emphasis. The diagrams presented in this chapter should not be considered fixed, but mutable to varying degrees. At present, for governments at various levels, positioning means control of ethnic autonomy, in which they can exercise control on the culture and identity of ethnic groups. By contrast, tourists on Hainan occupied a neutral position vis-à-vis ethnic autonomy because few understood what constitutes 'authentic' aspects of ethnic culture. For ethnic community members, such as dance performers involved in the folk villages, tourism provided economic opportunities to many who were able to perform on stage. Job security and a steady income were their priority. For village businesses, commodification led to the changes of themes of the villages. Their interests seemed to lie with a complete open field for shaping ethnic cultures to maximize income from tourists.

Clearly, the stakeholders discussed here provide only a partial perspective on the issue of authentication. Questions central to a discussion of ethnic tourism (e.g. 'who uses tourism attractions?' 'who manages those attractions?' 'who benefits from the economic gain of the attractions?' and 'what represents authentic ethnic culture, and who defines it?') are all inextricably linked. This book provides a composite answer, but not a complete one. On Hainan, ethnic tourism is a fundamental economic activity, an industry that commodifies ethnic culture and identities, and trades culture and identity for gain that can be measured in jobs, profits and incomes. The ambition of creating interactive, cross-cultural and authentic experiences that enrich and educate tourists has never been fulfilled. Folk villages are daring experiments for showcasing ethnic cultures through a form of commodification. There is no clear answer on how best to address the issue of authenticity, but I clearly believe that the best path to understanding authenticity is to examine the process through which authentication take place. Authentication is a self-balancing system involving different stakeholders and assessed by various yardsticks. The search for equilibrium will take longer but each works both ends.

Epilogue: Lo auténtico aún existe (Reprise)

At the beginning of her book, *Sounding Indigenous: Authenticity in Bolivian Music Performance*, Michelle Bigenho (2002) depicted a scene of Bolivian musicians sweating under heavy wool ponchos in the summer sun. Music and dance were moving sonorously and energetically through city streets. The performance was presented as an 'original' Italaque, set in a region of the highland Bolivian indigenous culture. The Bolivian performers' visible ethnic costume and beautiful chanting, dancing and movement were impressive and received a warm reception from the street spectators. However, these musicians, known in Bolivia as 'music of the Masters', performed their rendition of authentic indigenous music not in Bolivia, but in France as a part of the parade for the international folklore festival in the town of Saintes.

The discontinuities occurred because the musicians' concern for authenticity extended beyond their mere appearance in native dress while playing panpipes. In order to produce a performance that felt authentic, the Bolivian musicians had to feel the music deeply and move to it in specific ways. Bigenho (2002: 2) observed that 'while the French desired an authentic *representation* of Bolivian music, they were not concerned with the authentic *feeling* of this performance'. In other words, French spectators at the festival paid more attention to the appearance of the performance than its underlying emotional substance. These activities, which Bigenho called 'feelingful', did not translate well to 'meaningful' activities for French spectators. Furthermore, these musicians have traveled around the world, performing on the road. They have appeared on television and featured in the mass media. To some extent, these widespread locations suggest that their performance should not be considered authentic, but adapted for the entertainment of a wider audience. Bigenho (2002: 16) called this kind of change 'unique authenticity', in which the new form tends to be innovative and distinctive. Very often, such change engenders a brand new entity and identity. Bigenho asserted that despite the controversy generated by the process of authenticating ethnic musical performance, unique authenticity still matters; or *lo auténtico aún existe* (authenticity still exists), an appealing promotional slogan created by Tourism Bolivia.

Bigenho's study of the authenticity of musical expression in Bolivia's multicultural encounters with tradition and modernity provides an ideal epilogue to conclude my study of ethnic tourism on Hainan. My empirical research of the ethnic Li largely focused on the presentations of folklore, history, music and dance, regarded as an integral part of ethnic tourism. For example, I have observed the bamboo-beating dance in a variety of locations, ranging from the primitive folk villages to luxury hotel lobbies. The clapping sound of bamboos, colorful costume and the smiling faces of the performers were presented as a part of a genuine encounter with the Li culture. To some extent, the original meaning of the dance has gone through an evolution that makes it virtually impossible for an outsider to make a judgment of its authenticity. Often, the complex issue of authenticity confused me as I watched the performances. It seemed that I was watching a *trompe l'oeil* as the performance unfolded. Questions of whether these performers were Li and whether the performance truly represents the 'feelingful' culture of Li communities remained unan-swered. This is not to say that there is no such thing as a Li identity, or that people in Li communities do not feel distinctive. Rather, it is to say that Li identity may be understood and expressed in different ways in the external gazes of various stakeholders, including me as a participant observer – a tourist and a tourism researcher.

In private, I have spoken back stage to ethnic Li performers and community members. Some of these individuals secretly questioned their own Li authenticity, wondering if ethnic policies, modernity and commodification had deprived them of a sense of real identity. Like music and dance, culture has been reproduced and standardized to an extent that authenticity is destroyed. The rise and fall of folk villages along the highways further increased the complex interplay of Li culture. Given the constantly shifting character of Li identity, it is extremely difficult to assert that there is any continuing, uniform Li culture. An examination of ethnic tourism on Hainan reveals that the transformation of tradition and the emergence of a new mode of being and becoming, is a process that blurs any attempt to construct a definitive ethnic identity.

I have witnessed the dramatic economic development of the island for a decade. In 1999, the streets of Haikou and Sanya had very few traffic lights, but by 2009, both cities had become the most sophisticated tourist destinations in China with a wide array of five-star hotels lining the beaches. However, ethnic tourism has followed a different path: the majority of folk villages along the highways have disappeared in the past 10 years, with only two still in existence. The reasons for this decline have been discussed from different stakeholders' perspectives in several chapters. Clearly, in contrast to mass packaged tourism, ethnic tourism on Hainan has experienced a downward spiral.

During my field trips, I have seen and talked to many people, visited small villages and observed many different types of ethnic presentations. I must confess that searching for authentic Li is like playing a guessing game in a blind alley, reminding me of the Japanese film 'Rashomon' (1950), directed by Akira Kurosawa. The central event of the movie, the rape of a young bride and the murder of her noble husband as they were riding through a forest in 9th century Kyoto, was re-enacted four times from four differing points of view: the bride, her husband, the bandit, and a woodcutter who witnessed the crime. At the end of the film, the unreliability of evidence is explored and the question 'what is truth?' is posed. The 'Rashomon effect' is an allusion to the flickering nature of truth, and perhaps to our inability ever to know the real truth (Cole & Lass, 1991).

In a similar vein, Ryan and Hall (2001) have argued that the pursuit of truth is akin to peeling away the layers of an onion – different 'truths' are encountered as one moves deeper. The debate on authenticity results from lack of a set of criteria with which to measure, compare and deconstruct. Like an onion, inasmuch as there is a truth, it is the total onion, not the core of the separate layers alone. Lowenthal (1996: 129) has observed that 'out of some legendary kernel of truth, each corporate group harvests a crop of delusory faiths... that sustains (it)' and Du Cros (2004: 154) asserted that 'truth can be relative, and having someone else's truth forced upon you as either a tourist or host can be unpopular'. Authenticity reflects the 'Rashomon effect', while authentication is akin to peeling away an onion. Each layer represents different angles of truth as experienced by (in the Hainan context) four identified stakeholders.

This book will fill a gap by answering questions pertaining to the authentication of ethnic tourism in an island setting. However, there is still a great deal of room for additional research on various aspects of ethnic tourism in developing and developed countries. Questions of authenticity can be examined in a more fruitful manner by focusing on the process of social construction, and by recognizing that there are multiple levels of social presentation of reality (Guyette & White, 2003). The view of authentication presented here explores the multiple layers of reality, experienced by stakeholders using different yardsticks. As noted in Chapter 8, each stakeholder exhibits a differing position regarding the nature of authentication. I believe that the success of ethnic tourism and cultural survival on Hainan will, ultimately, be determined by the four stakeholders investigated in this book. They will influence future changes as the search for equilibrium continues. The conceptualization of authentication presented here draws attention to major stakeholders of ethnic tourism that might otherwise be overlooked. I have organized much of the information on, and examined many of the concepts pertaining to, ethnic tourism relative to a broader perspective. This will result in an approach that will be useful for decision making in a variety of locations.

This book has focused on Li folk villages and the Indonesian Village on Hainan. Other ethnic minorities, e.g. the Miao and Hui, reside on the island. Although their involvement in tourism seems to be much less significant than that of the Li or the diasporic Indonesians, future research should extend to these people to determine if the issues and dynamics observed at the Li and Indonesian villages are the same, or differ. Furthermore, this book analyzes cultural evolution as it relates to dance performance, customs and folklore. However, as noted previously, the majority of ethnic minority participation in tourism occurs in the informal sector with the selling of souvenirs and tropical fruit. This suggests that other cultural elements, such as craft souvenirs, merit research in the future.

I have compared four key Hainan stakeholders with regard to the tensions that exist when cultural resources are authenticated. The role that such other stakeholders as non-governmental organizations (NGOs) and international organizations play in authentication could also be identified. Although these groups may not play roles as important on Hainan as the four identified stakeholders, research examining their impact would add valuable knowledge about how the private sector and NGOs are involved in authentication and the potential for their collaboration with the more prominent stakeholders.

Hainan is an interesting laboratory in which to undertake research to understand ethnic tourism development. The conceptual framework presented in this book could be applied to other situations. Academic interest in such studies may include learning whether or not this conceptual framework and its methodology is useful in understanding the authentication of ethnic tourism in other destination areas. In addition, this type of research could reveal similar or dissimilar constraints to the application of the framework to socio-cultural, political and economic environments in other parts of the world.

On the basis of the observations and discussions presented, it is possible to make the following recommendations for ethnic tourism on Hainan. These recommendations center on four stakeholders, in particular, the role played by governments. Various levels of government play a crucial role in tourism on Hainan. Thus, they merit more attention in the future development.

My first recommendation centers on the relative naiveté of the Li with regard to business and organizational understanding/skill. I would observe that such ignorance is the greatest barrier to effective participation by ethnic people in the development and management of tourism. For most Li people and local governments, urban business culture is an alien activity that has surfaced in their community: they are not in a position to compete with experienced operators who are already well connected, well funded and have access to planning and business acumen. Folk villages on Hainan are generally small-scale operations lacking proper planning and administrative support. Lack of business sophistication, as a barrier, is not restricted to the Li population alone; it also affects the planning machinery and the bureaucracy vested with the task developing and managing ethnic tourist sites. Considering the negative impact of such lack of sophistication, it is imperative that an ethnic policy be integrated into the tourism planning process. For example, the provincial and local governments should implement strategies mandating consultation with the ethnic communities and their representatives. This would increase the likelihood that minority people's interests will be protected and their active involvement in the tourism development process will be encouraged.

Also, it is increasingly recognized that balance, compromise and trade-offs between competing interests will need to be affected on Hainan. I would recommend that the provincial government initiate a 'round table' representing all tourism stakeholders so that dialogue and information exchange might be facilitated. Local government should also seek ethnic participation (or even grassroots participation) so that minorities might participate in the development of folk villages, and other ethnic attractions and products. Similarly, tourism developers ought to devote more attention toward ensuring a greater degree of participation by the ethnic minority. One effective way of doing this would be to initiate such programs as consultation and focus group discussion, designed to encourage Li involvement in the economic development and planning of the attractions. Some educational programs sponsored by local governments are needed to help Li people develop appropriate tourism products. The findings of this book can, I believe, form an appropriate departure point for such a discussion.

Another set of recommendations focuses on the process of commodification of ethnic culture, an important aspect of developing ethnic tourism attractions. The experiences provided to tourists by folk villages are created, bought, sold and consumed in distinct ways. The nature of these products and the details of their marketing profoundly impact both hosts and guests. The negative effects of such commodification have been discussed; however, the process can be used as a positive mechanism in the pursuit of sustainable tourism development. By using the commodification process appropriately, the competitiveness of folk village could be strengthened and their attractiveness as tourist destinations enhanced. Folk villages should make ethnic structures, events, festivals and art forms into living, interactive and animated programs without sacrificing their cultural integrity. I recommend that local government should set administrative guidelines for village development. The guidelines should include a set of criteria to regulate ethnic displays. For example, regulations relating to ethnic dance programs should require that the presentations maintain the integrity of the culture, folklore and music of the ethnic group. At the same time, tourism businesses, in partnership with other industries, should play an active role in providing more ethnic tourism products while maintaining the ethnic authenticity of those products. For example, village businesses could work with textile manufacturers to develop and promote ethnic craft souvenirs. Such strategic alliances could effectively promote ethnic tourism, present a broader picture of ethnic cultures and further stimulate local economies.

A third recommendation stems from the observation that strategies of economic development typically center on making the assets of an ethnic culture more marketable. This focus, however, does not necessarily center on the needs of the ethnic community and its unique interests or vulnerabilities. Furthermore, in pursuing economic development, village businesses are apt to embrace a fairly short-term perspective, which may undercut the long-term well-being of the host communities. Although folk village businesses typically do not focus on the long-term needs of the ethnic community, the ethnic community is profoundly interested in its long-term future in a general sense. Many dance performers expressed a strong desire to 'stay ethnic'. To respond to the needs of ethnic communities most effectively, ethnic tourism developers should forge long-term products and promote long-term ethnic involvement in order to ensure that equitable strategies and tactics are recognized and promoted. Also, long-term development strategies should be fostered by all levels of government. In particular, the provincial government should provide tax incentives or policy prefer- ences for village businesses. The goal of developing ethnic tourism should be emphasized in regional policies; for example, three- or five- year plans to ensure the sustainable development of folk villages might be developed. The longer that businesses can be encouraged to stay within the ethnic communities, the better it will be for those commu- nities. It is both morally proper and good business sense to take the long-term interests of the host culture into account when strategies are being developed. Further, these government stakeholders should demonstrate that authenticity of ethnic cultures can be better showcased in ways that make sense to the tourism businesses. Since a long-term opportunity is more cost effective than projects with a short life, a commitment to preserving and enhancing ethnic cultures is a wise and potentially lucrative strategy.

A fourth recommendation holds that efforts must be made to maintain the ethnic integrity of a tourism attraction. Tourism business can turn 'exotic cultures into commodities and individuals into amusing "objects" for tourist "consumption"' (Klieger, 1990: 38). As a result, encounters that are initially novel, gradually become routine for both tourists and the ethnic hosts, and cultural presentations become more and more removed from the reality of the hosts' everyday life. The related temptation to 'freeze' culture should also be avoided. As Greenwood (1982: 27) has noted, culture is not a static entity as all 'viable cultures are in the process of "making themselves up" all the time'. In addition to tourism, numerous other forces influence cultural change. Governments and tourism planners need to anticipate major trends and, most importantly, identify and involve the important stakeholders who authenticate ethnic cultural resources. As indicated above, the provincial government should, as a high priority, develop a forum that will bring stakeholders together to exchange information and discuss their concerns. Also, the local governments should highly recom- mend that village businesses provide tourists with a detailed introduction to Li culture. For example, presenting experiences centered on the origins of the Li people, the past and present of Li folk dance and the contemporary Li lifestyle would allow tourists to have a broader context within which to encounter the Li culture. In this way, tourists' appreciation for both the ethnic cultural displays and Li culture as a whole would be enhanced.

My fifth recommendation addresses the reality that one of the greatest paradoxes encountered in the folk villages is the contradiction between ethnic tradition and contemporary lifestyle. From a tourist's perspective, Li culture should be different from what can be called 'mainstream' culture. This, of course, does not mean Li culture is totally isolated from Mainland Chinese cultures. Owing to an unfortunate, but perhaps understandable, chauvinism, ethnic communities may feel that labels such as 'folk' or 'traditional' are degrading and insulting. However, these labels often have an economic value and can be used to sell tourism services and products to the larger world. Many significant and positive elements of ethnic cultures are basic and enriching, and benefits accrue both to members of the ethnic communities and to society in general when exchange occurs. Sharing 'traditional culture' has the potential of building bridges of mutual respect and understanding between ethnic communities and other groups. On the other hand, developers of ethnic tourism should be aware that some aspects of ethnic culture may be private and should not be cavalierly shared with the public without proper consent, management and planning. Governments should play an active role in encouraging the establishment of high-quality tourist attractions along the central highway. Such attractions could include folk villages, cultural interpretation centers and such other attractions as agricultural displays related to the tea and rubber plantations. Tourism products can also be diversified along the transport route. For example, the city of Haikou might arrange an ethnic culinary festival (e.g. bamboo rice cooking, brewing rice wine) to attract tourists just arrived from the mainland. Ethnic food might serve as a door that leads tourists to explore the authentic part of ethnic cultures. Such introductions could motivate tourists to visit folk villages. Finally, an appropriately organized tour in Sanya could provide an excellent opportunity for tourists to buy good quality ethnic souvenirs and related products. In this way, an 'ethnic tourism corridor' could be created in some of the poorer areas in the island where many minority people live.

Finally, I would observe that ethnic tourism itself introduces many enticing opportunities for progress and change within the minority culture. The presentation of Li culture is a dynamic business. Li people in the villages have adopted ethnic clothing as a type of business uniform. Even street vendors were observed wearing ethnic clothes, presumably so that they could be identified as part of the minority group and derive the associated benefits of perceived authenticity. Li culture is nested within a complex mosaic of tradition, society and culture. I would recommend that the role of governments should shift from tight control of ethnic autonomy to flexible policies. For example, Li communities should be allowed to develop their own cultural products without going through the red tape usually required for approval. Village businesses, in particular those along the central route of Hainan, should be encouraged to expand the current ethnic programs in Li Autonomous Regions. Governments at different levels should acknowledge that ethnic communities have a right to their culture and traditions as they become more economically interconnected with the mainstream world. Governments should play a central role in assisting minorities to cope with the profound challenges involved in making economic progress, while also maintaining the traditions that will allow them to survive as a coherent ethnic group. Investment in ethnic education and heritage preservation is necessary for wise sustainable development.

Ethnicity is a complex phenomenon and different stakeholders in ethnic tourism authenticate a particular culture in different and often contrasting ways (Cable, 2008). Without doubt, the Li culture will continue to evolve with time and this raises the issue of how best to present this changing culture to outsiders. What if authentic Li identity has already been destroyed by commodification and tourism development? What if there is no such thing as authentic Li culture, given that government policies and tourism have encroached on their characteristic life? And, finally, how can authentication be carried out when there is no such thing as authenticity? These questions are not easily answered, but they are central to determining the future direction of ethnic tourism on Hainan and elsewhere.

Hall (1990: 222) suggested that 'identity is not as transparent or unproblematic as we think. Perhaps instead of thinking of identity as already accomplished fact... we should think, instead, of identity as a "production"'. As ethnicity has become a hybrid and marketable product, various stakeholders play active roles in molding new identities for ethnic minorities. However, the ongoing process of identity formation is fraught with commodification and museumification dangers. Often, the uniqueness of identity becomes irrelevant, a scene littered with torn-up pieces of authentic artifacts. Hall (2001) raised a practical question – if identity *is* no longer, what does it mean *to become*? Authenticating ethnic identity confronts one with the possibility of conflicting perspectives, ranging from those of such exogenous forces as tourists and the tourism industry, to those flowing from such internal processes as economic development and cultural preservation. Since to be is to become, the distinction between authenticity and inauthenticity is virtually unidentifiable. Ethnic tourism treads in this uncharted territory where authenticity and identity remain fluid.

References

Abercrombie, N. and Longhurst, B. (1998) *Audiences: A Sociological Theory of Performance and Imagination*. London: Sage.

Altman, J. (1989) Tourism dilemmas for aboriginal Australians. *Annals of Tourism Research* 16, 449–456.

Anderson, B. (1991) *Imagined Communities*. New York: Verso.

Ap, J. (2003) An assessment of theme park development in China. In A. Lew, L. Yu, J. Ap and G. Zhang (eds) *Tourism in China* (pp. 195–209). Binghamton, NY: The Haworth Hospitality Press.

Asplet, M. and Cooper, M. (2000) Cultural designs in New Zealand souvenir clothing: The question of authenticity. *Tourism Management* 21, 307–312.

Bao, J. (1995) The development and influence of theme parks: A case study of Shenzhen (in Chinese). Unpublished PhD dissertation, Zhongshan University.

Barth, F. (1969) *Ethnic Groups and Boundaries*. Oslo: Norwegian University Press.

Barthel-Bouchier, D. (2001) Authenticity and identity: Theme-parking the Amanas. *International Sociology* 16 (2), 221–239.

Baudelaire, C. (1970) *Paris Spleen*. New York: New Directions Book.

Baudrillard, J. (1995) *Simulacra and Simulations*. Ann Arbor, MI: University of Michigan.

Bauman, Z. (2000) *Liquid Modernity*. Cambridge: Polity.

Belhassen, Y., Caton, K. and Stewart, T. (2008) The search for authenticity in the pilgrim experience. *Annals of Tourism Research* 35 (3), 668–689.

Best, S. (1989) The commodification of reality and the reality of commodification: Jean Baudrillard and post-modernism. *Current Perspectives in Social Theory* 9, 23–51.

Bhabha, H. (2004) *The Location of Culture*. London: Routledge.

Bigenho, M. (2002) *Sounding Indigenous: Authenticity in Bolivian Music Performance*. New York: MacMillan.

Boniface, P. and Fowler, P. (1993) *Heritage and Tourism in the Global Village*. London: Routledge.

Boorstin, D. (1961) *The Image: A Guide to Pseudo-Events in America*. New York: Harper & Row.

Bowden, J. (2005) Pro-poor tourism and the Chinese experience. *Asia Pacific Journal of Tourism Research* 10, 379–398.

Bredin, M. (1993) Ethnography and communication: Approaches to aboriginal media. *Canadian Journal of Communications* 18 (3), 297–313.

Brown, D. (1996) Genuine fakes. In T. Selwyn (ed.) *The Tourist Image* (pp. 33–47). New York: Wiley.

Bruner, E. (1994) Abraham Lincoln as authentic reproduction: A critique of postmodernism. *American Anthropologist* 96 (2), 397–415.

Bruner, E. (2005) *Culture on Tour: Ethnographies of Travel.* Chicago, IL: The University of Chicago Press.

Bruner, E. and Kirshenblatt-Gimblett, B. (1994) Maasai on the lawn: Tourist realism in East Africa. *Cultural Anthropology* 9 (4), 435–470.

Bruno, G. (1993) *Streetwalking on a Ruined Map: Cultural Theory and the City Films of Elvira Notari.* Princeton, NJ: Princeton University Press.

Burns, P. and Novelli, M. (2006) *Tourism and Social Identities: Global Frameworks and Local Realities.* Amsterdam: Elsevier.

Butler, R. (1980) The concept of a tourist area cycle of evolution: Implications for management of resources. *Canadian Geographer* 24, 5–12.

Bryce, D. (2007) Repacking Orientalism. *Tourist Studies* 7 (2), 165–191.

Bryden, J. (1973) *Tourism and Development: A Case Study of the Commonwealth Caribbean.* Cambridge: Cambridge University Press.

Cable, M. (2008) Will the real Dai please stand up: Conflicting displays of identity in ethnic tourism. *Journal of Heritage Tourism* 3 (4), 267–276.

Cadario, P., Ogawa, K. and Wen, Y. (1992) *A Chinese Province as a Reform Experiment: The Case of Hainan.* Washington: The World Bank.

Cairncross, F. (1997) *The Death of Distance: How the Communications Revolution is Changing Our Lives.* London: Orion.

Callero, P. (1994) From role-playing to role-using: Understanding role as resource. *Social Psychology Quarterly* 57, 228–243.

Carey, J. (2005) *What Good are the Arts?* London: Faber.

Casetti, F. (1998) *Inside the Gaze: The Fiction Film and its Spectator.* Bloomington, IN: Indiana University Press.

Cauquelin, J. (2004) *The Aborigines of Taiwan: The Puyuma from Headhunting to the Modern World.* New York: Routledge Curzon.

Certeau, M. (1984) *The Practice of Everyday Life.* Berkeley, CA: University of California Press.

Chambers, E. (1999) *Native Tours: The Anthropology of Travel and Tourism.* Prospect Heights, IL: Waveland Press.

Chang, J. (2006) Segmenting tourists to aboriginal cultural festivals: An example in the Rukai tribal area, Taiwan. *Tourism Management* 27 (6), 1224–1234.

Chang, J., Wall, G. and Tsai, C. (2005) Endorsement advertising in aboriginal tourism: An experiment in Taiwan. *International Journal of Tourism Research* 7 (6), 347–356.

Chhabra, D. (2005) Defining authenticity and its determinants: Toward an authenticity flow model. *Journal of Travel Research* 44, 64–73.

China Academy of Urban Planning and Design (CAUPD) (1997) *The Comprehensive Land Use Plan for Haikou.* Beijing: CAUPD.

Chua, C. (2004) Defining Indonesian Chineseness under the new order. *Journal of Contemporary Asia* 34 (4), 465–479.

Clark, I. (2009) Naming sites: Names as management tools in indigenous tourism sites – an Australian case study. *Tourism Management* 30, 109–111.

Clifford, J. (1986) Introduction: Partial truths. In J. Clifford and G. Marcus (eds) *Writing Culture: The Poetics and Politics of Ethnography* (pp. 1–27). Berkeley and Los Angeles, CA: University of California Press.

Clifford, J. (1988) *The Predicament of Culture: Twentieth-Century Ethnography, Literature, and Art.* Cambridge, MA: Harvard University Press.

Cohane, O. (2008) Conde Nast Traveler. On WWW at http://www.concierge.com/ideas/hotspots/articles/1685?page = 7.

Cohen, A. (2004) *Urban Ethnicity.* New York: Routledge.

Cohen, E. (1988) Authenticity and commoditization in tourism. *Annals of Tourism Research* 15 (3), 371–386.

Cohen, E. (1993) Introduction: Investigating tourist arts. *Annals of Tourism Research* 20 (1), 1–8.

Cohen, E. (2002) Authenticity, equity and sustainability in tourism. *Journal of Sustainable Tourism* 10 (4), 267–276.

Cole, S. (2006) Cultural tourism, community participation and empowerment. In M. Smith and M. Robinson (eds) *Cultural Tourism in a Changing World: Politics, Participation and (Re)presentation* (pp. 89–103). Clevedon: Channel View Publications.

Cole, S. (2007) Beyond authenticity and commodification. *Annals of Tourism Research* 34 (4), 943–960.

Cole, S. and Lass, A. (1991) *The Dictionary of 20th Century Allusions.* New York: Fawcett Gold Medal.

Collins-Kreiner, N. and Olsen, D. (2004) Selling diaspora: Producing and segmenting the Jewish diaspora tourism market. In T. Coles and D. Timothy (eds) *Tourism, Diasporas and Space* (pp. 279–290). New York: Routledge.

Connor, W. (1984) *The National Question in Marxist-Leninist Theory and Strategy.* Princeton, NJ: Princeton University Press.

Conran, M. (2006) Commentary: Beyond authenticity: Exploring intimacy in the touristic encounter in Thailand. *Tourism Geographies* 8 (3), 274–285.

Crang, M. (1999) Nation, region and homeland: History and tradition in Dalarna, Sweden. *Cultural Geographies* 6 (4), 447–470.

Crang, P. and Malbon, B. (1996) Consuming geographies: A review essay. *Transactions of the Institute of British Geographers* 21 (4), 704–711.

Cukier, J. (2002) Tourism employment issues in developing countries: Examples from Indonesia. In R. Sharpley and D. Telfer (eds) *Tourism and Development: Concepts and Issues* (pp. 165–201). Clevedon: Channel View Publications.

Culler, J. (1981) Semiotics of tourism. *American Journal of Semiotics* 1 (1–2), 127–140.

Damrosch, L. (2005) *Jean-Jacques Rousseau: Restless Genius.* New York: Mariner Books.

Daniel, Y. (1996) Tourism dance performances: Authenticity and creativity. *Annals of Tourism Research* 23 (4), 780–798.

Davies, E. and Wismer, S. (2007) Sustainable forestry and local people: The case of Hainan's Li minority. *Human Ecology* 35(4), 415–426.

Desmond, J. (1999) *Staging Tourism: Bodies on Display from Waikiki to Sea World.* Chicago, IL: University of Chicago.

Diamond, B., Cronk, M. and Von Rosen, F. (1994) *Visions of Sound: Musical Instruments of First Nations Communities in Northeastern America.* Chicago, IL: The University of Chicago Press.

Doorne, S., Ateljevic, I. and Bai, Z. (2003) Representing identities through tourism: Encounters of ethnic minorities in Dali, Yunnan Province, People's Republic of China. *International Journal of Tourism Research* 5, 1–11.

Doyle, P. (1976) The realities of the product life cycle. *Quarterly Review of Marketing* 1, 1–6.

Dredge, D. (2004) Development, economy and culture: Cultural heritage tourism planning, Liangzhu, China. *Asia Pacific Journal of Tourism Research* 9 (4), 405–422.

Du Cros, H. (2004) Postcolonial conflict inherent in the involvement of cultural tourism in creating new national myths in Hong Kong. In C.M. Hall and H. Tucker (eds) *Tourism and Postcolonialism: Contested Discourses, Identities and Representations* (pp. 153–168). New York: Routledge.

Dupre, L. (1983) *Marx's Social Critique of Culture*. New Haven, CT: Yale University Press.

Duval, D. (2004) Cultural tourism in postcolonial environments: Negotiating histories, ethnicities and authenticities in St. Vincent, Eastern Caribbean. In C.M. Hall and H. Tucker (eds) *Tourism and Postcolonialism* (pp. 57–75). London: Routledge.

Dyer, P., Aberdeen, L. and Schuler, S. (2003) Tourism impacts on an Australian indigenous community: A Djabugay case study. *Tourism Management* 24, 83–95.

Eco, U. (1986) *Travels in Hyperreality*. Orlando, FL: Harcourt & Brace.

Edensor, T. (1998) *Tourists at the Taj: Performance and Meaning at a Symbolic Site*. London: Routledge.

Edensor, T. (2000) Staging tourism: Tourists as performers. *Annals of Tourism Research* 27 (2), 322–344.

Eriksen, T. (2002) *Ethnicity and Nationalism: Anthropological Perspectives*. London: Pluto Press.

Erlmann, V. (1999) *Music, Modernity, and the Global Imagination: South Africa and the West*. New York: Oxford University Press.

Errington, S. (1998) *The Death of Authentic Primitive Art and Other Tales of Progress*. Berkeley, CA: University of California Press.

Evans-Pritchard, D. (1989) How 'they' see 'us': Native American images of tourists. *Annals of Tourism Research* 16 (1), 89–105.

Fan, C., Wall, G. and Clare, M. (2008) Creative destruction and the water town of Luzhi, China. *Tourism Management* 29, 648–660.

Farrell, B. and Twining-Ward, L. (2005) Seven steps towards sustainability: Tourism in the context of new knowledge. *Journal of Sustainable Tourism* 13 (2), 109–122.

Feng, C. (1999) Seeking lost codes in the wilderness: The search for a Hainanese culture. *The China Quarterly* 160 (1), 1037–1056.

Feng, C. and Goodman, D. (1997) Colonial and post-colonial Hainan: Communal politics and the struggle for identity. In D. Goodman (ed.) *China's Provinces in Reform: Class, Community, and Political Culture* (pp. 48–88). London: Routledge.

Finley, C. (2004) Authenticating dungeons, whitewashing castles: The former sites of the slave trade on the Ghanaian coast. In M. Lasansky and B. McLaren (eds) *Architecture and Tourism: Perception, Performance and Place* (pp. 109–128). New York: Berg.

Fjellman, S. (1992) *Vinyl Leaves and Walt Disney World America*. Boulder, CO: Westview.

Florida, R. (2002) *The Rise of the Creative Class*. Cambridge, MA: Basic Books.

Forster, J. (1964) The sociological consequences of tourism. *International Journal of Comparative Sociology* 5 (2), 217–227.

Foucault, M. (1976) The eye of power. In C. Gordon (ed.) *Power/Knowledge: Selected Interviews and Other Writings* (pp. 146–155). Brighton: Harvester.

Foucault, M. (1980) *Power/Knowledge: Selected Interviews and Other Writings, 1972–1977*. New York: Pantheon Books.

Friedberg, A. (1993) *Window Shopping: Cinema and the Postmodern*. Berkeley, CA: University of California Press.

Friedman, G. (1981) *The Political Philosophy of the Frankfurt School*. Ithaca, NY: Cornell University Press.

Gardner, R. (2005) Tradition and authenticity in popular music. *Symbolic Interaction* 28 (1), 135–144.

Geertz, C. (1973) *The Integrative Revolution: Primordial Sentiments and Civil Politics in the New States*. New York: Basic Books.

Geertz, C. (2000) *The Interpretation of Cultures: Selected Essays*. New York: Basic Books.

Gerry, C. (1987) Developing economies and the informal sector in historical perspective. *Annals of American Academy of Political and Social Science* 493, 100–124.

Ghai, Y. (2000) Ethnicity and autonomy: A framework for analysis. In Y. Ghai (ed.) *Autonomy and Ethnicity: Negotiating Competing Claims in Multi-ethnic States* (pp. 1–24). Cambridge: Cambridge University Press.

Gibson, C. and Connell, J. (2005) *Music and Tourism: On the Road Again*. Clevedon: Channel View Publications.

Giddens, A. (1984) *The Constitution of Society: Outline of the Theory of Structuration*. Berkeley, CA: University of California Press.

Gilroy, P. (2000) *Against Race*. Cambridge, MA: Harvard University Press.

Godley, M. (1989) The sojourners: Returned Overseas Chinese in the People's Republic of China. *Pacific Affairs* 62 (3), 330–352.

Goffman, E. (1959) *The Presentation of Self in Everyday Life*. New York: Doubleday.

Goldberg, D. (1994) *Multiculturalism: A Critical Reader*. Oxford: Blackwell.

Gotham, K. (2002) Marketing Mardi Gras: Commodification, spectacle and the political economy of tourism in New Orleans. *Urban Studies* 39 (10), 1735–1756.

Gotham, K. (2007) *Authentic New Orleans: Tourism, Culture, and Race in the Big Easy*. New York: New York University Press.

Graburn, N. (1984) The evolution of tourist arts. *Annals of Tourism Research* 11, 393–449.

Graham, B., Ashworth, G. and Tunbridge, J. (2000) *A Geography of Heritage*. London: Oxford University Press.

Grazian, D. (2003) *Blue Chicago: The Search for Authenticity in Urban Blues Clubs*. Chicago, IL: University of Chicago Press.

Greenwood, D. (1977) Culture by the pound: An anthropological perspective on tourism as cultural commoditization. In V. Smith and W. Eadington (eds) *Tourism Alternatives: Potential and Problems in the Development of Tourism* (pp. 129–138). Philadelphia, PA: University of Pennsylvania.

Greenwood, D. (1989) Culture by the pound: An anthropological perspective on tourism as cultural commodification. In V. Smith (ed.) *Host and Guests: The Anthropology of Tourism* (pp. 177–187). Philadelphia, PA: University of Pennsylvania Press.

Grossberg, L. (1992) *We Gotta Get Out of This Place: Popular Conservatism and Postmodern Culture*. New York: Routledge.

Gruffudd, P. (1995) Heritage as National Identity: Histories and prospects of the National Pasts. In D.T. Herbert (ed.) *Heritage, Tourism and Society* (pp. 49–67). London: Mansell.

Grünewald, R. (2002) Tourism and cultural revival. *Annals of Tourism Research* 29 (4), 1004–1021.

Grünewald, R. (2006) Pataxo tourism art and cultural authenticity. In M. Smith and M. Robinson (eds) *Cultural Tourism in A Changing World: Politics, Participation and (Re)presentation* (pp. 191–202). Clevedon: Channel View Publications.

Gu, K. (2002) Urban morphology of the Chinese city: Cases from Hainan. Unpublished PhD thesis in Planning, University of Waterloo.

Gu, K. and Wall, G. (2007) Rapid urbanization in a transitional economy in China: The case of Hainan island. *Singapore Journal of Tropical Geography* 28, 158–170.

Gunn, C. (1972) *Vacationscape: Designing Tourist Regions.* Austin, TX: University of Texas.

Gunn, C. (1994) *Tourism Planning: Basics, Concepts, Cases.* Washington, DC: Taylor & Francis.

Gustafsson, B. and Shi, L. (2003) The ethnic minority-majority income gap in rural China during transition. *Economic Development and Cultural Change* 51, 805–822.

Guyette, S. and White, D. (2003) Reducing the impacts of tourism through cross-cultural planning. In H. Rothman (ed.) *The Culture of Tourism, the Tourism of Culture: Selling the Past to the Present in the American Southwest* (pp. 164–184). Albuquerque, NM: University of New Mexico Press.

Hague, E. (2001) The Scottish diaspora. Tartan Day and the appropriation of Scottish identities in the United States. In D.C. Harvey, R. Jones, N. McInroy and C. Milligan (eds) *Celtic Geographies: Old Culture, New Times* (pp. 139–156). London: Routledge.

Hainan Statistical Yearbook (2007) *Statistical Yearbook of Hainan 2007.* Beijing, China: Statistical Publishing House (in Chinese).

Hall, C.M. (1996) *Tourism and Politics: Policy, Power and Place.* Chichester: John Wiley & Sons.

Hall, C.M. (1991) *Introduction to Tourism in Australia: Impacts, Planning and Development.* South Melbourne: Longman Cheshire.

Hall, C.M. (2007) Response to Yeoman et al: The fakery of the authentic tourist. *Tourism Management* 28, 1139–1140.

Hall, C.M. and Jenkins, J. (1995) *Tourism and Public Policy.* New York: Routledge.

Hall, C.M. and Tucker, H. (2004) *Tourism and Postcolonialism: Contested Discourses, Identities and Representations.* London: Routledge.

Hall, S. (1990) Cultural identity and diasporas. In J. Rutherford (ed.) *Identity, Community, Culture, Difference* (pp. 222–237). London, Lawrence & Wishart.

Hall, S. (2001) Introduction: Who needs identity? In S. Hall and P. du Gay (eds) *Questions of Cultural Identity* (pp. 1–17). London: Sage.

Handler, R. and Linnekin, J. (1984) Tradition, genuine or spurious. *Journal of American Folklore* 97, 273–290.

Handler, R. and Saxton, W. (1988) Dissimulation: Reflexivity, narration, and the quest for authenticity in living history. *Cultural Anthropology* 3, 242–260.

Hanson, A. (1989) The making of the Maori: Cultural invention and its logic. *American Anthropologist* 91 (4), 890–902.

Harkin, M. (2004) *Reassessing Revitalization Movements: Perspectives from North America and the Pacific Islands*. Nebraska: University of Nebraska Press.

Harrell, S. (1995a) *Cultural Encounters on China's Ethnic Frontiers*. Seattle, WA: University of Washington Press.

Harrison, D. (2005) Introduction: Contested narratives in the domain of world heritage. In D. Harrison and M. Hitchcock (eds) *The Politics of World Heritage: Negotiating Tourism and Conservation* (pp. 1–10). Clevedon: Channel View Publications.

Harron, S. and Weiler, B. (1992) Review. Ethnic tourism. In B. Weiler and C.M. Hall (eds) *Special Interest Tourism* (pp. 83–92). London: Bellhaven.

Hebdige, D. (1988) *Subculture: The Meaning of Style*. London: Routledge.

Hechter, M. (1999) *Internal Colonialism: The Celtic Fringe in British National Development*. New Brunswick, NJ: Transaction Publishers.

Heidegger, M. (2008) *Being and Time*. New York: Harper & Row.

Henderson, J. (2007) Communism, heritage and tourism in East Asia. *International Journal of Heritage Studies* 13, 240–254.

Heryanto, A. (1998) Ethnic identities and erasure: Chinese Indonesians in public culture. In J. Kahn (ed.) *Southeast Asian Identities* (pp. 95–114). Singapore: Institute of Southeast Asian Studies.

Hinch, T. and Butler, R. (1996) Indigenous tourism: A common ground for discussion. In R. Butler and T. Hinch (eds) *Tourism and Indigenous Peoples* (pp. 3–19). Cornwall: T.J. Press.

Hinch, T. and R. Butler (2007) Introduction: Revisiting common ground. In R. Butler and T. Hinch (eds) *Tourism and Indigenous Peoples: Issues and Implications* (pp. 1–14). Oxford: Butterworth-Heinemann.

Hitchcock, M. (1999) Tourism and ethnicity: Situational perspectives. *Progress in Tourism and Hospitality Research* 4, 1–16.

Hitchcock, M. (1998) Tourism, "Taman Mini" and national identity. *Indonesia and the Malay World* 26 (75), 124–135.

Hitchcock, M., King, V. and Parnwell, M. (1993) Tourism in Southeast Asia: Introduction. In M. Hitchcock, V. King and M. Parnwell (eds) *Tourism in Southeast Asia* (pp. 1–16). London: Routledge.

Hobsbawm, E. and Ranger, T. (1992) *The Invention of Tradition*. Cambridge: Cambridge University Press.

Hollinshead, K. (1992) 'White' gaze, 'red' people-shadow visions: The disidentification of 'Indians' in cultural tourism. *Leisure Studies* 11, 43–64.

Hollinshead, K. (1997) Heritage tourism under post-modernity: Truth and the past. In C. Ryan (ed.) *The Tourist Experience: A New Introduction* (pp. 170–193). London: Cassell.

Hollinshead, K. (1998) Tourism, hybridity, and ambiguity: The relevance of Bhabha's "Third Space" cultures. *Journal of Leisure Research* 30 (1), 121–156.

Hollinshead, K. (1999a) Surveillance of the worlds of tourism: Foucault and the eye-of-power. *Tourism Management* 20, 7–23.

Hollinshead, K. (1999b) Tourism as public culture: Horne's ideological commentary on the legerdemain of tourism. *International Journal of Tourism Research* 1, 267–292.

Hollinshead, K. (2004) Tourism and new sense: Worldmaking and the enunciative value of tourism. In C.M. Hall and H. Tucker (eds) *Tourism and Postcolonialism* (pp. 25–42). London: Routledge.

Huddart, D. (2006) *Homi K. Bhabha*. New York: Routledge.

Hughes, G. (1995) The cultural constraints of sustainable tourism. *Tourism Management* 16, 49–60.

Hunter, W. (2001) Trust between culture: The tourist. *Current Issues in Tourism* 4 (1), 41–67.

Hyder, R. (2004) *Brimful of Asia: Negotiating Ethnicity on the UK Music Scene*. Burlington, VT: Ashgate.

Ibrahim, A. (2008) The new flâneur: Subaltern cultural studies, African youth in Canada, and the semiology of in-betweenness. *Cultural Studies* 22 (2), 234–253.

Jack, G. and Phipps, A. (2005) *Tourism and Intercultural Exchange*. Clevedon: Channel View Publications.

Jackson, J. (2006) Developing regional tourism in China: The potential for activating business clusters in a socialist market economy. *Tourism Management* 27, 695–706.

Jackson, P. (1999) Commodity cultures: The traffic in things. *Transactions of the Institute of British Geographers* 24 (1), 95–108.

Jacques, D. (1995) The rise of cultural landscapes. *International Journal of Heritage Studies* 1 (2), 91–101.

Jamal, T. and Hill, S. (2004) Developing a framework for indicators of authenticity: The place and space of cultural and heritage tourism. *Asia Pacific Journal of Tourism Research* 9 (4), 353–371.

Jenkins, O. (2003) Photography and travel brochures: The circle of representation. *Tourism Geographies* 5 (3), 305–328.

Johnson, J. (2002) *Who Needs Classic Music? Cultural Choice and Musical Value*. New York: Oxford University Press.

Jonsson, H. (2000) Yan minority identity and the location of difference in the South China borderlands. *Ethnos* 65 (1), 56–82.

Jordan, F. (2008) Performing tourism: Exploring the productive consumption of tourism in enclavic spaces. *International Journal of Tourism Research* 10, 293–304.

Judd, D. (1999) Constructing the tourist bubble. In D. Judd and S. Fainstein (eds) *The Tourist City* (pp. 35–53). New Haven, CT: Yale University Press.

Kaeppler, A. (2004) Recycling tradition: A Hawaiian case study. *Dance Chronicle* 27 (3), 293–311.

Kaltman, B. (2007) *Under the Heel of the Dragon: Islam, Racism, Crime, and the Uighur in China*. Columbus, OH: Ohio University Press.

Kaplan, C. (1996) *Questions of Travel: Postmodern Discourses of Displacement*. Durham, NC: Duke University Press.

Kasfir, S. (1992) African art and authenticity: A text with a shadow. *African Arts* 25 (2), 40–53.

Kaup, K. (2000) *Creating the Zhuang: Ethnic Politics in China*. Boulder, CO: Lynne Rienner.

Kehoe, A. (1989) *The Ghost Dance: Ethnohistory and Revitalization*. New York: Holt, Rinehart & Winston.

Kim, H. and Jamal, T. (2007) Touristic quest for existential authenticity. *Annals of Tourism Research* 34, 181–201.

Kirshenblatt-Gimblett, B. (1998) *Destination Culture: Tourism, Museums and Heritage*. Berkerly, CA: University of California Press.

King, V. (2009) Anthropology and tourism in Southeast Asia: Comparative studies, cultural differentiation and agency. In M. Hitchcock, V. King and

M. Parnwell (eds) *Tourism in Southeast Asia: Challenges and New Directions* (pp. 43–68). Honolulu, HI: University of Hawaii Press.

Klieger, P. (1990) Close encounters: Intimate tourism in Tibet. *Cultural Survival Quarterly* 14 (2), 38–41.

Kolas, A. (2008) *Tourism and Tibetan Culture in Transition: A Place Called Shangrila.* Abingdon: Routledge.

Krutak, L. (2007) *The Tattooing Arts of Tribal Women.* London: Bennett & Bloom.

Lacan, J. (2006) *Ecrits: The First Complete Edition in English.* New York: W.W. Norton.

Lane, B. (1994) Sustainable rural tourism strategies: A tool for development and conservation. *Journal of Sustainable Tourism* 2 (1 & 2), 102–111.

Levine, H. (1999) Reconstructing ethnicity. *Journal of Royal Anthropology Institute* 5 (2), 165–180.

Li, J. (2003) Playing upon fantasy: Women, ethnic tourism and the politics of identity construction in contemporary Xishuangbanna, China. *Tourism Recreation Research* 28 (2), 51–65.

Li, J. (2004) Tourism enterprises, the state, and the construction of multiple Dai cultures in contemporary Xishuangbanna, China. *Asia Pacific Journal of Tourism Research* 9 (4), 315–330.

Li, Y. (2004) Exploring community tourism in China: The case of Nanshan cultural tourism zone. *Journal of Sustainable Tourism* 12 (3), 175–193.

Li, Y. (2006) Contradictions of modernization in China and the implications for community tourism development. In T. Liu (ed.) *Tourism Management: New Research* (pp. 41–63). Hauppauge, NY: Nova Publishers.

Li, Y. and Hinch, T. (1998) Ethnic tourism attractions and their prospect for sustainable development at two sites in China and Canada. *Asia Pacific Journal of Tourism Research* 2 (1), 5–17.

Li, Y., Lai, K. and Feng, X. (2007) The problem of "Guanxi" for actualizing community tourism: A case study of relationship networking in China. *Tourism Geographies* 9 (2), 115–138.

Liang, J-Y., Umezaki, M. and Ohtsuka, R. (2003) Advantageous and disadvantageous impacts of tourism development on the living of Li ethnic minority villagers in Hainan Island, China. *Journal of Human Ergology* 32, 1–7.

Lim, L. (2008) New lives, new ethnic identity for Chinese villagers. December. On WWW at http://www.npr.org/templates/story/story.php?storyId=98681734. Accessed 25.12.08.

Lionnet, F. (1995) *Logiques métisses*: Cultural appropriation and postcolonial representations. In S. Benstock and C. Schenck (eds) *Postcolonial Representations. Women, Literature, Identity* (pp. 1–21). Ithaca, NY: Cornell University Press.

Liu, A. and Wall, G. (2005) Human resources development in China. *Annals of Tourism Research* 32 (3), 689–710.

Liu, T. (2006) *Tourism Management: New Research.* Hauppauge, NY: Nova Publishers.

Liu, X. (1997) Space, mobility, and flexibility: Chinese villagers and scholars negotiate power at home and abroad. In A. Ong and D. Nonini (eds) *Ungrounded Empires: The Cultural Politics of Modern Chinese Transnationalism* (pp. 91–114). New York: Routledge.

Löfgren, O. (1999) *On Holiday: A History of Vacationing.* London: University of California Press.

Long, V. and Wall, G. (1995) Small-scale tourism development in Bali. In M. Conlin and T. Baum (eds) *Island Tourism: Management Principles and Practice* (pp. 237–257). Chichester: John Wiley & Sons.

Lowenthal, D. (1996) *Possessed by the Past*. New York: Simon and Schuster.

Luckin, B. (1990) *Questions of Power: Electricity and Environment in Inter-war Britain*. Manchester: Manchester University Press.

Lukes, S. (2005) *Power: A Radical View*. Basingstoke: Palgrave Macmillan.

Lumsdon, L. (1997) *Tourism Marketing*. London: International Thomson Business.

MacCannell, D. (1973) Staged authenticity: Arrangements of social space in tourist settings. *American Journal of Sociology* 79 (3), 589–603.

MacCannell, D. (1976) *The Tourist: A New Theory of the Leisure Class*. Berkeley, CA: University of California Press.

MacCannell, D. (1984) Reconstructed ethnicity: Tourism and cultural identity in third world communities. *Annals of Tourism Research* 11, 375–391.

MacCannell, D. (1992a) *Empty Meeting Grounds: The Tourist Papers*. New York: Routledge.

MacCannell, D. (1992b) Tradition's next step. In S. Norris (ed.) *Discovered Country: Tourism and Survival in the American West* (pp. 161–179). Albuquerque, NM: Stone Ladder Press.

MacCannell, D. (2008) Why it never really was about authenticity. *Society* 45 (4), 334–337.

Mackerras, C. (2003) *China's Ethnic Minorities and Globalisation*. London: Routledge Curzon.

Macleod, D. (2004) *Tourism, Globalization and Cultural Change: An Island Community Perspective*. Clevedon: Channel View Publications.

Maoz, D. (2005) The mutual gaze. *Annals of Tourism Research* 33 (1), 221–239.

Markula, P. (1998) Dancing with postmodernism. *Waikato Journal of Education* 4, 73–85.

Maruyama, N., Yen, T. and Stronza, A. (2008) Perception of authenticity of tourist art among Native American artists in Santa Fe, New Mexico. *International Journal of Tourism Research* 10, 453–466.

Mason, K. (2004) Sound and meaning in aboriginal tourism. *Annals of Tourism Research* 31 (4), 837–854.

Maurer-Fazio, M., Hughes, J. and Zhang, D. (2004) The Economic Status of China's Ethnic Minorities. International Research Conference: Poverty, Inequality, Labor Market and Welfare Reform in China, Canberra, Australia.

McIntosh, A., Hinch, T. and Ingram, T. (2002) Cultural identity and tourism. *International Journal of Arts Management* 4, 39–49.

McIntosh, A. and Johnson, H. (2005) Exploring the nature of the Maori experience in New Zealand: Views from hosts and tourists. *Tourism* 52 (2), 117–129.

McIntosh, A. and Prentice, R. (1999) Affirming authenticity: Consuming cultural heritage. *Annals of Tourism Research* 26 (3), 589–612.

McKean, P. (1989) Towards a theoretical analysis of tourism: Economic dualism and cultural involution in Bali. In V. Smith (ed.) *Hosts and Guests: The Anthropology of Tourism* (pp. 119–139). Philadelphia, PA: University of Pennsylvania Press.

McKercher, B. and Du Cros, H. (2002) *Culture Tourism: The Partnership Between Tourism and Cultural Heritage Management*. Binghamton, NY: The Haworth Hospitality Press.

McLaren, D. (2003) *Rethinking Tourism and Ecotravel*. Bloomfield, CT: Kumarian Press.

McLean, G. (1997) Ethnicity, culture and 'primordial' solidarities. In P. Peachey, G. McLean and J. Kromkowski (eds) *Abrahamic Faiths, Ethnicity and Ethnic Conflicts* (pp. 143–174). Washington, DC, Council for Research in Values and Philosophy.

Medina, L. (2003) Commoditizing culture: Tourism and Maya identity. *Annals of Tourism Research* 30 (2), 353–368.

Meethan, K. (2001) *Tourism in Global Society: Place, Culture, Consumption*. New York: Palgrave.

Meethan, K. (2003) Mobile cultures? Hybridity, tourism and cultural change. *Journal of Tourism and Cultural Change* 1 (1), 11–28.

Morgan, M. (1994) *Mutant Message Down Under*. New York: Harper-Collins.

Moscardo, G. and Pearce, P. (1999) Understanding ethnic tourists. *Annals of Tourism Research* 26 (2), 416–434.

Nagel, J. (2003) *Race, Ethnicity, and Sexuality: Intimate Intersections, Forbidden Frontiers*. Oxford: Oxford University Press.

Nederveen-Pieterse, J. (1995) *White on Black: Images of Africa and Blacks in Western Popular Culture*. New Haven, CT: Yale University Press.

Nederveen-Pieterse, J. (2001) Hybridity, so what? The anti-hybridity backlash and riddles of recognition. *Theory, Culture & Society* 18 (2–3), 219–245.

Netting, N. (1997) The deer turned her head: Ethnic options for the Hainan Li. *Bulletin of Concerned Asian Scholars* 29 (2), 3–17.

Nonini, D. (1997) Shifting identities, positioned imaginaries: Transnational traversals and reversals by Malaysian Chinese. In A. Ong and D. Nonini (eds) *Ungrounded Empires: The Cultural Politics of Modern Chinese Transnationalism* (pp. 203–227). New York: Routledge.

Nora, P. (2001) *Rethinking France: Les Lieux de Memoire*. Chicago, IL: University of Chicago Press.

Norberg-Hodge, H. (1991) *Ancient Futures: Learning from Ladakh*. San Francisco, CA: Sierra Club Books.

Notzke, C. (2004) Indigenous tourism development in Southern Alberta, Canada: Tentative engagement. *Journal of Sustainable Tourism* 12 (1), 29–54.

Nyaupane, G., Morais, D. and Dowler, L. (2006) The role of community involvement and number/type of visitors on tourism impacts: A controlled comparison of Annapurna, Nepal and Northwest Yunnan, China. *Tourism Management* 27, 1373–1385.

Nyiri, P. (2006) *Scenic Spots: Chinese Tourism, The State, and Cultural Authority*. Seattle, WA: University of Washington Press.

Oakes, T. (1992) Cultural geography and Chinese ethnic tourism. *Journal of Cultural Geography* 12 (2), 2–17.

Oakes, T. (1997) Ethnic tourism in rural Guizhou. In M. Picard and R. Wood (eds) *Tourism, Ethnicity, and the State in Asian and Pacific Societies* (pp. 35–70). Hawaii, HI: University of Hawaii Press.

Oakes, T. (1998) *Tourism and Modernity in China*. London: Routledge.

Oakes, T. (2006) Get real! On being yourself and being a tourist. In C. Minca and T. Oakes (eds) *Travels in Paradox* (pp. 229–250). Lanham, MD: Rowman & Littlefield.

Ooi, C. (2002) *Cultural Tourism & Tourism Cultures: The Business of Mediating Experiences in Copenhagen and Singapore*. Copenhagen: Copenhagen Business School Press.

Ouyang, T. (1999) Resort morphology and local economic development: Example from Hainan Province, China. Unpublished Master's thesis, University of Waterloo.

Page, S., Forer, P. and Lawton, G. (1999) Small business development and tourism: Terra incognita? *Tourism Management* 20, 435–459.

Palmer, C. (1994) Tourism and colonialism: The experience of the Bahamas. *Annals of Tourism Research* 21, 792–811.

Pang, K. (1996) Being Hui, Huan-nang, and Utsat simultaneously: Contextualizing history and identities of the Austronesian-speaking Hainan Muslims. In J. Melissa (ed.) *Negotiating Ethnicities in China and Taiwan* (pp. 183–208). Berkeley, CA: University of California.

Parker, A. and Sedgwick, E. (1995) Introduction: Performativity and performance. In A. Parker and E. Sedgwick (eds) *Performativity and Performance* (pp. 1–18). London: Routledge.

Parris, R. (1996) Tourism and cultural interaction: Issues and prospects for sustainable development. *UNESCO/AIEST Proceedings of Round Table, Culture, Tourism Development: Critical Issues for the 21st Century* (pp. 36–40). Paris: UNESCO/AIEST.

Phillips, R. and Steiner, C. (1999) Art, authenticity, and the baggage of cultural encounter. In B. Phillips and B. Christopher (eds) *Unpacking Culture: Art and Commodity in Colonial and Postcolonial Worlds* (pp. 3–19). Berkeley, CA: University of California Press.

Picard, M. (1990) Cultural tourism in Bali: Cultural performances as tourist attraction. *Indonesia* 49, 37–74.

Picard, M. (1996) *Bali: Cultural Tourism and Touristic Culture*. Singapore: Archipelago Press.

Pitchford, S. (1995) Ethnic tourism and nationalism in Wales. *Annals of Tourism Research* 22, 35–52.

Poole, M. (1997) In search of ethnicity in Ireland. In B. Graham (ed.) *In Search of Ireland: A Cultural Geography* (pp. 151–173). London: Routledge.

Potter, A. (2010) *The Authenticity Hoax: How We Get Lost Finding Ourselves*. New York: HarperCollins.

Preston, R. (1999) Reflections on culture, history, and authenticity. In L. Valentine and R. Darnell (eds) *Theorizing the Americanist Tradition* (pp. 150–162). Toronto: University of Toronto Press.

Reed, S. (1998) The politics and poetics of dance. *Annual Review of Anthropology* 27, 503–532.

Reisinger, Y. and Steiner, C. (2006) Reconceptualizing object authenticity. *Annals of Tourism Research* 33 (1), 65–86.

Reisinger, Y. and Turner, L. (2003) *Cross-Cultural Behaviour in Tourism: Concepts and Analysis*. Burlington, MA: Butterworth-Heinemann.

Richards, G. (1996) *Cultural Tourism in Europe*. Wallingford: CAB International.

Richards, G. and Wilson, J. (2006) Developing creativity in tourist experiences: A solution to the serial reproduction of culture. *Tourism Management* 27, 1209–1223.

Richter, L. (1989) *The Politics of Tourism in Asia*. Honolulu, HI: University of Hawaii Press.

Ritzer, G. and Liska, A. (1997) McDisneyization and post-tourism: Complementary perspectives on contemporary tourism. In C. Rojek and J. Urry (eds) *Touring Cultures: Transformation of Travel and Theory* (pp. 96–109). London: Routledge.

Robinson, M. (1999) Collaboration and cultural consent: Refocusing sustainable tourism. *Journal of Sustainable Tourism* 7 (3&4), 379–397.

Robinson, M. and Boniface, P. (1999) *Tourism and Cultural Conflicts*. New York: CABI Publishing.

Rodriguez, S. (2003) Tourism, difference, and power in the borderlands. In H. Rothman (ed.) *The Culture of Tourism, the Tourism of Culture: Selling the Past to the Present in the American Southwest* (pp. 185–205). Albuquerque, NM: University of New Mexico Press.

Rojek, C. and Urry, J. (1997) *Touring Cultures: Transformations of Travel and Theory*. London: Routledge.

Root, D. (1996) *Cannibal Culture: Arts, Appropriation, and the Commodification of Difference*. Boulder, CO: Westview.

Ryan, C. (1991) *Recreational Tourism: A Social Science Perspective*. London: Routledge.

Ryan, C. (2002) Equity, management, power sharing and sustainability – issues of the 'new tourism'. *Tourism Management* 23, 17–26.

Ryan, C. (2002) *The Tourist Experience*. London: Thomson Learning.

Ryan, C. (2002) Tourism and cultural proximity: Examples from New Zealand. *Annals of Tourism Research* 29 (4), 952–971.

Ryan, C. (2003) *Recreational Tourism: Demand and Impacts*. Clevedon: Channel View Publications.

Ryan, C. and Aicken, M. (2005) *Indigenous Tourism: The Commodification and Management of Culture*. Oxford: Elsevier.

Ryan, C. and Hall, C.M. (2001) *Sex Tourism: Marginal People and Liminalities*. New York: Routledge.

Ryan, C. and Higgins, O. (2006) Experiencing culture tourism: Visitors at the Maori arts and crafts institute, New Zealand. *Journal of Travel Research* 44, 308–317.

Ryan, C. and Huyton, J. (2000) Aboriginal tourism – a linear structural relations analysis of domestic and international tourist demand. *International Journal of Tourism Research* 2, 15–29.

Ryan, C. and Huyton, J. (2000) Who is interested in aboriginal tourism in the Northern Territory, Australia? A cluster analysis. *Journal of Sustainable Tourism* 8 (1), 53–88.

Ryan, C. and Huyton, J. (2002) Tourists and aboriginal people. *Annals of Tourism Research* 29 (3), 631–647.

Saïd, E. (2003) *Orientalism*. New York: Penguin Classics.

Samuel, R. (1996) *Theatres of Memory: Past and Present in Contemporary Culture*. London: Verso.

Sautman, B. (2002) Ethnic law and minority rights in China: Progress and constraints. *Law & Policy* 21 (3), 283–314.

Schein, L. (1997) Gender and internal Orientalism in China. *Modern China* 23 (1), 69–98.

Schein, L. (2000) *Minority Rules: The Miao and the Feminine in China's Cultural Politics*. Durham, NC: Duke University Press.

Schouten, F. (2006) The process of authenticating souvenirs. In M. Smith and M. Robinson (eds) *Cultural Tourism in a Changing World: Politics, Participation and (Re)presentation* (pp. 191–202). Clevedon: Channel View Publications.

Scott, D. (2005) Re-presenting Mormon history: A textual analysis of the representation of pioneers and history at Temple Square in Salt Lake City. *Journal of Media and Religion* 4 (2), 95–110.

Sharpley, R. and Telfer, D. (2002) *Tourism and Development: Concepts and Issues*. Clevedon: Channel View Publications.

Shaw, G. and Williams, A. (1994) *Critical Issues in Tourism: A Geographical Perspective*. Oxford, Blackwell.

Sheller, M. and Urry, J. (2004) *Tourism Mobilities: Places to Play, Places in Play*. London: Routledge.

Shepherd, R. (2002) Commodification, culture and tourism. *Tourist Studies* 2 (2), 183–201.

Silver, I. (1993) Marketing authenticity in third world countries. *Annals of Tourism Research* 20, 302–318.

Sirakaya, E. and Sonmez, S. (1999) Gender images in state tourism brochures: An overlooked area in socially responsible tourism marketing. *Journal of Travel Research* 38 (4), 353–362.

Smith, B. (1985) *European Vision and the South Pacific*. New Haven, CT: Yale University Press.

Smith, S. (1990) *Dictionary of Concepts in Recreation and Leisure Studies*. Westport, CT: Greenwood.

Smith, V. (1989) *Host and Guests: The Anthropology of Tourism*. Philadelphia, PA: University of Pennsylvania Press.

Sofield, T. and Li, F. (1998) Tourism development and cultural policies in China. *Annals of Tourism Research* 25 (2), 362–392.

Sofield, T. and Li, S. (2007) Indigenous minorities of China and effects of tourism. In R. Butler and T. Hinch (eds) *Tourism and Indigenous Peoples: Issues and Implications* (pp. 265–280). Oxford: Butterworth-Heinemann.

Solinger, D. (1977) *Regional Government and Political Integration in Southwest China, 1949–1954: A Case Study*. Berkeley, CA: University of California Press.

Sorkin, M. (1992) *Variations on a Theme Park: The New American City and the End of Public Space*. New York: Hill and Wang.

Spang, L. (2000) *The Invention of the Restaurant*. Cambridge, MA: Harvard University Press.

Stebbins, R. (1996) Cultural tourism as serious leisure. *Annals of Tourism Research* 23 (4), 948–950.

Stone, L. (1989) Cultural cross-roads of community participation in development: A case from Nepal. *Human Organisation* 48 (3), 206–213.

Stone, M. and Wall, G. (2004) Ecotourism and community development: Case studies from Hainan, China. *Environmental Management* 33 (1), 12–24.

Storey, R., Lyon, J. and Wheeler, T. (1999) *China: A Travel Survival Kit*. Australia: Lonely Planet Publications.

Strain, E. (2003) *Public Places, Private Journeys*. Piscataway, NJ: Rutgers University Press.

Su, Y., Wei, J. and Liang, D. (1994) *The Dictionary of Li Ethnic Minority*. Guangzhou: Zhongshan University.

Sun, W. (2002) *Leaving China: Media, Migration, and Transnational Imagination*. Boulder, CO: Rowman & Littlefield.

Suvantola, J. (2002) *Tourist's Experience of Place*. Hampshire: Ashgate.

Swain, M. (1989) Developing ethnic tourism in Yunnan, China: Shilin Sani. *Tourism Recreation Research* 14 (1), 33–39.

Swain, M. (1993) Women producers of ethnic arts. *Annals of Tourism Research* 20, 32–51.

Tambiah, S. (1995) The politics of ethnicity. In R. Borofsky (ed.) *Assessing Cultural Anthropology* (pp. 430–441). New York: McGraw-Hill.

Tao, T. and Wall, G. (2009) Tourism as a sustainable livelihood strategy. *Tourism Management* 30 (1), 90–98.

Taylor, J. (2001) Authenticity and sincerity in tourism. *Annals of Tourism Research* 28 (1), 7–26.

Teo, P. (2002) Striking a balance for sustainable tourism: Implications of the discourse on globalisation. *Journal of Sustainable Tourism* 10 (6), 459–474.

Timothy, D. (1999) Participatory planning – a view of tourism in Indonesia. *Annals of Tourism Research* 26, 371–391.

Tivers, J. (2002) Performing heritage: The use of live "actors" in heritage presentations. *Leisure Studies* 21, 187–200.

Tosun, C. (2000) Limits to community participation in the tourism development process in developing countries. *Tourism Management* 21, 613–633.

Tosun, C. (2006) Expected nature of community participation in tourism development. *Tourism Management* 27 (3), 493–504.

Trauer, B. and Ryan, C. (2005) Destination image, romance and place experience – an application of intimacy theory in tourism. *Tourism Management* 26, 481–491.

Tsui, B. (2009) The surf's always up in the Chinese Hawaii. *The New York Times*.

Tulloch, J. (1999) *Performing Culture*. London: Sage.

Turner, L. and Ash, J. (1976) *The Golden Hordes: International Tourism and the Pleasure Periphery*. London: Constable.

Urry, J. (2002) *The Tourist Gaze* (2nd edn). London: Sage.

Urry, J. (2006) Preface: Places and performances. In C. Minca and T. Oakes (eds) *Travels in Paradox* (pp. vii–xi). Oxford: Rowman & Littlefield.

Van den Berghe, P. (1994) *The Quest for the Other: Ethnic Tourism in San Cristobal, Mexico*. Seattle, WA: University of Washington Press.

Van den Berghe, P. and Keyes, C. (1984) Introduction: Tourism and re-created ethnicity. *Annals of Tourism Research* 11, 343–352.

Vergès, F. (2001) Vertigo and emancipation, Creole Cosmopolitanism and cultural politics. *Theory, Culture & Society* 18 (2–3), 169–183.

Wall, G. (1996) Perspectives on tourism in selected Balinese villages. *Annals of Tourism Research* 23 (1), 123–137.

Wall, G. (2007) Tourism in the coastal zone: Perspectives from Hainan, P.R. China. *Journal of Regional Analysis and Policy* 37 (3), 193–198.

Wall, G. and Xie, P. (2005) Authenticating ethnic tourism: Li dancers' perspectives. *Asia Pacific Journal of Tourism Research* 10 (1), 1–21.

Wallace, A. (1956) Revitalisation movements. *American Anthropologist* 58, 265.

Walle, A. (1996) Habits of thought and cultural tourism. *Annals of Tourism Research* 23, 874–190.

Walle, A. (1998) *Cultural Tourism: A Strategic Focus*. Boulder, CO: Westview Press.

Waller, J. and Lea, S. (1999) Seeking the real Spain? Authenticity in motivation. *Annals of Tourism Research* 26 (1), 110–129.

Wang, N. (1999) Rethinking authenticity in tourism experience. *Annals of Tourism Research* 26 (2), 349–370.

Wang, N. (2000) *Tourism and Modernity: A Sociological Analysis*. Kidlington: Elsevier Science.

Wang, Y. and Wall, G. (2005) Resorts and residents: Stress and conservatism in a displaced community. *Tourism Analysis* 10, 37–53.

Wang, Y. and Wall, G. (2007) Administrative arrangements and displacement compensation in top-down tourism planning – A case from Hainan Province, China. *Tourism Management* 28, 70–82.

Wang, Y., Yan, X., Wang, J., and Liu, Y. (1992) *The Social Investigation on Li Ethnic Minority in Hainan*. Guiling: Guangxi Ethnic Publishing.

Watson, G. and Kopachevsky, J. (1994) Interpretations of tourism as commodity. *Annals of Tourism Research* 3, 643–660.

West, C. (2000) *The Cornel West Reader*. New York: Basic Civitas Books.

Willis, S. (1994) Memory and mass culture. In G. Fabre and R. O'Meallly (eds) *History and Memory in African-American Culture* (pp. 178–188). New York: Oxford University Press.

Wilson, R.M.S., Gilligan, C. and Pearson, D.J. (1992) *Strategic Marketing Management: Planning, Implementation and Control*. Oxford: Butterworth-Heinemann.

Winthrop, R. (1991) *Dictionary of Concepts in Cultural Anthropology*. Westport, CT: Greenwood Press.

Wood, R. (1980) International tourism and cultural change in Southeast Asia. *Economic Development and Cultural Change* 3, 561–581.

Wood, R. (1997) Tourism and the state. In M. Picard and R. Wood (eds) *Tourism, Ethnicity, and the State in Asian and Pacific Societies* (pp. 1–34). Honolulu, HI: University of Hawaii Press.

Wood, R. (1998) Bali: Cultural tourism and touristic culture. *Annals of Tourism Research* 25 (3), 770–772.

Wu, X. (2000) Ethnic tourism: A helicopter from "huge graveyard" to paradise? *Hmong Studies Journal* 3, 1–33.

Wu, Y. (1991) *The History of Li Minority*. Guangdong, China: Guangdong Press.

Wynn, L. (2007) *Pyramids and Nightclubs*. Austin, TX: The University of Texas Press.

Xiao, H. (2006) The discourse of power: Deng Xiaoping and tourism development in China. *Tourism Management* 27 (5), 803–814.

Xie, P. (2003a) The bamboo-beating dance in Hainan, China: Authenticity and commodification. *Journal of Sustainable Tourism* 11 (1), 5–17.

Xie, P. (2003b) Managing aboriginal tourism in Hainan, China: Governmental perspectives. *Annals of Leisure Research* 3, 279–302.

Xie, P. (2004) Visitors' perception of authenticity at a rural heritage festival: A case study. *Event Management*, 8 (3), 151–160.

Xie, P. and Lane, B. (2006) A life cycle model for Aboriginal arts performance in tourism: Perspectives on authenticity. *Journal of Sustainable Tourism* 14 (6), 545–561.

Xie, P., Osumare, H. and Ibrahim, A. (2007) Gazing the 'hood: Hip-hop as tourism attraction. *Tourism Management* 28 (2), 452–460.

Xie, P. and Wall, G. (2000) *Proposal for the Creation of an Eco-province in Hainan*. Province of Hainan, China: Ministry of Environment and Resources.

Xie, P. and Wall, G. (2002) Visitors' perceptions of authenticity at cultural attractions in Hainan, China. *International Journal of Tourism Research* 4, 353–366.

Xie, P.F. and Wall, G. (2008) Authenticating visitor attraction based upon ethnicity. In A. Fyall, B. Garrod and A. Leask (eds) *Managing Visitor Attractions: New Directions* (pp. 132–147). Oxford: Butterworth Heinemann.

Xu, G. (1999) *Tourism and Local Economic Development in China: Case Studies of Guilin, Suzhou, and Bedaihe*. Surrey: Curzon.

Yang, L. and Wall, G. (2009) Authenticity in ethnic tourism: Domestic tourists' perspective. *Current Issues in Tourism* 12 (3), 235–254.

Yang, L., Wall, G. and Smith, S. (2008) Ethnic tourism development: Chinese government perspectives. *Annals of Tourism Research* 35 (3), 751–771.

Yang, M. (1995) Music loss among ethnic minorities in China: A comparison of the Li and Hui peoples. *Asian Music* 27 (1), 59–73.

Ying, T. and Zhou, Y. (2007) Community, governments and external capitals in China's rural cultural tourism: A comparative study of two adjacent villages. *Tourism Management* 28, 96–107.

Zeppel, H. (1998) Land and culture: Sustainable tourism and indigenous peoples. In C.M. Hall and A. Lew (eds) *Sustainable Tourism: A Geographical Perspective* (pp. 60–74). Essex, UK: Addison Wesley Longman Ltd.

Zhang, G. (2003) China's tourism since 1978: Politics, experiences, and lessons learned. In A. Lew, L. Yu, J. Ap and G. Zhang (eds) *Tourism in China* (pp. 13–34). Binghamton, NY: The Haworth Hospitality Press.

Zhang, H., Chong, K. and Ap, J. (1999) An analysis of tourism policy development in modern China. *Tourism Management* 20, 471–485.

Zhu, L. (1999) Lost in a changing time: Researchers debate folk arts and culture. *China Daily (Hong Kong)*, p. 13.

Index